Your Country Kitchen

Your Country Kitchen

Jocasta Innes

Garden Way Publishing
Charlotte, Vermont 05445

Editor/Designer:
Nonie Niesewand

Art Editor:
Jane Willis

Assisted by:
Piet Saag (design)
Jill Goolden (copy)
Pamela Todd (copy)
Antonia Demetriadi (indexer)

Photographer:
Christine Hanscomb

Illustrators:
Stewart Walton
Tony Kerins
Liz Butler

Your Country Kitchen is the Garden Way edition of a book
first published in the United States by William Morrow and Co. Inc.
under the title Notes from a Country Kitchen.
Text © Jocasta Innes 1979
Artwork and photographs © Frances Lincoln Publishers Ltd 1979.
Conceived, edited and produced by Frances Lincoln Publishers Ltd,
Apollo Works, Charlton Kings Rd, London NW5 2SB.

First Garden Way edition 1982
Reprinted 1983

ISBN 0-88266-306-2

Printed in Italy

Author's acknowledgments

Talking and listening has provided me with so much help in writing this book that I feel a list of acknowledgments should begin with a collective thank-you to all the people whose reminiscences helped to bring the old country ways to life.

My sincere thanks to Angela Cox, most indispensable of assistants, whose North country common sense and genuine love of good food were an unfailing support. I could not have done without the help and advice of George Carter and Peter Stickland, both wise in country ways. Bill Brown told me more about fish than I could have learnt from books. Mark and Rachel Helfer supplied me with Jersey milk which would inspire any amateur cheesemaker and Mr and Mrs Norman Stoate of Cann Mills in Dorset told me all I needed to know about stoneground flour. Among the many friends who helped me with ideas, recipes and encouragement, I would like to thank Lif, Mirdza, Bronnie and Sally. For their forbearance over books missing or overdue, thank you to the charming staff of Wareham Public Library.

Shaping the book for publication was definitely a team effort and here I must thank that vigilant and tactful trio: Pamela Todd, Jilly Goolden and especially Nonie Niesewand, who deciphered illegible notes, revised endless proofs. And finally, thank you to Jane Willis, Christine Hanscomb, Jean-Luc Bénard, Stewart Walton and Tony Kerins for making the book not just useful but beautiful.

Contents

The author's kitchen in the country

Your country kitchen

Everyone has a picture of how a country kitchen should look . . . it's a phrase as clustered with associations, as a berry bush with fruit. Usually it is an old settled place which comes to mind: a flagged floor smoothed into hollows by the passing of countless feet, vast plank table scoured to pale straw color, a round faced clock companionably ticking and set into the chimney breast, and that tyrant of the old style country kitchen, the cast-iron range whose needs, moods and eccentricities must be faithfully served if bread is not to scorch and kettles refuse to boil. Scrubbed, sanded, scoured, swabbed almost to colorlessness over the years, the gentle austerity of the place is brightened here and there by copper pans big enough to bath a baby in, burnished strings of onions, a bunch of dried herbs, the best china set out against the dark wood dresser. For comfort, a wooden chair eased by sagging cushions, and beneath it, a scuffed rag rug.

Some features of this imagined kitchen would change from one part of the world to the other, but not the essentials: a certain old fashioned air, the use of honest materials like brick, wood, stone, the sense of an ordered way of life linked to the changing seasons, the good feeling which comes off places where people are generously fed, warmed and cherished, and the squirrelling impulse to store good things away, tucked into pots and jars. But the quintessence of old country kitchens is their smell, a richly complicated experience for the nose in which new bread, frying onions, hot jam, muddy boots, vanilla, wet washing, smoke, herbs, dishwater have all somehow merged their differences over the years.

This archetypal country kitchen is frankly a nostalgic creation. By comparison the typical modern country kitchen is smart, colorful and briskly labor saving. And why not? Stainless steel sinks and drainers are hygienic and practical and you can wipe them down in a moment which certainly was not the case with the old porcelain sink and wooden draining boards. Yet links with the old traditions survive in a contemporary kitchen. Ropes of onions, shallots and garlic still hang by the stove, parsley and chives sprout from pots on a sunny windowsill, the unmistakable smell of working yeast shows that a batch of dough is rising in the big earthenware jar beside the range, bundles of dried herbs from the garden are pinned close to the worktop and there is possibly a keg of homebrew propped on bricks in one corner. Not merely decorative accessories chosen to lend a touch of homeliness to streamlined plastic laminates, but signs of a peaceful revolution going on in more and more homes as people discover that they can have the best of both worlds. So they make use of the time and energy saved by modern appliances to rediscover the culinary skills known to their forebears.

First and foremost, the sharpened appetite and relish which comes from eating fresh, homemade, unadulterated food, honest loaves made from flour and yeast, beer and ales of a strength and heartiness since vanished from commercial products, jams, jellies and preserves which still retain the fragrance of summer. Then there is the enjoyable glow with which one chooses a jar of pickled peaches to perfectly complement a plate of cold ham, or home-made pâté. A kitchen cupboard stocked with jars of homemade preserves, jams, jellies, fruit butters and cheeses must be one of the country cook's deepest satisfactions. Quite apart from economy and superlative flavor – straight from the garden to the pan is the rule for the best flavors – homemade preserves look so beautiful, especially the translucent jellies like quince, rowan, apple and mint. I have rediscovered the delights of preserving with old-fashioned recipes that use both fruits of hedgerow and woodland, like the cut gooseberry preserve flavored with elderflowers to resemble muscatels, and the orchard fruits like the dumpsideary jam. One good thing often leads to another. It is not such a big step from baking bread to making the cheese to eat with it, or from cooking meat in terrines, pâtés and galantines to preserving it by curing and smoking it yourself. Disentangled from the folk lore which is apt to grow up around these old skills, the basic processes prove to be uncomplicated. It is an interesting fact too that brewing, baking, bottling, salting and smoking your own food provide a pleasure as direct, simple and nourishing to the spirit as bread is to the belly.

Nor must you live in the country to enjoy countrified pleasures. Certainly, it is less trouble for country dwellers with a kitchen garden, an orchard and wild foods for the picking to explore new ways of using and preserving them. But one of the most countrified kitchens I ever knew was in the sooty heart of London, a basement room below pavement level that relied on windowboxes and tubs for greenery. Green beans scrambled up from windowboxes like living sunblinds, the tomato salad came from a plastic grow-bag and was sprinkled with fresh chopped basil from a pot on the windowsill. Stacked in kegs along a wall was an impressive choice of fruit and flower wines, much of it picked on London's wilder heaths and parkland. There is no yard, however small or ill-favored, where something cannot be coaxed to grow; a Bing cherry tree against a shaded wall, herbs in a raised bed to catch the sun, strawberries in pots. Even if you live on the fiftieth floor of a concrete tower, never deny yourself the thrill of growing something edible. Houseplants are decorative and pleasing, but to tend, harvest and finally eat a crop of anything – no matter if it is only a plate of bean sprouts – is a keen delight to that bit of frustrated farmer in us all. More practically, with bulk buying proving an economical way of getting in fruit and vegetables, not to mention meat, cereals and legumes, even the most urbane of urbanites will find it useful to 'put them up' before they perish. It is no more difficult to make epicurean delicacies like damson cheese, spiced beef, apple butter, raspberry vinegar, than it is to fill a few jars with marmalade or jam, but it is a lot more interesting, rewarding and fun.

This book is intended to encourage those cooks who value such things and who have thought they would like to try making sausages . . . or smoking kippers . . . or brewing their own beer . . . or making fruit liqueurs to give away as Christmas presents, if they could only find detailed practical instructions and information on the equipment needed, how long the process takes and whether the product is finally worth the effort and trouble. Nostalgia for the sake of nostalgia has been avoided because gadgets do save time and effort if you can afford them. After all, it is the flavor of your sausage filling that counts, not whether it was pushed into the casing mechanically or by human hand.

Food for all seasons

Spring

Spring sweeps the countryside like a green fire, puffs of white blossom rising behind like smoke. The sharp young greens are a tonic to the eye and to the system, eaten when still acrid with newness. You can taste the old earth minerals in dandelion and hawthorn leaf; use them as our ancestors did in 'sallets', later picking the flowers for wine.

Spring is when the provident cook turns gardener, pricking out, sowing and planting for the year ahead. Sturdy winter vegetables, cauliflowers, cabbages, the worthy root family are making way for catch crops of radishes, the first spinach, lettuce nursed under cloches against spring frosts. As the season advances, sprouting broccoli, or 'poor man's asparagus', makes way for the other sort which you need patience, not riches, to enjoy. Spring fruit is scarce, so value the first young sticks of rhubarb for light fine wine and jam set with ginger and marrow. But the first spring gooseberries, hard, green and acid are the true spring fruit, best for jams, canning and wine. Gooseberry wine is like a good hock.

Early spring sees the end of the white fish season, a good time to buy halibut, cod for drying and salting, herring for pickling and smoking. By mid-spring, the breeding season is well under way so game is taboo apart from the odd rabbit. However, as the months pass, lobster and crab – 'game of the sea' – take over from oysters, mussels and scallops.

Summer

Everywhere summer oozes richness: cattle, fed on lush grass yield the year's richest milk for cheesemaking, or to eat as clotted cream with the season's soft fruit, first gooseberries then strawberries, currants, loganberries and raspberries, best eaten fresh before making into the delectable jams, jellies, syrups and cordials. Elder blossom makes a fragrant wine.

Even the fish of the season are sappy, rich with oil like mackerel and trout. Freshly caught fish can be smoked in the simplest metal box to eat later with all the crisp salad vegetables, lettuce, cucumber, peppers, early tomatoes or pound shrimp with butter and pot it for spreads. The best meat is young – veal, lamb, chicken, duckling – good to make up into refined pâtés and galantines. Venison is back in midsummer, buck not roe, as the herds are being culled. It is excellent home-cured to eat with a sharp currant or rowan jelly, or made into hearty sausages.

As summer draws to a close, a glut of vegetables – zucchini, squash, watermelon, tomatoes – sets one rooting among pickle and chutney recipes. Green beans should be salted down each week for winter use; tomatoes canned for pasta sauces. Collect herbs to dry and store, or to flavor your pickles. Late summer brings cherries, plums, apricots, peaches, all excellent dried, or canned to make lavish preserves, fruity wines and unbeatable home-made liqueurs, like cherry shrub which uses brandy as a preservative for fresh cherries.

Fall

This is the season that sees the most bustle and stir in country, and countrified, kitchens. Crops are harvested daily. Begin with a glut of late vegetables by plaiting, for drying into coppery strings, onions, shallots, garlic. A profusion of late plums, pears, damsons, quinces can be made into jams, preserves, fruit cheeses and butters to eat later.

By mid fall, the wild fruits, berries and nuts, are ready for picking – blackberries, sloes, crab apples, elderberries, rosehips. These yield some of the freshest tasting, most evocative preserves and wines. Wild hazelnuts and American chestnuts will be just right for Christmas eating.

Field mushrooms and puffballs, most mysterious earth fruit of all, are there for the persevering rambler. Surplus mushrooms–excepting puffballs–can be dried to add savor to winter soups and casseroles. For winter legumes, dry beans, peas and store them in a cool place.

Traditionally, fall is when the family pig was killed to make hams, bacon, brawns, sausages and blood pudding to be stored for winter use. It is still practical to cure and smoke hams and sausages now so they can mature and mellow during the winter when there is least danger of bacteria spoiling your handiwork. Also, with Christmas in mind, meat can be put up in various ways. A good time too to smoke herring, which is plentiful now.

Winter

Stormy, sodden or frosted with stars, winter nights are long enough to oppress the spirit, and it needs human resourcefulness to make them homely with such comforts as bright fires, good food and warming drinks. Nothing is more fortifying than a steaming mug of spiced, mulled elderberry wine or a hot raspberry cordial to drive away the cold.

It is also now that the provident cook really scores with so many good things put by. Some industrious cooks may find time to pickle the first hard cabbages in brine to eat with Christmas goose, or begin fermenting their parsnip wine. Now is a good time to make sausages, bland or spicy, to dry, freeze or smoke. Game is back and plentiful for layering into terrines, flavored with port and brandy, spices and herbs, or for eating spiced, cured or pickled.

Stored fruit and vegetables, fresh and dried, need checking to weed out moldy ones. As winter hardens, your stores are raided in earnest to flavor the heartening soups and casseroles and add variety to meals threatened by monotony. As the last stored apples come to an end, all the citrus fruits reach their peak in time for marmalade making, row upon row of tawny pots to last the year's breakfasts.

Just when spring seems further away than ever, snowdrops pierce the frozen ground, a glow surrounds the budding elms and the whole cycle, sowing and reaping, birth and death, nature's gifts and man's industry is poised to begin again.

Cereals

The staff of life

All the maincrop cereals so vital to feeding the world's hungry millions belong to the botanical family of *Graminaciae*, grasses, along with reeds, rushes and lawns. Corn (a word for the seed of grass) in the old days signified grain in general, meaning oats to the Scots, wheat, rye or barley to the English, maize or corn in the U.S. It might be eaten whole, boiled up into cereal, roughly crushed into groats to make a more digestible gruel, split into flakes, ground into flour of varying degrees of fineness. Often the grain could be fermented to make alcoholic drinks, both mild and potent. Before factory milling and cheap transport brought 'fine whete' flour within everyone's reach, dishes of strong local character were invented to use the corn, or cereal ... consider the way Mexicans, early Americans and Italians variously explored the possibilities of cornmeal, mixing it with hot chiles, or molasses or cheese with utterly different results.

It may come as a surprise to learn that the Western world still relies to a large extent on basic cereals – wheat primarily, also rice and oats. Nutritionists' surveys indicate that cereals account for one *quarter* of the daily calorie intake in the average Western diet. The significance of this, from the health point of view, only becomes clear once you realize how much cereals, in particular wheat and rice (the most widely eaten), vary in food value according to whether they have been refined, polished, bleached or otherwise commercially processed.

In their unrefined state all the cereals are valuable foods, providing good protein, a rich source of B vitamins and many essential minerals. Wheat germ is the richest natural source of vitamin E, which is involved in the health of muscles, skin and all tissues. When wheat grain is milled to produce refined white flour most of the B vitamins, in the outer husk, are removed and *all* the wheat germ, because wheat germ oil can turn flour rancid if it is stored for any length of time. True, two of the lost B vitamins, plus calcium and iron, are partially restored, but who knows whether the lost vitamin E may not count for more in the subtle biochemistry of the human body? Similarly with rice, the nutrients are concentrated in the brown husk, which is entirely removed to produce polished white rice.

It is not just what commercial processing takes out, but what it puts *in* which needs thinking about. The wheat grains used to make flour have been subjected to all manner of interference, from sprays used on the growing crop, through bleaches used to brighten white flour, to 'improvers' used to achieve the standard commercial loaf.

Without becoming too diet conscious, it seems sensible to make sure that the cereals which form a large part of your family's diet should be as rich in all their natural nutrients as possible.

Begin with bread, which is the cereal food most people, especially children, eat in largest quantities. Half the battle is won if you switch from white to wholewheat bread, by which I mean bread made from stoneground, compost grown, wholewheat flour. Wholewheat flour delivers all the goodness in wheat intact, while stoneground ensures an even distribution of the precious wheat germ oil. Buy your own flour by the sack from a reputable miller and make and bake the bread yourself. This is both economical and satisfactory. If the family are gluttons for white loaves, begin with a half and half mixture of wholewheat and bread flour, and step up the wholewheat content gradually. Reluctant children can be tempted by adding enough sweetener – molasses, malt or honey – to make a slightly sticky loaf. The chewy texture of wholewheat bread is due to the bran content, which, in many doctors' opinions, is one of its most important contributions to health. A generous dollop of bran daily is one of the best ways of adding roughage.

Try making some of the simpler cookies, cakes, and tea breads with wholewheat flour mixed with white. All sorts of things can be added to make them more nourishing as well as more delicious: nuts, seeds, dried fruit, cracked corn, eggs, honey, fats. These not only bring their own quota of protein, calcium and iron but also help the body to assimilate the cereal nutrients more efficiently. Yeast is a potent source of B vitamins and much else. Keep an airtight tin of wheat germ handy too, and add a spoonful wherever its faintly nutty taste seems appropriate.

Perhaps the most flexible, popular health food of our time is muesli. Health conscious people have discovered that the basic formula of rolled oats and raw grated apple is endlessly adaptable. You can add fresh fruit in season, or dried milk powder, wheat germ or a little bran. It can be eaten with milk, cream, yogurt, and sweetened with honey or condensed milk. Some people like a savory version with grated cheese and herbs. But the most instantly popular variant is 'granola', which uses your favorite basic muesli mix, turned over with a little corn oil and honey and toasted in a low oven until slightly crisped and golden.

Rolled oats are the cereal richest in minerals and oils and old fashioned oatmeal needs no introduction. Any food with vitamin C eaten with the oats helps to make use of the iron more effectively. So give your children a glass of orange juice with their porridge and eggs for a warming, impeccably nutritious winter breakfast, or try hot oat cakes eaten with fresh butter, followed by fresh fruit.

According to nutritionists, the best way to get full protein and vitamin value from cereal, is to eat as many different types as possible during the course of the day. So, muesli for breakfast, wholewheat bread with lunch, nut bread for a snack, rice with supper, and so on. Keep a supply of the less conventional cereal foods such as millet, buckwheat, cornmeal, brown rice and barley on hand and experiment with different ways of using them. Be tactful; if you overdo the health side of things you run the risk of making healthy eating seem downright dull and penitential. Instead, try brown rice in soups, cold and well seasoned as a basis for salads or fried up with soy sauce, shrimps and scallions, Chinese style. Buckwheat is delicious when cooked in any of the traditional Russian ways, with mushrooms, hard-cooked eggs and sour cream. Millet can be used to make light and delicious gnocchi. Rye mixed with wholewheat flour makes a sophisticated dark bread, with a sour flavour which contrasts particularly well with good cheese, radishes and pickles. Add barley to soups, stews and casserole dishes, or use it instead of rice with game dishes. Try substituting cooked barley, millet or buckwheat, well seasoned, for rice in stuffings for vegetables and poultry. Chase up traditional peasant recipes which rely on cereals and try them out. Adding more fiber to your diet will benefit you.

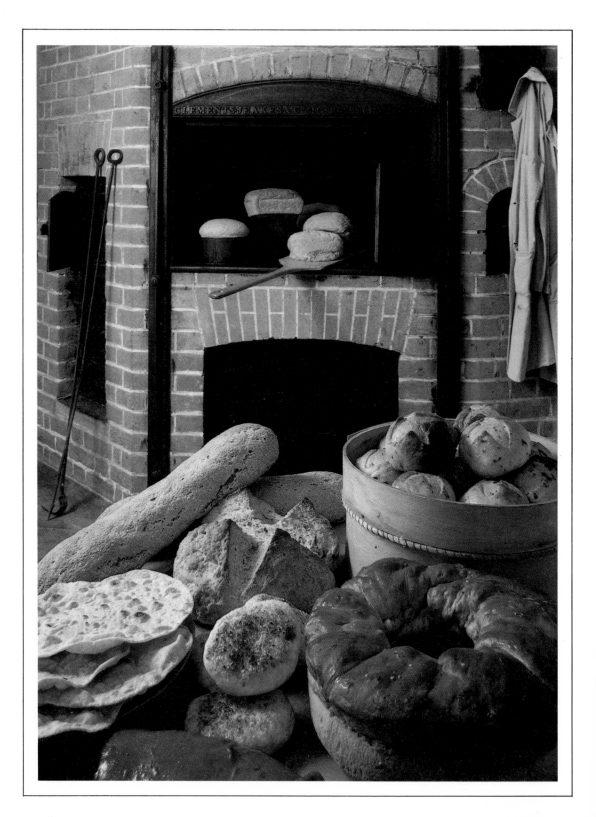

Bread

'The smel of new breade is comfortable to the heade and to the herte'

Anon 1400

How one's heart goes out across the centuries to the unknown person who felt it worth recording such a touchingly simple truth. For he – or she – was quite right: the smell of new bread is incomparable; rich, warm and yeasty, it makes the kitchen a place of true comfort.

Bread making is one of those basic skills, like being able to light a fire or ride a bicycle, which everyone should master. When bread strikes loom, or public holidays strip store counters bare, it is a relief to know you have only to reach for the flour and the dried yeast to fill the gap. Baking your own bread regularly saves money and it is reassuring that the loaves contain only what you have put into them. Freshly baked loaves, buns and croissants can be frozen successfully, so freezer owners can organize one massive baking session every two weeks. The rest of us can get by with baking once a week and wrapping the loaves in foil or wax paper, to keep them from drying out.

The best argument for making bread is simply that it is altogether pleasurable. The sensuous glee to be found in working up a sticky flour and water mess with your fists, is capped only by the wonder of the rising dough, puffing itself up steadily in the warm, sleek as a mushroom. Finally, there is the crowning moment when the oven door is opened and out come the steaming loaves, so rounded, golden and immaculate it is hard to believe they could be the work of your own hands.

Compared with precision cooking, which depends on timing and judgment to come out right (béarnaise sauce, soufflés, batters) making bread is easy. It uses few ingredients and the simplest equipment and once you have had a couple of trial runs, you will find that the stages follow upon each other as inevitably as ABC. If you are in a hurry the process can be speeded up so that the bread is on the table in $1\frac{1}{2}$ hours flat. Alternatively the rising period can be extended by anything up to 48 hours by leaving the dough to rise in progressively cooler temperatures often with better results. Begin with a foolproof recipe like the one for daily bread, but don't be afraid to experiment with more elaborate ones – they may look complicated but this is simply because they contain more ingredients – the basic formula of yeast, flour and liquid still remains. You can add honey, malt, treacle for sweetness, wheat germ for extra vitamins, seeds, herbs, spices for relish, and shape the loaves in many ways to add variety to your bread doughs.

At the bakehouse oven, the miller's loaf and rising daily bread. In the flour sifter (foreground) hot cross buns and (clockwise) glazed Swedish Christmas bread in both ring and stick shapes, Chinese sesame seed buns, unleavened chapatis, two sticks of rye bread and, center, Irish soda bread.

Flour

Wheat flour is the universal choice for regular baking because it makes lighter bread. Hard wheat (mostly winter wheat grown in Canada) is richest in gluten, the protein substance which gives dough enough strength and elasticity to expand and contain the furiously multiplying yeast cells (and to remain that way after oven heat has killed off the yeast). Milled, 'hard' wheat gives a strong flavor which absorbs more liquid, makes a springier dough and bakes into a larger loaf. Soft wheat flour, usually milled from a local crop, is less absorbent and results in a denser, shorter textured crumb. The color, texture, nutritional content and flavor of wheat flour is established by the degree to which it has been milled and refined (that is, sifted and bolted) to remove bran or wheat husk. As milling proceeds, the flour becomes milder and paler.

Stoneground wholewheat: the coarsest and healthiest. It makes a dark, chewy, strongly flavored bread that is close in texture.

Wholewheat or graham: falls between stoneground wholewheat and bread flour. It is wholewheat with a varying proportion of the bran or the wheat husk sifted out – the extraction rate varies from 81% to 90%. However, it retains a wheaty flavor and makes a softer, lighter bread and more spicy solid types of cakes, buns or cookies.

Bread flour: is available bleached (white) or unbleached (creamy). This flour contains an extra high proportion of hard wheat and gluten, and rises well, making a loaf with an elastic, spongy texture and a good flavor. Use it wherever springiness matters: pizzas, rolls, buns, cakes, puff and flaky pastry, Yorkshire puddings and batter in general.

All-purpose flour: whiter than white, bleached, bran free, 'soft' and satisfactory for general cooking, thickening sauces, making cakes, cookies and quick tea breads (self-raising flours make these even quicker).

Many people keep a supply of wholewheat and bread flour, mixing the two wherever a wheatmeal effect is needed. It is most economical to buy wholewheat flours in bulk from a miller who grinds – stone grinds usually – his own on the premises. It is also possible with the aid of an electrical gadget or a hand-operated mill, to mill your own flour in small quantities. All flour should be stored in a cool, dry place. Plastic wastebaskets with lids are clean, neat and mouseproof, even if not things of great beauty.

Finally, a brief word about other cereal flours:

Rye, on its own, or mixed with white flour, gives a sharp flavor which is ideal for sour dough techniques and for snacks of the smorgasbord variety. It contains less gluten than wheat flour.

Barley flour is hard to come by (try health food stores) but a couple of ounces mixed into a wholewheat dough will give a distinctive, nutty taste to your bread.

Oat flour, or fine meal, is also hard to find outside traditional oat growing areas, but a handful of medium oatmeal (not the hot cereal type) can be added to wholewheat bread for a pleasant change in flavor. It can also be used to make oatcakes which taste delicious eaten with cheese.

Yeast

The yeast you buy, whether fresh or dried, is made by cultivating and processing selected strains of wild yeast, colorless, microscopic fungi present in the air about us. In a moist, warm environment and fed with a little sugar, yeast starts multiplying furiously, converting sugar into carbon dioxide and, ultimately, alcohol. The word yeast is derived from the Sanskrit *yas*, to seethe, which neatly describes what you see when you peer into a bucket of homebrewed beer. Scrape the sludge off the bucket and mix a cupful into your next batch of bread. It raises the dough slowly and leaves a slight 'hoppy' bitterness which makes an appealing change.

Hoping to settle the controversy about the respective merits of fresh and dried yeast, I made up a loaf using each. The fresh-yeast dough made a spectacular start, doubling in size faster than its fellow, and maintaining its lead when they went into the oven together, on the same shelf. Unexpectedly, things leveled out during the baking, and there was less than $\frac{1}{2}$ inch in height between the cooked loaves, the fresh-yeast loaf being fractionally lighter textured and perhaps a little sweeter tasting than the other. From this I concluded that fresh yeast is slightly stronger but you can still make excellent bread from the dried. Fresh yeast will keep for a week stored in a screwtop jar or plastic bag, in a cool place; the potency of dried yeast will decline once the tin has been opened. When baking, remember you will need to use twice as much fresh yeast as dried, because dried yeast is concentrated and so more powerful. Two other factors affect the amount of yeast needed: the density of the dough (wholewheat flour needs more yeast, as do fancy breads enriched with fruit and nuts) and the length of time allowed for raising it. The longer you leave it the more dough a given amount of yeast will raise, producing lighter bread every hour.

Activating yeast
Yeast cells respond to a little encouragement so warm the flour, bowl and the liquid before use. Never knead the dough in a drafty place. Salt inhibits yeast, though improving bread flavor and crisping the crust, so use *less* salt for quick breads. Sugar boosts yeast growth – a pinch is enough to reactivate fresh yeast. Or you can crumble the yeast into the liquid or rub it straight into the flour. To reactivate dried yeast, add a pinch of sugar to about $\frac{1}{2}$ cup of warm water, stir in the yeast granules and leave for 10 minutes until frothy.

Yeast culture
Thrifty souls might like to try keeping their own yeast culture going between baking sessions. Keep aside a small piece of unrisen dough when next baking and store it in a screwtop jar in a cool place. Look at it every few days and sprinkle on a little sugar if it shows signs of wilting. Before your next bake, bring it back into the warm, add a little warm water and sugar to it and sprinkle a little flour on top. At bedtime transfer it into a bowl, add about $\frac{1}{2}$ cup of flour, mix together and leave overnight to rise. It can now be kneaded into the rest of the flour as if it were ordinary yeast. Remember to subtract the flour you used and to keep a little dough back for the next time. This method does not work every time but is worth trying.

Bread making

Flour, water and yeast are mixed to a dough which is kneaded to distribute the working yeast and force in air and then left for a varying period to allow the yeast cells to expand and develop. The dough is then punched down and rapidly kneaded again before being shaped into loaves or put into pans. These loaves are left to rise once more for a short time before they are baked. Some simpler bread recipes cut out the punching down and second rising stage which saves time but results in a much less uniform texture. Thanks to modern technology, there are now a number of gadgets designed to do some of the work of kneading, and yeast boosters like ascorbic acid to speed up the rising time, but, essentially, the old methods stand unaltered.

Mixing and kneading

Sift a measured amount of flour and salt into a mixing bowl and warm slightly. The water or milk used for mixing should also be hand-hot. Start with a little more liquid than the recipe requires to save having to fumble about with sticky hands if the flour proves unexpectedly absorbent, but add it gradually and have the flour bag handy to dust the table top and your hands if the dough becomes too sticky to manage. All the ingredients for fancy bread recipes should be measured out into bowls and close at hand to save confusion. The reactivated yeast should also be ready, frothing in a small bowl.

Make a well in the warmed flour and pour in the yeast and some of the liquid. Use your hand to draw the flour into the liquid, stirring it around and adding water cautiously until the bulk of the flour feels moist and is beginning to stick together. Use both hands now to collect the sticky mess into a lump and roll it around to collect the last of the loose flour. Add a little more water if needed. It is possible to do all the kneading in the bowl but I prefer a flat table top, the surface lightly floured to prevent sticking. Smack down the dough lump, push it down and away from you with the heels of both hands, fold it back towards you and push it away again. This traps the air and the rhythmic back and forth motion soon becomes instinctive. If the dough remains obstinately sticky, after a minute's kneading, shake a handful of flour over it. If you can spare the time, knead the dough for between 10 and 20 minutes or until the dough springs up smoothly leaving a print which fills up in a second when poked with a finger. One-rise, or quick breads, benefit from an extra long kneading which compensates for the shorter time spent developing the yeast.

Electric mixers with dough hooks

If you are using one of these to make bread, put the yeast and liquid in the bowl, sift in the dry ingredients, set to lowest speed and mix for a couple of minutes until a dough is formed. Increase the speed slightly and mix for another 2 or 3 minutes to knead the dough. Most mixers will not hold more than 4 cups of flour at a time but they make dough so quickly, you can make two or three batches in less time. Add the liquid gradually in an electric mixer, as you may find the dough needs less liquid than normal.

Making plain white bread: first stage

This quantity of dough divides conveniently into one large loaf and one smaller one which can be mixed with fruit and eggs to make a sweet tea bread.

1. In a small bowl, mix 2 teaspoons active dry yeast and 1 teaspoon sugar or honey with a little warm water and leave it until it foams. Sift 6 cups flour with 2 teaspoons salt into a warmed bowl, then tip onto a floured working surface. Make a well in the center and pour in the yeast mixture. Use your hands to draw the flour into the liquid. Keep adding warm water a splash at a time (up to 1 pint), until the liquid binds the flour.

2. Draw in all the flour until a doughy lump forms which feels firm and does not stick to the surface. Roll it around to collect the last of the loose flour.

3. Begin kneading. Using both hands, push the dough down and away from you with the heels of both hands. Kneading must push air into the dough, unlike kneading clay for pottery which drives air out.

4. Fold it back towards you and push it away again and so on in a rhythmic back and forth motion that traps in the air. After a few minutes you will notice the dough changing from an inert lump, acquiring smoothness, even texture. It is shaping up.

5. Knead the dough for anything between 10 and 20 minutes – the longer you knead, within reason, the lighter the bread – until it springs elastically, leaving a print which fills up in a second when prodded gently with a finger.

Rising and punching down

Smear a drop of oil over the dough (to stop a crust forming) and either put it back in the mixing bowl under a clean, thick cloth or into a lightly tied and oiled plastic bag. For rapid rising, place it somewhere warm, near the stove with the oven turned down to the lowest setting for instance, or to one side of a solid old fashioned range if you are lucky enough to own one, or near the boiler. Never allow it, or the container, to touch anything hot because this will check, if not destroy, the budding cells. What you are aiming for is an even warmth.

For slower rising, 2 to 4 hours, leave the dough at room temperature, covered or wrapped as before. For an overnight rising, place the dough in a cool place like a pantry. For a 48-hour rising, leave it in the lower half of the refrigerator.

Wheat flour has risen sufficiently when doubled in size; rye and barley, however, will always rise less, even when mixed with wheat flour. Never leave dough rising in a warm place for hours on end because yeast tends to die back gradually when it has reached its capacity. This will result in hard, bitter-tasting bread. If, for some reason, you have to break off in the middle of the rapid rising routine, remember to shift the dough into a cooler spot first. If already well risen, quickly punch it down, shape it and leave to rise again at room temperature.

Punching down means exactly that. Punch the puffy surface of the dough, which collapses like a burst paper bag, scrape it up into a lump and knead quickly for a minute or two. Shape the dough into loaves by hand, or pat into well greased or oiled pans, not more than half full as the dough will double in size again before cooking. Leave to rise.

One-rise bread is put straight into pans, or onto a greased baking sheet, after the first kneading and put into a hot oven as soon as it has doubled in size.

Baking

Always preheat the oven for 5 minutes to the given setting as bread dough needs to be started off at a brisk heat to kill the yeast and set the loaves.

The baking time varies with the size of the loaves – about 40 minutes for 1 pound loaves, 1 hour or more for larger loaves. When the tops are crisp and hard and the loaves make a hollow sound when tapped, the bread is cooked. If in any doubt, take them out of their pans and return them to the oven, upside down, for 5 minutes. Brush a little melted butter over the loaves while still hot to give an attractive glazed finish. If you want to press seeds, nuts or cracked wheat over the top, take the loaves out 10 minutes before they are done, brush with beaten egg, or milk, press the seeds on top and replace them in the oven. The seeds can scorch if you do this at the start.

Storing

Always allow the loaves time to become completely cold on a cake rack, before storing. Warm bread will go moldy if imprisoned. Wrap the loaves in foil or wax paper for longer storing. If any mold appears, either scald the bin or box or swab it out with a potassium metabisulphite solution (see wine making).

Making plain white bread: second stage

6. Put the dough in a mixing bowl, smear a drop of oil over it to stop a crust forming, and put a thick clean cloth over the bowl. Choose a rising time which suits your schedule: for rapid rising set the bowl near the oven, for overnight rising, leave in a cool place, or for really slow rising – 48 hours – put the dough in the refrigerator.

7. Depending on the rising time you have chosen, the loaf is ready for punching down when it has doubled in size. Quicky do this by punching it with your fists.

8. Scrape the dough in a lump and knead it on a floured working surface for a minute or two. Take two-thirds of the dough for a cottage loaf and keep aside one-third for a fruit loaf.

9. To shape the cottage loaf, lightly roll out the piece of dough and make a division in the center with the edge of your hand. Lift the dough, set it on end and in the lifting twist the top bit slightly to make the divide more marked. Let the top and bottom sections down into each other and secure with a central punch. Place the shaped loaf on a greased baking sheet and bake at 425 degrees for 10 minutes. Lower the temperature to 375 degrees and continue baking for 30 to 40 minutes.

10/11. Add $\frac{1}{3}$ cup seedless white raisins, $\frac{1}{4}$ cup currants, $1\frac{1}{2}$ tablespoons chopped candied peel, 1 tablespoon brown sugar and a pinch of allspice to the remaining piece of dough, place it in a fruit loaf pan, already warmed and greased, and leave to rise for another 30 minutes. Bake according to fruit loaf recipe (p. 30) until the bread is firm and has shrunk away slightly from the sides of the pan.

Plain breads

Use wholewheat, for health and flavor, and bread flour for bounce and texture. Some bread recipes call for fat or milk as these give a richer, moister dough with good lasting qualities.

Daily bread
As the name suggests, this is a good loaf for everyday eating. It requires only one rising made up for by generous kneading.

8 cups wholewheat flour
4 cups bread flour
1 tablespoon salt
1 teaspoon sugar or honey
1 quart warm water
4 packages active dry yeast

Mix the two flours and salt together in a large bowl and warm slightly. Dissolve the honey or sugar in $\frac{1}{2}$ cup of the warm water, stir in the yeast and leave for 10 minutes until frothy. Add the yeast to the flour and mix, adding the rest of the water gradually until the dough forms a lump and leaves the sides of the bowl clean. Transfer the dough to a floured board or table and knead for at least 15 minutes. Place in greased pans or shape into loaves on a greased baking sheet. This amount will make two large 2 lb loaves or four smaller ones. I usually make one big loaf to wrap and keep, and two smaller ones to eat during the next day or two. Slip the loaves into a large oiled plastic bag and leave to rise for 45 minutes to 1 hour in a warm place or 2 to 3 hours at room temperature. When the loaves have doubled in size put them into the oven preheated to 425 degrees and bake for 10 minutes, then turn down to 375 degrees and bake for another 30 to 50 minutes, depending on the size of the loaves. Turn out and leave to cool.

The miller's loaf
This wholegrain bread recipe comes from the miller who supplies my stoneground flour whose mill is illustrated on page 14. His family have been millers since the early 19th century – the mill is still driven by water – and having experimented with a number of different flours they stick with plain wholewheat flour 'for flavor'. The fat makes a much moister loaf.

2 teaspoons sugar or honey
1 quart warm water
2 oz cake compressed yeast or 3 packages active dry yeast
4 tablespoons margarine or lard
12 cups wholewheat flour, preferably stoneground
1 level tablespoon salt

Stir the sugar or honey into about $\frac{1}{2}$ cup of the measured water, crumble the compressed yeast on top (or sprinkle dry) and leave to froth up. Meanwhile work the fat and salt into the warmed flour with your fingers, as if making pie pastry. Combine the yeast mixture with the flour, adding about three-quarters of the remaining water and start mixing. Add the rest of the water slowly until the dough begins lumping together nicely – it should be on the soft side, but not sticky. Sprinkle on more flour if tacky.

Transfer to a floured table and knead for 5 to 10 minutes. Leave to rise under cover, or in a plastic bag, in a warm place until the dough has doubled in size – about 1 hour. Punch down, knead for 3 minutes and divide into pieces that half fill your loaf pans. Shape the dough into loaves on baking sheets. Leave, covered with plastic wrap, in a warm place until the dough has doubled in size again. Bake the loaves at 425 degrees for 15 minutes, then turn down to 375 degrees and bake for a further 30 to 45 minutes, depending on the size of the loaves. Turn out onto a rack and leave until cold before storing.
Note: For a stronger version, add 1 tablespoon of molasses at the stage when you stir the sugar into the water before adding the yeast.

Swedish rye bread
A simplified rye bread, this has the typical rye tang, but is nothing like so sour or dark as the sourdough recipe using wild yeast that follows. Also it is made in one operation, though with more than the usual number of risings. It is particularly good used for open sandwiches in true Scandinavian style.

Do not expect this bread to rise dramatically

after proving the dough – rye flour dough only increases by one-third – because rye flour has little gluten, a protein substance that gives dough enough energy and strength to expand.

1½ cups scalded milk
½ pint water
2 teaspoons honey or sugar
3 teaspoons active dry yeast
2 cups rye flour
3½ cups bread flour
2 teaspoons salt
1 tablespoon caraway seeds (optional)

Scald the milk by heating it until it rises up the pan, then leave it to cool until lukewarm. Into warm water stir the honey or sugar, then the yeast and leave until frothy. Mix the flours and salt together and warm slightly. Add the yeast to the flour, then add the milk, gradually working up to a moderately stiff dough. Mix in the caraway seeds. Turn the dough onto a floured surface, knead for 10 to 15 minutes. Leave in a bowl or bag to rise until it has doubled in size. Punch down, then leave to rise again until it has doubled in size. (This extra punching/rising is to get the most from the rye flour, but can be skipped.) Punch down a second time, knead for a few minutes until firm then fill into oiled pans. Leave to rise once more, then bake at 375 degrees for 40 minutes.

   Sliced thinly, this loaf makes the ideal base for open sandwiches of the smorgasbord variety.

Naturally fermented rye bread

Try this once, if only for a graphic demonstration of how to make a sour, dark, well-risen loaf using the mysterious powers of wild yeast. The recipe was given to me by a Latvian friend and makes the most distinctive continental rye bread I have ever tried. It tastes delicious with cheese and pickles or, more unexpectedly, toasted with honey. It takes 5 days to get a sufficiently strong wild yeast culture – but the wait is justified.

6 cups wholewheat flour
2 cups rye flour
a pinch of salt and sugar
1 pint water

Measure out 1 cup of each flour into a small bowl and mix together with a pinch each of salt and sugar and enough warm water to make a sloppy dough. Leave, uncovered, in a warm place to ferment for 3 days. Add the same amount again of both flours, plus enough water to make a slack dough and another small pinch each of salt and sugar. Leave for another 2 days uncovered and then transfer to a large bowl and mix in the remaining 4 cups of wholewheat flour and 1 teaspoon of salt. Add enough warm water to make a firm but pliable dough. Knead on a floured surface until smooth and springy, shape into French-type loaves pointed at both ends and slip onto a greased baking sheet. Then place them in an oiled plastic bag and leave to rise. This can take all day, but they will rise steadily by about one-third to one-half. Bake at 375 degrees for 45 minutes or until the loaves sound hollow when tapped.

Note : Add 1 tablespoon of caraway seeds with the last amount of flour for extra pungency. If you want to press seeds, nuts or cracked wheat over the top, take the loaf out of the oven 10 minutes before it is done, brush with beaten egg or milk, press on seeds and replace in the oven.

Semolina bread

Semolina (a protein-rich durum wheat flour) gives a close, firm bread nicest eaten warm with butter. Unless cooked in round cakes, the middle remains raw.

1 teaspoon honey
1½ cups warm water
2 teaspoons active dry yeast
2⅔ cups fine semolina
a pinch of salt
1 tablespoon oil

Dissolve the honey in ½ cup of the warm water, then stir in the yeast and leave to froth. Mix the semolina, salt and oil in bowl. Add the yeast mixture, stir, then gradually add more of the warm water and mix to make a soft dough.

   Shape into two round flat cakes, score the tops lightly and then leave to rise in a warm place in an oiled plastic bag. When the cakes are well risen, bake for approximately 30 minutes at 400 degrees.

Emergency and unleavened breads

A speedier leavening agent such as baking powder, or baking soda with buttermilk and cream of tartar will cut down on rising time. Unleavened breads are mostly quick to prepare and are excellent blotting paper for all spicy, juicy, seasoned dishes.

Soda bread

This Irish recipe is the most distinguished of hasty loaves. It is as delicious hot with butter and sharp fruit jelly as it is cold with cheese. Use wholewheat flour if you can.

4 cups wholewheat, or bread, or all-purpose flour
1 teaspoon salt
1 teaspoon cream of tartar
1 teaspoon baking soda
2 tablespoons lard or margarine
1½ cups buttermilk or sour milk

Note: Fresh milk can be soured by stirring in 1 teaspoon of lemon juice or vinegar.

Sift the dry ingredients (flour, salt, cream of tartar, baking soda) into a bowl, rub in the lard or margarine and make a well in the middle. Pour in the liquid a little at a time, mixing until a soft dough forms. Turn onto a floured board, knead lightly for a minute, then pat out into a round about 1½ inches thick and place on a greased baking sheet. Cut a cross on top with a sharp knife and bake at 400 degrees for 35 minutes. Eat hot, warm or cold.

Sesame seed rolls

Chinese in origin, these are easy to make and excellent to serve at an impromptu party.

4 cups all-purpose flour
1 teaspoon baking powder
2 teaspoons sugar
a pinch of salt
1 cup water
¼ cup sesame seeds
1 tablespoon oil, sesame oil preferably

Sift the flour and baking powder together into a bowl. Stir in the sugar, salt and water with a wooden spoon. Collect into a ball with both hands, knead quickly until smooth, then roll out into a salami sized sausage. Cut into 2 inch slices and pat flat into rounds. Moisten one side of each round with water, turn and press with the damp side facing down into a plate of sesame seeds. Heat a large, heavy skillet, or griddle, and wipe over with a film of sesame seed oil. Put the rounds in, plain side downwards, and cook for about 5 minutes or until lightly browned. Move to the broiler, not too near the heat, and cook for a few minutes, until the seeds start to toast. Serve hot.

Pitta bread

This needs ascorbic acid (vitamin C) and fresh yeast but is the quickest route to properly leavened bread. Rolls or *pittas* made this way are best eaten hot. Yeast battens on vitamin C, as any winemaker knows, cutting rising time to a minimum.

1 25 mg ascorbic acid tablet
1½ cups warm milk
1 oz (¼ cake) compressed yeast
2 tablespoons margarine or lard
4 cups bread or all-purpose flour
1 teaspoon sugar
1 teaspoon salt
beaten egg to brush over tops (optional)

Crush the tablet and stir into ½ cup of the milk with the crumbled yeast. Rub the fat into the sifted flour, mix in the sugar and salt, make a well in the middle and add the yeast mixture. Stir, adding the rest of the milk gradually to make a firm dough. Turn this onto a floured surface and knead well for about 10 minutes until smooth and springy. Leave to rise in a bowl in a warm place. Knead again for 1 minute, then divide into 12 pieces. Shape these into round balls or flattened ovals (*pittas*) and arrange well apart on a greased baking sheet. Put them all into an oiled bag and leave to rise in a warm place until doubled in size. Brush with the beaten egg, and bake at 400 degrees for 10 to 15 minutes.
Note: Poppy seeds can be sprinkled over the egg glaze, before replacing in the oven. The seeds scorch if you do it at the start.

Baking powder bread

Use this dough to make speedy bread for hungry people.

4 cups all-purpose flour
1 tablespoon baking powder
1 teaspoon salt
2 tablespoons butter or margarine
1 pint warm milk

Sift together the flour, baking powder and salt and rub in the fat. Stir in the milk, mixing quickly with a wooden spoon. Turn onto a floured board, shape into a round, cut a cross on the top and place on a baking sheet. Bake at 400 degrees for 30 to 40 minutes.

Corn pones

Cornmeal is the basis of many endearingly homely types of bread like this 'low down corn pone' to quote Huckleberry Finn in Mark Twain's novel of the same name.

3 cups cornmeal
1 teaspoon baking powder
1 teaspoon salt
1¼ cups warm water and milk mixed
2 tablespoons finely chopped onions (optional)

Sift the cornmeal and baking powder into a bowl, add salt. Stir the liquid gradually into the flour, adding a little onion as you go. The dough should be soft but not sloppy. Turn onto a floured surface, flour both hands and shape pieces of dough into 'pones', oblong cakes about the size of a small envelope, and ¾ in thick. Put onto a greased baking sheet, brush tops with milk and bake at 400 degrees for 20 to 30 minutes, or until golden brown. Eat hot, dripping with butter.

Chapatis

The simplest Indian bread, unleavened and earthy tasting with a pleasantly dry homespun texture. The only problem in making chapatis is to judge the cooking heat so that they cook but do not scorch and smoke out the kitchen. They can be buttered on one side for a richer flavor before wrapping in a cloth to keep them warm before serving.

2 cups wholewheat flour
2 cups bread flour
1 teaspoon salt
1½ cups water

Sift the flours together with the salt. Add the water gradually to make a stiff but workable dough. Knead thoroughly until pliable, adding a drop more water if necessary. Cover with a damp cloth and leave for 2 to 3 hours. Knead again. Pinch off egg-sized lumps, roll between your palms into round balls, flatten on a floured surface and roll out very thinly to about the size of a side plate. Heat a heavy cast iron skillet over a moderate flame, put in a chapati, and cook for 1 minute until brown spots appear underneath. Turn over and repeat, pressing it gently with a cloth to make it puff up. As each chapati is done, put into a clean cloth, wrapping them to keep hot and soft.

Simit

Unleavened bread shaped in decorative rings, sprinkled with sesame seeds. In Turkey they are peddled through the streets slung on poles.

2 cups all-purpose flour
1 teaspoon salt
4 tablespoons margarine
1 tablespoon oil
1 tablespoon milk
1 tablespoon water
1 egg
approx 3 tablespoons sesame seeds

Mix the flour and salt in bowl and make a well in the middle. Melt the margarine over gentle heat, mix with oil, milk, water and beaten egg and stir this into the flour. Mix to a dough – it will feel slippery but can be worked quite easily. Knead for a minute or two. Shape with floured hands into rings about the diameter of a saucer, arrange on a greased baking sheet. Brush over with milk and sprinkle with sesame seeds. Bake at 400 degrees for about 30 minutes or until golden brown.

Simit makes a delicious breakfast bread and because of its quick mixing, kneading and baking, can be made in time for an early morning start.

Fancy breads

Traditionally a fancy bread would be made with odd pieces of dough left over from the weekly bread baking. By adding an egg, sugar and a handful of dried fruit the plain dough became a sweet loaf or small rolls.

Christmas bread

Traditional fare over the Christmas period, this fragrant but not over-sweet bread is made with a mixture of rye and all-purpose flour, moistened with stout. In Sweden this bread is flavored with cardamom, a deliciously scented spice, that has been popular in Scandinavia since the Vikings.

1 teaspoon sugar
¾ cup warm milk or water
2 packages active dry yeast
2 tablespoons butter or margarine
1½ cups stout or dark beer
⅔ cup light corn syrup
3 cups rye flour
3 cups bread flour
finely grated rind of 1 large orange
1 tablespoon caraway seeds or seeds from 8 cardamom
  pods
a pinch of salt

Dissolve the sugar in the milk or water, stir in the yeast and leave for 10 minutes until frothy. Melt the fat, beat in the stout and continue beating until lukewarm, then beat in the syrup and mix until smooth. Sift both flours together, and divide into three bowls, so that you have 3 cups in one, 1¾ cups in the next, and 1¼ cups in the last.

Add the stout mixture to the 3-cup bowl of flour, beat well, add the yeast mixture and beat again until thoroughly blended. Now add the grated orange rind, caraway or cardamom seeds and a pinch of salt and beat in the 1¾ cups of flour a little at a time. When the dough is thoroughly blended, with a shiny appearance, leave to rise under cover or in an oiled plastic bag until almost doubled in size. Shake the last bowl of flour over the work top and tip the dough out on top, kneading it so as to pick up all the loose flour. Divide in half and shape into two long French-type loaves on a greased baking sheet. Cover again with plastic and leave until well risen. Bake at 350 degrees for 45 minutes. After 30 minutes glaze the tops of the loaves quickly with some syrup or honey diluted with a little water. When cooked, leave to cool on racks, re-glaze the tops, and, when cold, wrap in clean dishtowels to keep the crust soft until the bread is eaten.

Fruit loaf

This delicious sweet bread is a traditional Celtic recipe, known as Bara Brith in Wales and Barm Brack in Ireland.

I usually bake a fancy loaf at the same time as I bake plain breads. See page 25 for the illustrated instructions.

2 tablespoons brown sugar
1½ cups lukewarm milk
2 packages active dry yeast
4 cups bread or wholewheat flour or a mixture of both
⅔ cup seedless white raisins
½ cup currants
3 tablespoons chopped candied peel
4 tablespoons margarine or butter
a pinch of ground allspice
a pinch of salt
1 egg

Dissolve a little of the sugar in half the milk, add the yeast, stir and leave for 10 minutes until frothy. Warm the sifted flour slightly in one bowl and the fruit and peel in another. Rub the fat into the flour, then stir in fruit, peel, spice, remaining sugar and salt and mix well. Beat the egg. Make a well in the flour, add the yeast mixture and the egg, then as much of the remaining warm milk as is needed to make a soft dough. Cover and leave to rise in a warm place for 2 hours.

Turn out onto a floured board and knead for 5 minutes. Put into a greased, *warmed* 9 × 5 × 3 inch loaf pan and place in an oiled plastic bag to rise for 30 minutes. Bake at 400 degrees for 20 minutes; lower the heat to 325 degrees and bake for a further 20 to 30 minutes, or until the bread is firm and has shrunk away slightly from the sides of the pan. Turn out and brush the top with a spoonful of honey to glaze. Slice and eat cold.

Shaping your loaf

1. Naturally fermented rye bread: like French-type loaves, it is made by rolling out the dough to the length required with the palms of your hands. If you want a crusty loaf, score it like this to get as much crust as possible. Also bake one smooth and plain to keep longer.

2. Hot cross buns: light, spicy fruit dough is divided after kneading into a dozen buns, placed on greased baking sheets and marked on top by a knife with the shape of a cross (the buns are traditionally eaten on Good Friday). After rising again for 30 minutes, the buns are baked for 15 minutes. When cool, they are glazed with sugar dissolved in milk.

3. Onion and herb bread: plain bread can be dressed up for savory loaves. Add herbs to a plain dough, punch it into a round flat shape, brush with beaten egg, then top with overlapping fried onion rings, sprinkle with coarse salt and bake.

4/5. Swedish Christmas bread: a fancy shape for a fruit bread, with two twists of bread dough pinched together at the top then twisted around each other loosely. Coiled into a greased Savarin or tube pan, the dough is left to rise for 30 minutes, then baked.

6. Plain white bread: roll out a long strip of bread dough, and cut two vertical lines almost to the top to separate the dough into three strands. Braid these and pinch together the dough ends top and bottom before baking. Ten minutes before baking time is up, brush with beaten egg and sprinkle with poppy seeds.

Apple bread

Serve this German version of the fruit loaf, with the added juiciness of a paving of sliced apple on top, as a dessert, warm, with cream.

3 cups bread flour
a pinch of salt
1 heaping teaspoon sugar
1½ cups milk
2 packages active dry yeast
4 tablespoons margarine or butter
1 egg
⅔ cup seedless white raisins
3 or 4 tart dessert apples
sugar and ground cinnamon to sprinkle on top

Sift together the flour and salt and warm slightly. Stir a little sugar into the milk, add the yeast, mix and leave for 10 minutes until frothy. Melt the fat over a gentle heat. Make a well in the flour and stir in first the yeast, then the well-beaten egg, and finally the melted fat. Beat this mixture well with a spoon and leave in a warm place to rise until doubled in bulk. Turn onto a floured board and knead for a few minutes, or until smooth, then work in the raisins and knead again to distribute them evenly. Press the dough into a well-greased 8 or 9 inch cake pan. Peel, core and thinly slice the apples. Press the slices into the dough.

 Brush over the surface with water, sprinkle thickly with sugar and a little cinnamon and leave for 20 minutes in an oiled plastic bag to rise. Bake at 350 degrees for 45 minutes. Serve warm with whipped cream or ice cream.

Onion and herb bread

Plain bread dough can, of course, be dressed up for savory, as well as sweet loaves. If your tastes incline that way, try this simple but tasty bread using about half the quantity of dough made according to the plain white bread recipe. On page 31 this bread is illustrated.

½ quantity white bread dough (see p. 23)
1 teaspoon dried white thyme, marjoram or dill seeds
2 onions
oil or margarine for frying
beaten egg
coarse salt

At the punching down stage, mix the dried herbs well into the dough. Leave to rise for 20 to 30 minutes. Meanwhile, fry thinly sliced onion rings in a little oil or margarine until softened and drain on paper towels. Just before baking, brush the top of the loaf with beaten egg and spread with overlapping onion rings, pressing them down slightly. Sprinkle coarse salt all over. Bake as for plain white bread, but check after 20 minutes to see if the onions are browning. If so lay a piece of buttered or oiled baking paper on top. Can be eaten hot or cold.

Note: You can of course vary the selection of herbs according to what you happen to have in your storecupboard.

Hot cross buns

These are made and eaten, by ancient custom, on Good Friday to mark the crucifixion. They only need to be made without the cross mark on top to become light spicy fruit buns to eat any day of the year.

¾ cup milk
¼ cup plus 1 teaspoon sugar
1 package active dry yeast
3 cups bread or all-purpose flour
1 teaspoon salt
2 tablespoons butter or margarine
1 teaspoon mixed spices (ground ginger, cinnamon,
 cloves and grated nutmeg)
⅔ cup currants
1 egg

Warm the milk slightly, stir in 1 teaspoon of sugar and sprinkle the yeast onto it. Leave it for 10 minutes, until frothy. Sift the flour and salt, rub in the fat and stir in the spices, remaining sugar and fruit. Mix in the well beaten egg and the yeast mixture. Beat until smooth, adding a little more milk if needed – the dough should be soft. Turn onto a floured board and knead until springy and smooth. Leave the dough inside an oiled plastic bag at room temperature until doubled in size. Knead again lightly until firm, then divide into 12 pieces and set these out – not too close – on greased baking sheets. Mark a cross on the tops with a knife, then leave for about 30 minutes to rise again. Touch up the crosses and then bake at 425 degrees near the top of the oven for about 15 minutes. If they seem in danger of scorching, lower the oven heat to 400 degrees after 10 minutes. Glaze the tops by brushing them with 1 tablespoon of sugar dissolved in 1 tablespoon of milk.

Note: For extra light buns, leave the dough to rise overnight in a cool place before you add the sugar, spices and fruit. The next day, add them and proceed with a second rising and the rest of the steps, as above. The crosses can be made with a little frosting, if you prefer.

Croissants

Anyone who makes their own puff pastry will find no difficulty producing excellent croissants, essentially rolls made with a leavened puff pastry. Nothing is more delicious, and you can make a dozen for the price of two in the bakery. Better still, if you have a freezer, make three times that number in one session and freeze the surplus.

1 teaspoon sugar
1¼ cups warm water
2 packages active dry yeast
1 egg
2 tablespoons lard
4 cups all-purpose flour
2 teaspoons salt
12 tablespoons margarine
beaten egg to glaze

Dissolve the sugar in the water, stir in the yeast and leave for 10 minutes until foaming. Add the egg, well beaten, to the yeast mixture. Rub the lard into the sifted flour and salt. Mix in the yeast mixture, then knead for 5 to 10 minutes, until smooth. Roll out the dough on a lightly floured surface to make a rectangle of approximately 20 × 8 inches and ¾ inch thick. Take one-third of the margarine, break it up into small pieces and dot the pieces evenly over two-thirds of the dough rectangle. Fold the plain third over towards the center, then cover with the remaining 'dotted' third and press the edges down with the rolling pin to seal.

Repeat this twice, rolling out the strip to the same size, dotting it with margarine, folding and sealing. By now you will have used up all the margarine. Chill the dough in the refrigerator for

1 hour, then do three more rollings and foldings but without adding any fat. Return to the refrigerator for 30 minutes to 1 hour, or until firm and cool.

Roll out on a lightly floured surface to make a sheet 29 × 15 inches, trim the edges and cut into 6 inch equilateral triangles. Roll up the triangles from base to point, bending them into the characteristic horseshoe shape. Place them on greased baking sheets, brush with egg glaze and leave uncovered to rise for 30 minutes in a warm place. Brush again with egg glaze and bake at 425 degrees for about 20 minutes.

For freezing, bake the croissants until they are light brown then remove from the heat promptly. Otherwise leave 2 to 3 minutes longer, until golden brown.

To freeze. Cool, pack in rigid containers, store for up to 2 months.

To thaw. Bake the croissants at 350 degrees for 15 minutes.

Croissants, rolls made with leavened puff pastry, are shaped by cutting the dough into 6 inch equilateral triangles. Roll up the triangles from base to point, bending into the horseshoe shapes, illustrated above. Place on ungreased baking sheets, brush the tops with egg glaze and leave to rise for 30 minutes. Brush again with egg glaze and bake at 425 degrees for 20 minutes.

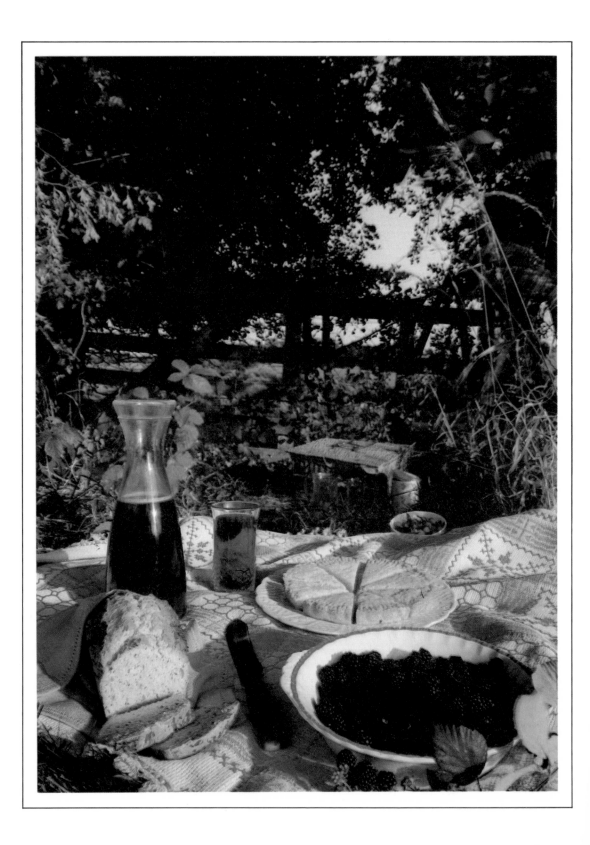

Cakes &
Cookies

...her mistress ... now sat in state,
pretending not to know what cakes were sent up,
though she knew, and we knew, and she knew that we knew,
and we knew that she knew that we knew,
she had been busy all morning
making tea-bread and sponge-cakes.'
Cranford   Elizabeth Gaskell   1853

Baking cakes and cookies and suchlike confections has always provided good cooks with a chance to shine. Indeed, the best of them made quite a name for themselves in their day. Mrs Macnab, for instance, a 19th-century Scottish farmer's wife, was so famous for her fine baking that she enticed royalty to tea from nearby Balmoral castle, bringing with them such distinguished guests as King Frederick of Prussia. What drew the royals was not some rococo cake, sumptuously frosted and oozing cream, but a plain – though perfect – scone. I came across an almost identical recipe recently, described as 'Queen Victoria's favourite scone' which suggests that the formidable little lady was as quick as the next housewife when it came to wheedling a good recipe out of a friend. Refined simplicity is the hallmark of the best traditional recipes, which brings them right into line with contemporary tastes in food. I find children who are not concerned with 'eating for health' will devour a plateful of the plainest homemade water biscuits with a sprinkling of coarse salt. But simplicity is not a rigid rule as birthdays would not be the same without a sticky chocolate cake. So I have included a recipe for this and one or two more fanciful confections for special occasions. To enjoy really delicious cakes you simply have to make them yourself – all but the most expensive commercial confectionery proves sickly and synthetic tasting. None of the recipes in this section should prove too difficult, even for beginners, but remember that cake, roll and cookie making is something of an exact science. All the minor details like accurate measuring, the right oven setting, conscientious beating and creaming really do *matter*. Make cakes when you are in a calm, confident frame of mind and have the kitchen to yourself for a couple of hours. If the worst happens and the cake sinks in the middle, do not rage or panic – cut out the gooey bit, fill it with whipped cream and serve it as a pudding.

Late summer blackberry picnicking: shortbread wedges made with ground rice to give a light, short texture, ideal for picnics as it keeps well in a pan, caraway tea bread, sliced and eaten with butter, and blackberry cordial to mix with sparkling soda.

Baking

Cakes

A firm grasp of the basic principles helps in cake making. The object of the laborious beating and creaming is to force as much air into the batter as possible and so make the cake rise. Most recipes, though not all, also require a leavening agent like baking powder (self-rising flour has its baking powder built in) or baking soda plus cream of tartar. These agents react with liquid and heat to produce a gas, carbon dioxide, which expands and makes the cake rise as it cooks. But don't expect them to raise your cake unaided. Probably the commonest mistake in cake making is to imagine that you can cut down on the creaming or beating if you double up on the baking powder. As a result the cake rises like a hot-air balloon, then drops like a balloon with a puncture, and you are left with something dry, crumbly and heavy. *Moral:* get an electric mixer, or stick to scones, rolls and tea breads which do not need beating.

Always make sure before leaping into action that everything you will need in the way of equipment and ingredients are close to hand, and, if possible, ready for use: pans greased, oven preheated, eggs separated.

For light mixtures sift the flour with the baking powder *three* times, to aerate it. A metal spoon should be used to fold flour into a beaten mixture as a wooden spoon will squash those vital air bubbles. The secret of a foolproof cake is to use extra egg yolks as they emulsify the mixture better and keep it stable during cooking. One or two tablespoons of hot water mixed into a well-beaten – especially electrically beaten – batter at the last minute will make a moister cake. The grated rind of an orange or lemon mixed into the batter will transform a plain cake. If you want the flavor of almonds, use the whole variety, lightly toasted and then chopped. However, bought ground almonds can be added to rich fruit cakes to prevent the fruit from sinking. If you are using cocoa to flavor cakes, mix a little boiling water into it first to take the raw taste off. Spirits, which are expensive, are best poured over the cooked cake, not mixed into the batter. That way you will keep all the flavor and bouquet (heat volatilizes alcohol) and the alcohol will help preserve the cake.

Baking times

Baking times vary according not only to the recipe, but the size and shape of your container and the idiosyncrasies of your oven. Deep cakes keep better but need longer cooking at a lower setting. Don't open the oven door before the end of the recommended cooking time as a rush of cold air may make the cake sink. To test if a cake is done press lightly with a finger, and it will spring back when ready. If in doubt insert a skewer or knife down the center; if it comes out clean, the cake is ready. Leave it to cool in the pan for five minutes before turning out on a cake rack.

Cookies

For crisp, short cookies use block not tub margarine, so they do not spread everywhere, and 3 to 4 tablespoons of ground rice or cornstarch in place of some of the wheat flour. If the mixture is crumbly, bind it with an extra egg yolk. Again, do not handle them too much, or the fat will soften, resulting in leathery biscuits. Do not store cookies in the same tin as cakes, or they will absorb moisture and soften. Stored in a separate tin they should remain crisp for several weeks.

Equipment

A hand-held electric beater takes the ache out of cake making and is more useful than the fixed kind because it can be moved from the work top to the stove for different purposes. A fine meshed strainer or sieve – wire or plastic – is essential. Save time by measuring out the dry ingredients beforehand, very carefully on kitchen scales, either spring balanced or the old-fashioned kind with separate weights. A set of measuring spoons is also essential – too much baking powder is as disastrous to the end result, as too little. One large bowl and several smaller ones are essential for mixing and separating eggs. Wooden spoons are required for beating and creaming the cake mixture if you do not own an electric blender. The non-stick variety of cake pan is more expensive but it does save time spent greasing and flouring. For deeper cakes, pans with detachable bottoms are useful. Grease the pans by brushing them over with a pastry brush dipped in oil or melted lard. Tip a little flour into the pan as a further guard against sticking and shake until evenly coated. Tube pans, plain or fancy, add glamour to brioche-type cakes. Cookies may be cut with a cup or glass, but children love the more amusing cut-out shapes and these are available in tin or rigid plastic. Foil is essential for wrapping cakes for long storage (fruit cakes and Christmas cakes) but use a layer of wax first, then foil, or the acid in the fruit will eat through the foil and leave you wondering whether mice have got there first. Store cakes and cookies in *separate* airtight tins or plastic containers with lids. Light spongy cakes do not keep well so eat them fast. Rich fruit cakes and moist, sticky teabreads like the gingerbread on the next page, however, improve with keeping.

Tin cookie cutters like these can be used with a short crisp cookie mixture like Dutch butter cookies to cut fancy shapes before baking: just press the mix into the pan to bake, and cool biscuits before turning out and frosting. Roll the mixture thinly to make the crinkle-edged cookies, more thickly to decorate a Christmas tree with heart and star shapes.

Cakes and tea breads

A clutch of plainish cakes for everyday eating and a few lavish ones for birthdays or to round off a dinner party. Beginners should tackle the tea breads first as the essence here is a simple loaf whereas the fluffier cakes require conscientious beating.

Caraway tea bread

Tea bread in this case means a plain cake which should be baked in a loaf pan, to be sliced and eaten with lots of butter. The caraway seeds – beloved of Victorian cooking – give it a unique flavor.

3 cups all-purpose flour
2 teaspoons baking powder
¾ cup sugar
6 tablespoons butter or margarine
about ¾ cup scalded milk
1 egg
1 tablespoon ground caraway seeds

Sift the flour and baking powder twice, add the sugar and lightly rub in the butter or margarine. Mix the milk, which has been left to cool a little, with the well-beaten egg and ground caraway seeds. (To achieve the best flavor, lightly heat the seeds in a skillet for a minute and then pound in a mortar or whizz in an electric coffee grinder.) Stir the milk and egg mixture into the dry ingredients, beat until well mixed, then turn onto a floured board and knead quickly. Put into a $9 \times 5 \times 3$ inch loaf pan. Bake at 375 degrees for 60 minutes, or until it feels firm on top. If in doubt, cover the top with buttered baking paper to prevent scorching, and bake for another 10 minutes.

Mrs Macnab's featherweight scones

Mrs Macnab was a 19th-century Scottish farmer's wife whose fine baking enticed royalty to tea. Best eaten with jam and cream as illustrated on page 78.

4 cups all-purpose flour
1 teaspoon baking soda
2 teaspoons cream of tartar
1 teaspoon salt
4 tablespoons butter
1 egg
1½ cups sour milk or buttermilk

Note: Use fresh milk soured by stirring in $\frac{1}{2}$ teaspoon lemon juice, or milk which has just 'turned' naturally, but *not* milk 3 days old and bitter tasting. Buttermilk, if you can get it, is best of all as the acid in it reacts with the leavening agents to produce a lighter texture.

Sift the flour with the soda, cream of tartar and salt. Sift again. Rub in the butter. Stir in the well-beaten egg, then the sour milk or buttermilk. Keep stirring until the dough collects in a lump, then turn it onto a floured surface and knead for a few seconds until smooth. Break off little pieces and flatten them with your knuckles on a greased baking sheet to form a roughly round shape. Do *not* roll. Prick with a fork. Bake at 425 degrees for 8 to 10 minutes, or until just colored on top. Wrap the scones in a clean cloth to keep warm and soft.

Nutcake

A characteristically sophisticated Austrian confection, rich but not sickly thanks to the stiffening of chopped nuts. Walnuts, hazelnuts or almonds (or a mixture) can be used with varying effect. Observe that the cake uses no flour, only breadcrumbs.

1 cup dry white breadcrumbs (see below)
1 tablespoon rum
⅔ cup sugar
5 eggs, separated
1¼ cups chopped nuts
1¼ cups whipping or heavy cream

Make the breadcrumbs by whizzing up stale bread in a grinder. Put them in a low oven for a few minutes to dry out. To make the cake, first mix half the rum with the breadcrumbs. In a bowl over a pan of hot water beat the sugar and egg yolks together until thick, creamy and a trail of the mixture dropped on top holds its shape for a few seconds. Beat the egg whites until stiff then, using a metal spoon, gently fold the egg whites, breadcrumbs and nuts into the fluffy beaten yolk mixture, trying not to crush the mixture as you blend. When well blended spoon gently into a greased and floured 8 inch cake pan and bake at 375 degrees for between 45 minutes and 1 hour. Test with a skewer down the middle – if it comes out clean, the cake is done. Cut into two layers and sandwich with slightly sweetened whipped cream flavored with 1 tablespoon of rum and the same amount of chopped nuts. Serve this as a dessert, accompanied for a lavish effect by a dish of peaches or apricots preserved in brandy.

Mary Ball Washington's gingerbread

We owe this most sumptuous of dark, spicy, sticky gingerbreads to the mother of the first President of the United States. One or two slight modifications such as nutmeg in place of mace have been made to tone it down a little for modern palates, but essentially it is just as it was served to an appreciative Marquis de Lafayette close on 200 years ago.

8 tablespoons butter
⅔ cup dark brown sugar
3 cups all-purpose flour
1 teaspoon cream of tartar
1 cup seedless white raisins
¾ cup warm milk
¼ cup sherry
2 tablespoons ground ginger
2 teaspoons ground cinnamon
1 tablespoon freshly grated nutmeg
⅔ cup light corn syrup
⅓ cup molasses
3 eggs
1 large orange
1 teaspoon baking soda dissolved in 2 tablespoons warm
  water

Grease two oblong pans (about $8 \times 7 \times 2\frac{1}{2}$ inches) and line them with baking paper. In one bowl cream the butter with the sugar until soft, light and non-gritty. Sift the flour and cream of tartar into a second bowl and add the raisins. In a third bowl mix together the milk, sherry, spices, syrup, molasses and beaten eggs. Add the flour mixture alternately with the milk and spice mixture to the basic creamed butter and sugar. Beat thoroughly until well mixed. Finally beat in the orange juice and grated rind, plus the dissolved baking soda.

Pour into the pans and bake at 325 degrees for 30 minutes, then reduce to 275 degrees, and bake for another 30 to 40 minutes. Leave to cool before removing from the pan. Sliced thinly and buttered, this gingerbread is delicious.

Sticky chocolate cake with fudge frosting

Children and men adore this – ladies on a diet must just look the other way. It makes a splendidly archetypal birthday cake which can be jazzed up with silver balls, piped messages, candles or what you will.

2 cups all-purpose flour
2 tablespoons cocoa powder
1 teaspoon baking soda
⅔ cup light corn syrup
¾ cup milk
½ cup sugar
8 tablespoons margarine
1 egg

Sift the flour, cocoa powder and baking soda into a bowl. Melt the syrup, together with the milk, sugar and margarine over a gentle heat, stirring until blended. Cool a little and then add the beaten egg to this mixture. Now add the liquid ingredients gradually to the flour, beating all the time. Pour the mixture into a greased and paper-lined 7 inch square cake pan or $9 \times 5 \times 3$ inch loaf pan. Bake at 300 degrees until it feels firm to the touch. Frost with fudge mixture while still warm for the best flavor and texture.

Fudge frosting

2 cups confectioners' sugar
2 tablespoons cocoa powder
6 tablespoons shortening
6 tablespoons granulated sugar
3 tablespoons milk
1 teaspoon vanilla extract or coffee powder

Sift the confectioners' sugar with the cocoa into a bowl. Melt the shortening and granulated sugar in a pan, add the milk and flavoring and bring to a boil. Tip into the bowl containing the confectioners' sugar and beat until fluffy – about 1 minute – with a wooden spoon. Pour quickly over the cake.

Crackers and cookies

Ground rice or cornstarch can be added in place of all-purpose flour to make cookie textures light and short. If the mixture is too crumbly, you can add an extra egg yolk.

Oatcakes

Useful when you run out of bread as they are quick to make. Oatcakes freeze well.

1 cup fine or medium oatmeal (not cereal oats)
½ cup sifted all-purpose flour
½ teaspoon salt
¼ teaspoon baking soda
3 tablespoons butter, margarine or lard
2 tablespoons boiling water

Mix the dry ingredients (oatmeal, flour, salt, soda) together in a bowl. Melt the fat in the boiling water, add to the dry mixture and knead lightly (adding a drop more water if needed to give a firm dough). Then roll out thinly on a surface floured with a handful of oatmeal and cut into triangles with a knife. Bake on a greased baking sheet at 400 degrees for 15 minutes until crisp in a hot oven. Leave on a rack in a warm place to dry out until crisp.

Shortbread

A particularly good version of the Scottish classic as the ground rice gives a light, short texture. These keep well in a tin.

1 cup all-purpose flour
⅔ cup ground rice
8 tablespoons butter or margarine
½ cup sugar
1 beaten egg yolk
2 tablespoons cream or half-and-half

Sift the flour and ground rice together into a bowl and rub in the butter or margarine quickly as for pie pastry. Mix in the sugar, then stir in the egg yolk and the cream to make a stiff dough. Roll out on a lightly floured surface until approximately $\frac{1}{4}$ inch thick. Cut out with a cookie cutter, glass or cup, lay on greased baking paper on a baking sheet and bake at 350 degrees for 15 minutes or until golden brown. Cool on a cake rack.

Grissini

These are the crisp bread sticks you nibble in Italian restaurants.

2 cups all-purpose flour
¼ teaspoon baking powder
½ teaspoon salt
1 tablespoon butter or margarine
2 to 3 tablespoons boiling water

Sift the dry ingredients (flour, baking powder, salt) into a bowl, rub in the fat finely and add just enough water to make a stiff dough. Turn onto a floured board, knead until quite smooth, then roll small lumps between both palms until just thicker than a pencil and about 9 inches long. Lay on a greased baking sheet and bake at 325 degrees for 40 minutes or until hard and lightly tanned. Leave to cool before eating or storing in an airtight tin.

Crackers

These are ridiculously easy to make, cheaper than the bought kind, and extremely delicious with cheese.

2 cups all-purpose flour
1 teaspoon baking powder
a pinch of salt
4 tablespoons margarine or lard
¾ cup water
ground coarse salt

Sift together the flour, baking powder and salt and rub in the fat finely. Add just enough water to mix to a firm dough. Roll out thinly on a lightly floured surface with a floured rolling pin. Stamp out rounds, prick them all over with a fork, sprinkle with ground coarse salt and bake on a lightly greased baking sheet at 325 degrees for 20 minutes or until golden and crisp. Cool on a rack and store in an airtight tin. Crisp up, if necessary, in a warm oven for 3 or 4 minutes before eating.

Brandy snaps

These look impressive with their lacy texture, but they are easy to make. You don't *have* to use brandy, they are tasty without – some people fill them with whipped cream.

¼ cup sugar
3 tablespoons light corn syrup
4 tablespoons butter
½ cup sifted all-purpose flour
½ teaspoon ground ginger
½ teaspoon grated lemon rind
1 teaspoon brandy (optional)

Melt the sugar, syrup and butter together in a pan, then stir in the flour, ginger, lemon rind and brandy and mix well. Drop the mixture a teaspoon at a time onto a greased baking sheet, leaving a space of 3 inches between each. Bake at 275 degrees for about 10 minutes. Leave on the sheet to 'set' for a few minutes, then detach and roll around the handle of a wooden spoon to make the characteristic tube shape. Cool before storing.

Dutch butter cookies

Short, crisp and pretty with their whole almond decoration, these are good cookies to make and store (they will keep excellently in a tin) for all contingencies. For a change add ½ teaspoon of your favorite spice to the mixture.

8 tablespoons butter
⅔ cup raw sugar
2 cups all-purpose flour
1 egg
½ cup whole blanched almonds

Cream the butter with the sugar until fluffy, then mix in the sifted flour. Bind with the beaten egg. Roll out thinly and cut into small 2 inch rounds. Brush over with milk, press one whole almond onto each round and bake at 350 degrees for 15 minutes until the almonds are lightly browned.

Cheese biscuits

Nicest eaten hot and peppery from the oven.

½ cup sifted all-purpose plain flour
¼ teaspoon cayenne pepper
¼ teaspoon salt
4 tablespoons butter or margarine
½ cup grated cheese (Cheddar or Parmesan)
1 egg yolk mixed with 1 teaspoon of water

Sieve the flour and seasonings, rub in the butter finely, then mix in the grated cheese. Stir in enough of the egg mixture to make a stiff, dryish paste. Knead lightly, roll out on a floured surface until ¼ inch thick, prick well with a fork, then stamp into rounds or cut into fingers. Put on a greased baking sheet and bake at 375 degrees for 7 to 10 minutes.

For brandy snaps, drop teaspoonfuls of the mixture onto a greased baking sheet, spacing 3 inches apart. Bake at 300 degrees for 10 minutes. Leave on the sheet to set for a few minutes, detach and roll around a wooden spoon handle to make the tube shapes. Cool.

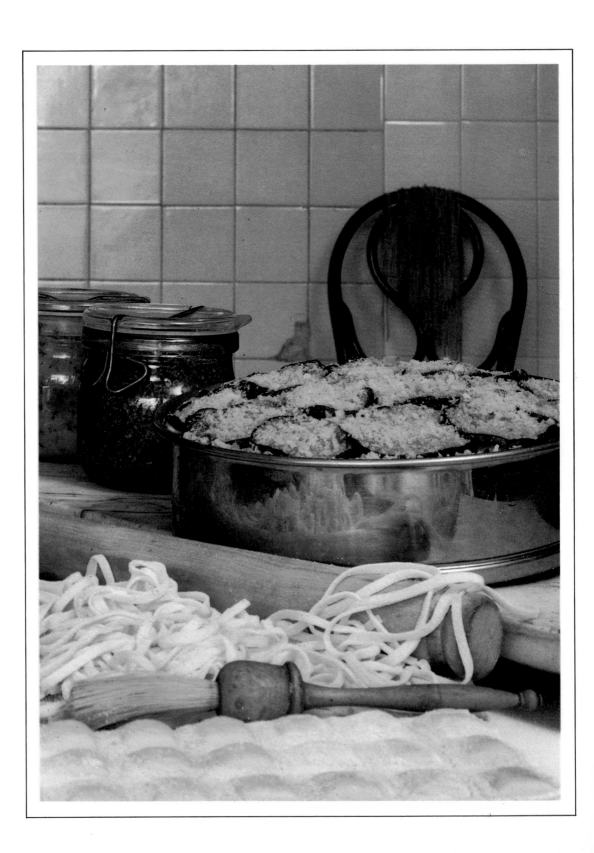

Pasta

'The angels in Paradise eat nothing but vermicelli al pomodoro'
Duke of Bovino, Mayor of Naples 1930

Some say Marco Polo, the 15th-century explorer, brought the first pasta back from the Grand Cham's court, others that he introduced it there. Whatever the truth, the fact remains that pasta in some shape or other – Italians have by far the widest and shapeliest – is eaten almost everywhere in the world. Essentially, pasta uses bread flour, with eggs added for richness and sometimes spinach for flavor and color. Durum wheat is used commercially for its keeping properties. Health buffs will use wholewheat flour but this has the disadvantage of being harder to work.

It ranks alongside mankind's most ancient foods like bread, lentils and rice, sharing their characteristics of extreme simplicity, versatility and convenience. With just a little flour and water, perhaps an egg or two, and a pot on the boil, you had the makings of a substantial meal, which could be filled out with cheese, herbs, meat or vegetables, as available. It was first heard of 6,000 years ago in China, reappeared on the menus of Imperial Rome and was carried by Mongol herdsmen in their saddlebags, conveniently frozen by the bitter winter weather. Over the centuries, pasta has undergone all the refinements and elaboration that imaginative chefs could devise. This delightfully plastic substance has lent itself to hundreds of dishes, ranging from the hearty peasant dishes of the Abruzzi, eaten with *pecorino*, a pungent sheep's milk cheese, to a sophisticated *timballo*, or pastry crust filled with richly stuffed pasta and seasoned with fresh truffles. But, of course, all this is mere top dressing for essentially, pasta today retains the sturdy simplicity of its humble origins.

All pasta connoisseurs, Italian, Chinese or whatever, agree that the best pasta, in point of flavor and texture, is fresh, homemade pasta made with eggs. This is known as pasta *al uovo*, or *mien* in China. There are many varieties of commercial dried pasta, or pasta *secca*, on display in good Italian grocery stores, or delicatessens but, when made well, fresh pasta has a clean delicate flavor and bite which makes commercial pasta taste stodgy and heavy by comparison. A plate of homemade *fettuccine* (narrow noodles) eaten with the simplest of sauces – sour cream, *pesto*, sesame seed sauce, or nothing more than a lump of butter and chopped fresh herbs – is a noble dish. The first step is learning to make good pasta, and for this you need the simplest ingredients and equipment, time, muscle and a little perseverance. Your first batch of tagliatelle may resemble a bunch of rubber snakes, but, with practice, you will be able to produce paper thin noodles in 20 minutes flat.

Fresh ribbons of tagliatelle beside ravioli sheets filled with savory beef, ready to cook and serve with one of the sauces in jars, either fresh tomato sauce or the green pesto made from fresh basil and, right, eggplant and pasta pie made with tagliatelle.

Pasta making

The rule of thumb every Italian girl learns is an egg and a small pinch of salt to 1 cup of flour. This makes a generous portion for one person, so if you are making pasta for six, 5 cups of flour and 5 large eggs will be ample. Some recipes advocate using a little oil too, for extra suppleness. Bread flour, as sold for baking, gives the most flavor. Wholewheat flour is impossibly crumbly. Commercial pasta, or pasta *secca*, uses durum wheat flour, or semolina, which has a high gluten content. If your dough stays too dry to make a nice lump you can use another egg or – cautiously – a little water to make up the moisture content. Purists groan at this, but I do not think it hurts the pasta as long as you do not overdo it. Pasta *verde*, or green pasta, is made by adding a small amount – approximately $\frac{1}{2}$ cup per 4 cups of flour – of cooked, squeezed, sieved or puréed spinach to the flour at the same time as the eggs, and one egg is usually left out of the above formula because the spinach contributes some moisture of its own.

When rolling by hand, divide your dough into fist-sized lumps and begin rolling vigorously from the middle outwards in all directions. At first, unless you are muscled like a gorilla, it will fight back, springing back 1 inch for every 2 you stretch it. Patience. Suddenly it starts to give, grows thinner and wider. Roll it as thin as you can – Italians claim you should be able to read the headlines through it, but this takes practice – flouring the pasta, the rolling pin and the work top occasionally to prevent sticking. Do not worry if it tears. Lay the sheet on a floured cloth, or anywhere handy, to dry off while you tackle the next lump of dough. This makes it much easier to cut, otherwise the dough is apt to stick together again.

A machine will do some of the kneading and rolling business for you. The gadget works like a tiny mangle.

To cut the pasta, roll up, or concertina fold, your lightly floured sheet and slice across to the width you want, remembering that the pasta will swell up in the pot. $\frac{1}{4}$ inch slices give a nice slim, but not stringy, noodle. Cut postcard-sized pieces for lasagne. When cutting with the gadget, insert rollers grooved to the width you want and turn the handle.

If you can spare the time, leave the cut pasta for 15 to 20 minutes longer, giving it time to rest and dry a little more. Pile it into little loose heaps, or spread it out for lasagne-type sheets.

To cook, heat the required amount of water to boiling, salt it and drop in the pasta, a handful at a time so as not to take the water off the boil. A dash of oil helps to stop the water from boiling over. Italians estimate 1 quart of water to $\frac{1}{4}$ lb uncooked pasta. Stir briefly to separate the pieces. Bear in mind that homemade pasta cooks much faster than the dried sort. For the finest noodles – *fettuccine, mien* – start tasting after 3 to 4 minutes, for the others, after 5. When it is tender but still firm and tastes not at all of flour, tip the pasta into a colander over the sink and shake off the water. Return it to the pan, or a hot dish, with a pat of butter or drop of oil to put on a nice sheen. Lasagne is usually parboiled before baking although I find it cooks perfectly well when layered raw with a Bolognese and strong white sauce and sprinkled with Parmesan cheese, then baked in a hot oven at about 400 degrees for an hour, till the dish is hot and bubbly, and the cheese melted.

Making fresh pasta

1. Having sifted 6 cups of flour and a pinch of salt onto a floured work surface, make a well in the center and break into it 5 eggs or, for pasta *verde* (green pasta), 4 eggs and 3 oz of puréed spinach. Using two fingers, draw the flour into the eggs until it lumps together.

2. Slap the lump down and attack with the heels of both hands using a scrubbing action which stretches the dough away from you. Gather up and repeat the process for not less than 15 minutes. Then divide the dough into lumps.

3. Flatten each lump by rolling vigorously with a floury rolling pin, from the middle outwards in all directions. At first it will spring back but suddenly it will grow thinner, wider. Roll out thinly then lay on a cloth over the back of a chair.

4. A pasta machine can save you this last step. Pass the dough through the mangle and it will stretch it finely, though not to any great width. To make pasta ribbons – or tagliatelle – set the machine with grooved rollers to slice to the width you want: $\frac{1}{4}$ inch gives slim noodles.

5. Pasta comes in all shapes and sizes. For the ravioli below, roll out a rectangle of fresh pasta. Divide one half into lightly marked squares and spoon meat filling into the center of each square. Moisten the other half of the pasta dough, fold it over the meat-filled squares and press down firmly by hand. Lightly cut out the squares.

45

Pasta sauces

Everyone has their own version of the classic Bolognese and Napolitana sauces, but some of the following recipes are less familiar and can be used with homemade noodles of any width you please. Yield: 6 servings.

Onion sauce

Simple, warming and surprisingly good, this recipe provides a winter equivalent to the tomato and basil sauce. It is traditionally eaten without Parmesan cheese.

6 medium sized onions
¼ cup oil
1 heaping tablespoon tomato paste
a pinch of salt, black pepper and sugar

Slice the onions very finely and put them in a heavy pan with the oil (I sometimes add a little butter for flavor). Cover, and cook over a very low heat, until they are reduced to almost a purée. They must not burn, so shake the pan occasionally. After 30 minutes, mix in the tomato paste, seasonings and a little water. Simmer for another 5 to 10 minutes.

Pesto sauce

A Genoese invention that provides the most delicious way of using fresh – but it must be fresh – basil and Parmesan cheese. If you cannot get fresh Parmesan, to grate yourself, use ¾ cup of packaged Parmesan and 1 cup of freshly grated Gruyère cheese.

6 big handfuls of fresh basil
6 tablespoons olive oil
1 cup pine nuts
3 cloves garlic
1½ cups freshly grated Parmesan cheese
a pinch of salt and black pepper

Lightly chop the washed, drained basil and place in the blender with all the other ingredients. Blend until smooth. Use a few tablespoons of pasta cooking water to warm and dilute the sauce. When the pasta has been cooked and drained, put it in a large serving dish. Add the sauce, mix well and serve at once.

   Any surplus sauce can be stored in a jar in the refrigerator with a layer of olive oil on top.

Fresh tomato and basil sauce

The simplest of all, a perfect high-summer complement to your own fresh pasta. Both the tomatoes and the basil must be fresh. If basil is out, try chopped chives and a little marjoram.

2 lb tomatoes
1 large handful basil leaves
1 large clove garlic
5 tablespoons olive oil
a pinch of salt, pepper and sugar

Dip the tomatoes in boiling water for 1 minute then skin. Remove the seeds and chop roughly. Drain off the juice, by leaving in a strainer for 1 minute. Put in a large dish, mix gently with the finely chopped basil, garlic, olive oil and seasonings. Serve with a large mound of hot pasta. Do not add cheese.

Fukien sesame seed sauce

If you like the flavor and breath-taking aroma of toasted sesame seeds, you will find this sauce compulsive eating. Peanut butter may be substituted in which case the sauce resembles Indonesian *sate*.

¼ cup sesame seeds
2 tablespoons soy sauce
1 tablespoon sesame oil
1 tablespoon Hoisin sauce
1 tablespoon tomato paste
2 teaspoons sugar
2 tablespoons sherry
¾ cup stock (or ½ bouillon cube plus water)

To make the sesame paste heat the sesame seeds in a heavy skillet over a low heat for about 3 minutes until lightly colored and fragrant. Put in an electric coffee grinder and whizz to a powder. Mix with all the other ingredients in a small pan and stir over a low heat until smooth and thick. Serve with plain noodles and bowls of chopped scallions.

Tuna fish and anchovy sauce

This classic sauce is usually served with spaghetti and also makes an invaluable contribution to a variety of baked pasta dishes.

1 small can of tuna fish
3 anchovies
2 tablespoons butter
1¼ cups chicken or meat stock
chopped parsley
a pinch of salt and pepper

Chop the tuna and anchovies together, heat in the melted butter in a small pan (this can be done while the pasta is cooking) and add the stock, the parsley and seasonings. Stir well and simmer for a minute or two. Pour over cooked pasta, mix lightly and serve at once.

Sugo or Bolognese sauce

Just open a couple of cans any time of the year to rustle up this tasty sauce.

1 large onion
1 medium can of peeled tomatoes
2 cloves garlic
1 carrot
1 stalk celery
½ lb ground beef
¼ cup wine or wine vinegar
chopped fresh parsley
a pinch of salt and black pepper

Slice the vegetables finely and fry together with the ground beef. When golden brown, add the liquid, herbs and seasonings and cook for a further 15 minutes.

Pasta fillings

If you want to spoil your dinner guests, there is a wealth of more elaborate pasta dishes, some stuffed, some baked, which only someone working at home with loving patience can raise to perfection.

Lasagne verde with Bolognese sauce

If you make up the sauces the night before, this dish can be ready to serve in a few minutes.

1¼ lb green pasta
1 cup grated Parmesan cheese
slices of mozzarella (optional)
1½ cups thick white sauce
nutmeg
2½ cups rich Bolognese sauce
butter

Roll the green pasta out thinly and cut into half postcard-sized rectangles. Have ready the grated Parmesan and, if possible, slices of mozzarella. Starting with white sauce, well seasoned with nutmeg, layer lasagne alternately with the two sauces, including a layer of mozzarella and sprinkle of Parmesan between every layer. The dish should finish with white sauce thickly sprinkled with Parmesan. Dot with butter and bake at 400 degrees for 20 minutes.

Lasagne with chicken livers and truffles

A more expensive version of the dish.

¼ lb chicken livers
8 tablespoons butter
1¼ cups thick meat gravy (or juice from a casserole)
1 canned black truffle
1¼ lb lasagne
1¼ cups grated Parmesan cheese
a pinch of salt and black pepper

Lightly fry the chopped livers in half of the butter, then add the gravy and simmer for 30 seconds. Keep warm. Cut the truffle into strips. Fill a 9 inch diameter baking dish with layers of lasagne, gravy and liver, and cheese, truffle and seasonings. Repeat the layers until the dish is full, ending with a thick layer of cheese. Now leave for 12 hours, to allow the truffle aroma to permeate. Dot with butter, bake for 20 minutes at 400 degrees.

Ravioli

Envelopes of fine white flour, lukewarm water and egg can be filled with a variety of stuffings for a hearty meal.

4 cups sifted flour
5 eggs
1 tablespoon olive oil

Combine the flour, eggs and oil as described in pasta making. When the pasta reaches the proper consistency divide into two roughly equal pieces. Roll these out separately and as thinly as possible into rectangular sheets of roughly equal size. Brush one sheet with a pastry brush dipped in cold water to dampen it, then with a knife mark out into 2 inch squares. Put 1 teaspoon of stuffing in the middle of each square. Lay the other pasta sheet carefully on top and press firmly down around stuffing. Cut down and across the sheets to make raviolis 2 inches square using a pastry wheel or sharp knife. Lower into a pan of boiling water and cook for 5 minutes.

Piedmontese filling for ravioli

1 medium can of peeled tomatoes
2 tablespoons oil
1 stalk celery
1 clove garlic
1 small onion
½ lb lean ground beef
½ cup white wine
¼ lb piece cabbage
a pinch of salt, black pepper and grated nutmeg
2 eggs
½ cup grated Parmesan cheese

Pour off the liquid from the canned tomatoes and remove the seeds. Heat the oil in a skillet and gently fry the chopped vegetables (except the cabbage) until softened. Stir in the ground beef and cook gently until light brown, breaking up any lumps with a fork. Add the wine, tomatoes, chopped cabbage, seasoning and nutmeg. Bring to a boil, then cover the pan and simmer for 30 minutes. The mixture should now be thick and dryish, the right consistency to fill the ravioli envelopes. When cool, add the beaten eggs and cheese and mix together thoroughly. Stuff the ravioli, cook and serve with melted butter and grated Parmesan.

Pork filling for ravioli

½ lb spinach
1 bunch watercress or about ¼ lb beet tops
½ lb pork sausage meat
¼ lb ground veal
2 tablespoons butter
1 clove garlic
¾ cup grated Parmesan cheese
a pinch salt, black pepper and grated nutmeg

Wash the greens, do not shake off the water, cover and cook for 3 minutes. Squeeze out all moisture, purée and cool. Lightly fry the meats in the butter for 5 to 8 minutes with the chopped garlic. Mix with the greens and cheese and add nutmeg and salt and pepper to taste. Stuff the ravioli with the mixture and cook for five minutes.

Vegetarian filling for ravioli

1 lb spinach
1 cup grated Parmesan cheese
½ lb ricotta (or use ¼ lb cottage cheese and ¼ lb cream cheese)
1 tablespoon finely chopped marjoram or basil
3 egg yolks
2 tablespoons butter
a pinch of salt and black pepper

Cook the spinach as above, then blend with the other ingredients. Fill the ravioli envelopes, cook and serve with melted butter and thick cream poured over them and sprinkled generously with Parmesan. Heat under the broiler until golden.

Stuffed Chinese dumplings

These are not *won ton*, but the Northern *giaotze*. They are larger and more garlicky ravioli. The paste, or dough, is made without eggs.

¾ cup cold water
2 cups sifted all-purpose flour
2 pinches of salt
½ lb Chinese, or savoy, cabbage
1 leek
1 lb finely ground lean pork
2 cloves garlic
1 teaspoon grated fresh ginger root
1½ tablespoon sesame oil
1 tablespoon soy sauce

Make a smooth, stiff dough by working the water into the flour and half the salt. Knead it for a few minutes. Leave to rest for 30 minutes covered with a damp towel. The stuffing is not pre-cooked. Finely chop the cabbage and leek (washed well, hard green part removed) and – this is important – wring them in a clean cloth to extract all moisture. Add to the other ingredients and mix together well by hand. Make the dumplings by rolling out the dough into a thin sheet on a lightly floured surface. Keep a damp cloth over the sheet while you work. Using a glass, stamp out a circle of dough, put a rounded teaspoon of uncooked stuffing in the center, then moisten and join the outer edges of the circle, making a little pleat or two to give a crescent-shaped, fat little dumpling. Place on a floured surface, under a floured cloth. Repeat until all the dough is used up. To cook *giaotze*, bring a large pan of salted water to a boil, drop in six or eight dumplings at a time, return to a boil, add a cup of cold water. Repeat this twice then lift out, drain and serve at once. These are eaten dipped in bowls of soy sauce mixed with a dash of white vinegar.

Eggplant and pasta pie

Eggplants have a rich flavor and this pie can substitute successfully for a meat dish.

1 lb tagliatelle
4 small eggplants
salt
olive oil for frying
1 lb fresh tomatoes or 1 medium can of peeled tomatoes
3 cloves garlic
4 tablespoons butter
black pepper
1 handful fresh basil (or parsley, thyme or marjoram)
100 g (4 oz) Parmesan cheese
¼ cup dried homemade breadcrumbs

Cook the tagliatelle for 3 to 4 minutes so they are firm. Drain and set aside in a warm place.

Thinly slice the unpeeled eggplants, salt lightly and leave for 10 minutes to sweat. Deep fry, a few slices at a time, in olive oil until golden brown, then drain on paper towels. Continue until all the eggplant is cooked.

Skin the tomatoes, remove seeds, chop roughly and transfer to a colander to drain. Chop the garlic and lightly fry in a little oil and 1 tablespoon of the butter until golden, then add the tomatoes, salt and pepper and simmer for a few minutes. Chop the basil, minus stalks, or other herbs, quite finely. Mix the herbs, tomato mixture and most of the grated cheese together with the cooked tagliatelle. Now butter a deep cake pan generously (it must be big enough to take the noodle mixture and eggplants) and coat it evenly all over with half of the breadcrumbs. Fill the pan with one layer of the pasta mixture, then one layer of eggplants, and so on until all the ingredients are used up. Top with the remaining cheese and breadcrumbs, then dot with the rest of the butter and bake at 425 degrees for 30 minutes. Unmold onto a dish to serve.

Note: For grand occasions you can substitute a pastry case, with lid, for the crumb case.

Use a pie pastry and bake unfilled for 15 minutes. Bake a lid of the same pastry, decorated with pastry leaves, on a sheet of foil at the same time. Check after 10 minutes. This is a *timballo*.

Tagliatelle cake

A sweet version of the eggplant and pasta pie. The macaroons, almonds and cocoa give a delicate flavor to the fresh pasta base.

4 cups sifted all-purpose flour
4 egg yolks
½ cup sweet vermouth
1⅛ cups sugar
1¾ cups cocoa powder
1 cup almonds
2 large macaroons
drop of vanilla extract
8 tablespoons butter

Make a pasta dough using the flour, egg yolks and enough vermouth to stick it together. Knead as usual, roll out, dry and cut into the thin ribbon strips for tagliatelle. Mix together the sugar, cocoa, blanched, peeled and chopped almonds, crushed macaroons and vanilla. Butter a deep cake pan with half the butter, then flour it. Arrange alternate layers of tagliatelle (uncooked) and the cocoa, ending with the cocoa mixture. Dot with the remaining butter and bake in the pan at 375 degrees for about 40 minutes.

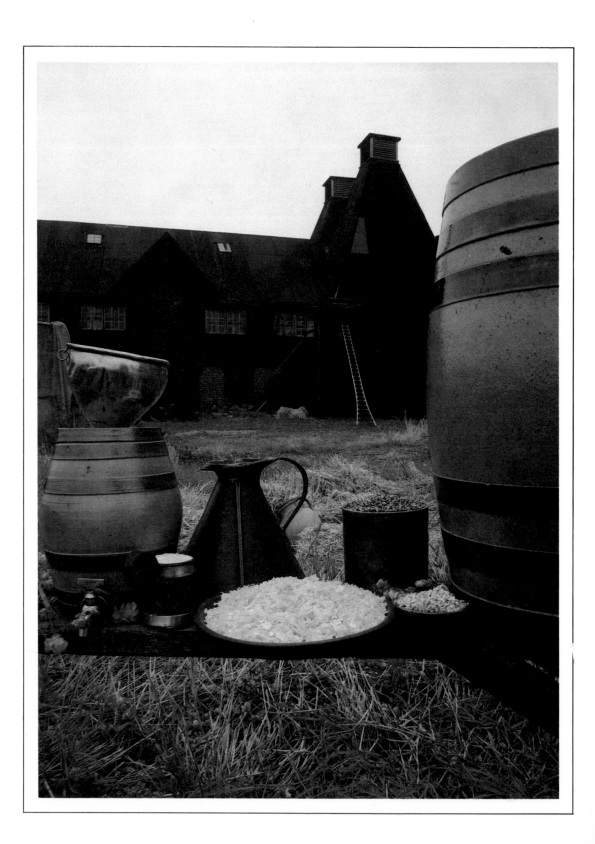

Malts
& Beers

'*My two large Piggs, by drinking some Beer grounds
taking out of one of my Barrels today,
got so amazingly drunk by it that they were not able to stand
and appeared like dead things almost . . .
I never saw Piggs so drunk in my life,
I slit their ears for them without feeling.*'

Diary of a Country Parson   Rev James Woodforde   1778

Ale and beer are interchangeable words today, but there is a distinction between them. Ale, the forerunner, was a drink made from the fermented liquor extracted from malted grain which could be rye, millet, wheat and barley and soon established itself as the best for the purpose. Around the 15th century ale was flavored with local herbs and plants: sweet gale, nettles, spruce tassels. When Flemish traders first introduced their own 'bier' to Britain, a brew flavored with hop flowers, there was a storm of protest.

 Turkeys, Heresies, Hops and Beer
 All came to England in one Year

Resistance soon crumbled, however, when the 'hopped' bitterness proved itself on lengthier and thirstier acquaintance to add the very thing the old ales needed, a brisk astringency which perfectly complemented the sweet, rich flavor of malt. So beer came and stayed, ousting the older brews in all but the remotest country districts. The noble title of 'ale' is only used nowadays to describe the finest oldest vintage beer.

During the 19th century beer brewing was a normal part of household routine, a chore housewives undertook along with baking, raising poultry and curing meat for the winter months. They brewed fine ale for special occasions, 'small' or weak beer for harvesters, and strong stouts for expectant and nursing mothers. Indeed, beer was so nourishing that William Cobbett, in 1825, lists it along with bread and meat as essential to a farm laborer's diet.

Home brewing is becoming more and more popular because it is cheap, easy and good – such a paragon of a drink, in fact, that it can only be deep-seated human laziness which keeps the breweries in business.

Hops stored in an oast house in Kent, England, and malt in barrels, both essential to brewing: grains added to give body and flavor are, center, golden flaked corn and, right, flaked barley, both for brewing light ale, and right, roast crystal malt to sweeten nutbrown ale.

Brewing

The ingredients

The basic ingredients for beer are simple: malt, hops, water, yeast. As with most simple formulas, little changes make a lot of difference. By using a different color of malt or more hops, or hard or soft water, a completely different beer is produced. Then there are what brewers call 'adjuncts', flavorings such as cracked corn, rice, sugar which enrich, smooth or otherwise modify the basic character of beer.

Malt is available in grain form, or as powdered or liquid malt extract. Grain malt comes in most varieties. Depending on the time and temperature in the kiln, it emerges pale or crystal (used in light and pale ales and bitters), amber or brown (for milds, browns and stouts), or chocolate to black (used to give color and flavor to some dark beers). These malts are used for all brewing from the grain and in conjunction with malt syrup or extract in some recipes to give more strength and flavor. Malt syrup or extract is available in only two forms: light and dark. For the home brewer who does not have much time or space it is very convenient.

Use ordinary brewers' yeast, sold as dried granules. Lager, which is a bottom-fermenting beer, uses a special lager yeast.

Water is another essential ingredient in beer making. I have read of fanatics making beer with distilled water, but ordinary tap water is fine for most beers. But try and suit the beer you make to your local water supply: hard water is best for light beers and bitters and soft water areas are famous for their stouts. However you can change the nature of your water supply by adding a little gypsum to soft water to make it more suitable for light beers, and a little common salt to hard water.

Equipment

Start small. A $5\frac{1}{2}$ gallon white plastic bucket with a lid is most convenient for fermenting. It is worth investing in a sacrometer or beer hydrometer to measure when the brew has fermented out, i.e. the yeast has converted all the sugar into alcohol. A pressure cooker can be used to extract maximum flavor from the hops.

A near relation of the controversial *Cannabis indica*, the hop plant – or its female flowers – contributes to beer both bitterness and aroma, as well as preservative and other chemical properties. Several varieties are grown: Hallertau is favored for lager, Fuggles for browns and stouts and Goldings for light ales and bitters. To infuse the hops the green, cone-shaped flowers are boiled for 1 hour or more in the wort, either loose or tied in cheesecloth. Hops should not be kept too long before use because they lose their potency as they dry out. All these varieties are available from specialist brewing stores.

(This is an unorthodox method but it does work.) One extra large ($5\frac{1}{2}$–11 gallon) pan (such as a metal laundry tub), or several smaller ones, will be needed to bring the water to a boil.

For beers brewed from the grain, a 'mash tun' (a container fitted with a flanket or spigot) in which the grain can be mashed or steeped, and the water then drained off, is also required. The mash must be kept at a temperature of 150 degrees so an insulating cabinet, as sold for camping, or, at a pinch, a thick fiberglas blanket is required. There is a special all-purpose plastic boiler fitted with a thermostat and heating element on the market and this does make the whole business much easier though it is fairly expensive. For 'sparging' or spraying the mash, pour over buckets of boiling water, or, more efficiently, siphon hot water from a keg through a simple shower attachment. A long-handled wooden spoon, cheesecloth and potassium metabisulphite, used in solution with water for sterilizing the equipment, are also essential. Finally, a good thermometer, able to stand immersion in hot water, is vital. A jam thermometer is suitable.

The kit
The last word in convenience, neatly boxed beer kits supply the wherewithal for making a range of beers and ales. They include a suitably flavored and colored hop-flavored malt syrup or extract which needs only water, sugar and, usually, yeast added. It is the most expensive way to make home brew but the results are very drinkable and quick to mature. Two weeks are sufficient in many cases.

Storage
Bottle or store the finished brew under pressure for carbonated beer, with a foaming head and 'fine bead' (tiny bubbles). Use solid glass beer bottles, such as those you get in Canada, with caps which can be put on with a bottle capper (available at hardware stores). *Note:* Beer goes through its secondary fermentation at considerable pressure so make sure all bottles are in perfect condition, free from chips or hairline cracks. Flat or non-fizzy brews can be stored in sealed gallon jugs, bottles or wooden kegs. All storage containers must be kept clean and sweet – rinse out with hot water immediately after use, scrub and swill out with a potassium metabisulphite solution. This is the dull part of home brewing but it is necessary if your beer is not to pick up sour flavors or the odd unwelcome infection.

Brewing from the grain
Brewing from the grain is the purists' method, beginning with the malted grains (fanatics even malt their own barley) as our great-grandmothers might have done. The advantage is a cleaner flavored beer with more guts and character. The snag is time: it takes longer, involving many processes spread over several days. It needs more, and larger, equipment but it is still the cheapest and most authentic way to brew. I recommend it to perfectionists in search of a hobby who have lots of space (a basement) and plenty of helpers. See the recipe for light ale.

Brewing: the malt extract method for nutbrown ale

1. Wash and rinse a $5\frac{1}{2}$ gallon white plastic bucket. Pour in 2 lb malt extract and 5 lb (10 cups) granulated sugar, then add a kettleful of boiling water. Stir with a long-handled spoon until dissolved. Cover with a lid.

2. Gently heat 2 oz roast crystal malt in a heavy skillet until golden brown. The smell is delicious.

  Malts are obtainable from specialist stores and are used to give the beer more strength and flavor.

3. Put the roast crystal malt with 2 oz Goldings hops into a cheesecloth bag and cook in 1 quart of water in a pressure cooker for 20 minutes.

  If you do not have a pressure cooker or disapprove of short cuts, cook for 1 hour in 5 quarts of water.

4. After removing the cheesecloth bag, add the liquid from the pressure cooker to that in the white bucket and make up the liquid content to $5\frac{1}{2}$ gallons, using tap water.

5. When tepid, sprinkle one package of brewers' yeast over the top. Stir thoroughly, then cover, but not tightly, so the air can circulate. Leave overnight. By the next morning a vigorous fermentation will be well underway.

6. After 2 days skim off any 'rocky head' or discolored froth, just the top layer. After 6 or 10 days, depending on the weather and room temperature, the fermentation will have stopped and the beer should have fermented out, giving a hydrometer reading of SG 1000.

7/8. For a carbonated, bubbly beer, siphon off the brew into bottles. The bottles must be solid glass, such as those you get in Canada with caps which can be tapped into place with a special gadget (available in hardware stores) once the beer has been 'primed' with sugar to encourage secondary fermentation.

Note: Beer goes through its secondary fermentation at considerable pressure so make sure all the bottles are in perfect condition – no chips or hairline cracks.

Prime the beer by adding sugar at a rate of 1 generous teaspoon per quart of beer.

9. Fit the caps and store upright at room temperature for 3 or 4 days. Then transfer to a cooler spot and store until the beer has cleared save for a dark line of yeasty sediment at the bottom. This clearing can take between 4 and 10 days, depending on the temperature.

Note: When pouring out bottled beer take care not to shake up the yeast sediment. Hold the bottle up to the light to gauge this and pour steadily, without shaking, into a jug, stopping just before the dark sludge slides out. Then scrub and swill out the bottle with a potassium metabisulphite solution to prevent any infection.

9

7/8

5

6

Beers

In these recipes there are examples of malt extract beers and grain-mashed beers, with a simple gingerbeer thrown in for those of you too thirsty to wait for the others to mature. These recipes will yield about $5\frac{1}{2}$ gallons of home-brew.

Mild ale
Crisp, light beer for everyday drinking made by the malt extract method of brewing.

2 oz hops (Fuggles or Progress)
6 oz crystal malt
2 oz roasted barley grain
2 teaspoons brewers' gypsum
6 cups sugar
2 lb malt extract
1 package of brewers' yeast

Bring 5 quarts of water to the boil. Put the hops, crystal malt and roast barley grain (you can roast your own by heating it until golden brown as with crystal malt, see previous page) into a cheesecloth bag, tie up and add to the boiling water with the gypsum. Boil hard for 1 hour. Tip in the sugar and malt extract and stir until melted. Remove the bag, tip your wort into a clean fermentation bucket, and add cold water to make up to $5\frac{1}{2}$ gallons of tepid liquid. Pitch in the yeast granules, stir and cover. Keep at room temperature for about 1 week, until fermentation stops and the hydrometer registers SG 1000. After 48 hours, skim off the head.

Siphon into bottles, leaving 1 inch headroom at the top and 'prime' at the rate of 1 generous teaspoon of sugar per quart. Screw on tops, secure caps and store in a cool place for 2 weeks, until the ale 'falls bright'.

Lager
Light and sparkling but with a marked hop flavor, lager is made by the malt extract method, and uses special lager yeast.

2 lb malt extract
2 oz hops (Hallertau or Saaz)
1 lb lager malt or 1 lb pale malt plus 2 teaspoons
  gypsum
6 cups sugar
lager yeast
water

Note: Lager yeast is best started beforehand by adding it to a little tepid water mixed with 1 teaspoon malt extract in a clean bottle, and leaving it a few hours or until it starts frothing vigorously.

The method is the same as for mild ale except that the liquid should be only just tepid when adding the yeast.

The fermentation bucket should be kept in a cool place (like an unheated room) for a week or so until the fluffy 'head' sinks from the top. Siphon off into bottles, prime with $\frac{1}{2}$ teaspoon of sugar per $1\frac{1}{4}$ pint, secure caps or screw tops and keep the bottles in a cool place until the lager is bright and clear. Drink well chilled.

Bitter

A good strong traditional brew.

$\frac{1}{4}$ lb Goldings hops
1 lb crystal malt
4 cups granulated sugar
3 cups raw sugar
2 lb can malt extract
2 teaspoons brewers' gypsum (if you have soft water)
1 package brewers' yeast

Boil the hops and crushed malt (either buy it already crushed or crack the grains with a rolling pin) with 5 quarts of water for 45 minutes. Then stir in sugars, malt extract and gypsum (if used). Add enough cold water to make $5\frac{1}{2}$ gallons of tepid liquid and sprinkle 1 package of brewers' yeast over. Tie a small handful of hops in a cheesecloth bag and drop this into the bucket to infuse during fermentation. This is called 'dry hopping' and will sharpen the flavor. Cover and ferment at room temperature. Siphon off into bottles and prime at the rate of 1 generous teaspoon of sugar per quart. Secure caps or screw tops and leave for at least a month to mature in a cool place. This makes good strong beer, with a malty richness.

Light ale

This recipe is brewed from the grain. The addition of flaked barley and corn gives extra flavor and richness. Both can be obtained from specialist home-brew shops.

The answer to mashing the grain is to buy an all-purpose boiler, thermostatically controlled to boil the water and hold the temperature. These boilers have only a $5\frac{1}{2}$ gallon capacity which does not give long before the entire long-winded process needs to be gone into again. This is why some purists still prefer a 'mash tun' container fitted with a spigot.

6 gallons water
$\frac{1}{4}$ lb cracked corn
4 lb crushed pale malt
$\frac{1}{4}$ lb flaked barley
$1\frac{1}{4}$ cups brown sugar
2 oz Goldings hops
1 package brewers' yeast

Either buy ready crushed malt or crush it roughly yourself with a rolling pin. Heat $4\frac{1}{2}$ gallons of water to boiling point, then cool to around 160 degrees. Add the corn, crushed malt, flaked barley and brown sugar. Stir. Check the temperature. When it has settled at 150 degrees leave to mash (in an insulated container or under a fiberglas blanket, if you don't have an all-purpose boiler) for 2 hours. Strain off the wort into a $5\frac{1}{2}$ gallon fermentation bucket. Use a further 1 to $1\frac{1}{2}$ gallons of hot water to 'sparge' or spray the sodden mash left behind in the receptacle, collecting this extra liquid in the fermentation bucket as it runs through. If the mash is 'set' and the water refuses to run through, stir it up a bit with a spoon. Now boil up the 'wort' plus the hops (added loose for maximum effectiveness). The wort will rise up in the container when boiling so it might be safer to divide the wort and hops between $4\frac{1}{2}$ gallon containers. When the wort has boiled for 1 hour, strain it off into a plastic fermentation bucket. Rinse the hops with a kettleful of cold water to remove the last traces of wort and add this water to the wort. The object now is to cool the wort as fast as possible to the tepid stage yeast likes. You could put it outside or try putting it in a cold bath. When the temperature is right add the yeast (preferably 'started' in a bottle but straight from the package will do) and stir well. Leave to ferment for about a week, skimming off the top layer of foam after 48 hours. Now leave covered for 3 days for the sediment to settle. Siphon into bottles or barrel. Add 'priming' sugar at the rate of $\frac{1}{2}$ teaspoon per 3 cups of beer. Leave in a warm place for 4 days to get the secondary ferment going, then transfer to cool place for storage. Drink when clear.

Gingerbeer

Strictly speaking, this is not a beer at all, but a fermented lemon drink hotted up with ginger. Fresh ginger gives a much fresher flavor as well as a delicious smell.

Traditionally gingerbeer or 'pop' was relegated to children, but do not knock it back like lemonade – it has quite a kick to it. For hot summer days it makes a delicious, refreshing drink, and it is ready to drink in less than a week!

Note : Use beer bottles with caps if you are going to drink it fast. Otherwise for safety's sake use bottles with corks as this ensures that if the pressure builds up too much you will only have spilt beer to deal with, not broken glass. Ideally, gingerbeer should be drunk within a week of bottling and under these circumstances I have never had any problems using capped bottles, solid glass beer bottles, such as those you get in Canada with caps put on with a bottle capper.

1 oz fresh ginger or 1 tablespoon ground ginger
2 cups sugar
5 quarts boiling water
2 lemons
$\frac{1}{4}$ oz cream of tartar
1 teaspoon brewers' yeast

Grate fresh ginger (or alternatively pound it in a mortar) and put it in a bucket with the sugar. Pour on the boiling water and stir well to dissolve the sugar. Squeeze the lemons and add the juice and the rinds to the liquid, plus the cream of tartar, dissolved in the lemon juice. When cooled to a tepid temperature sprinkle the yeast over. Cover with a plastic garbage bag and leave for 2 days. Strain the contents into a clean bucket, then siphon off into bottles and cap. It can be drunk after 3 days.

The Dairy

The fat of the land

Homer meant nothing but praise, I am sure, when he gave to mild-eyed Hera, consort of Zeus, the attributes of a cow. The cow is something of a goddess among domestic animals, gentle, comely, overflowing with milk – that generous stream of life which we skim for cream, churn to butter, curdle and press to make cheese. Silly sheep and pretty shepherdesses decorate the urban poet's Arcadia; the true countryman has always known better.

I know no writing where the poetic and commonplace of country life are more vividly counterpoised than the chapters by Dorset born Thomas Hardy which describe his heroine Tess working in a dairy 'amid the oozing fatness and warm ferments of the Frome Vale, at a season when the rush of juices could almost be heard below the hiss of fertilization.' Milking at dawn in misty fields, scouring pastures for wild garlic which has 'tainted' the butter, skimming and churning in the cool dimness of the dairy – with such details as these Hardy recreates the routine of a Victorian dairy hand's life.

Free milk, cream, butter, cheese are an attractive prospect in an inflationary age, and more and more people are trying their hand at dairying in a small way, keeping a cow or goats on such grazing as is available, which they milk by hand as did Tess and everyone else until about 80 years ago. The price of self-sufficiency, as usual, is loss of freedom. Cows – and goats – need regular milking twice daily, or they dry up – 'go azew' as Tess's master dairyman boss puts it. Buying a cow with calf helps, as a suckling calf drains off enough milk to let the owners take an occasional weekend off. In summer a good cow may give over 3 gallons of milk daily, a nanny goat maybe 1 gallon. Goat's milk is less rich than cow's, with a faintly chalky taste that you need to adapt to, but it is very digestible and makes excellent yogurt and cheese. Goats undoubtedly score over cows in that they are hardy, unfussy about grazing and their milk yield just about keeps pace with an average family's needs. Goat and ewe milk cheeses, like the Greek *feta*, have a sharp, salt tang to them.

All the milk sold commercially is pasteurized – that is 'flash' heated momentarily, then cooled – to destroy bacteria, a sound policy where huge quantities of milk from innumerable sources are involved. Untreated milk ('raw' milk straight from the cow) is sold in many parts of the world, subject to stringent checks on the herds for brucellosis, and T.B. Kept clean, it sours naturally and pleasantly in a few days where pasteurized milk and cream usually go bitter and inedible, being more vulnerable to bacterial invasion and 'taints'. Homogenized milk is pasteurized milk processed to redistribute the fat content evenly, making it structurally similar to goat's milk. Like goat's milk, too, it is good for making yogurt and certain cheeses. You can sterilize milk, by processing a stage further to make it keep longer. Fairly nasty to drink, it remains a useful standby and can also be used to make yogurt. None of these special processed milks can produce cream, or butter, which is solidified cream with the water spun off.

As a glance at pasteurized milk reveals, cream rises – fat being lighter than water. The creaminess of commercial milk varies according to how much of the fat, or cream, is removed. If curiosity prompts you to try making cream and butter for yourself, from bought milk, get several quarts of whole milk and gently heat it for several hours to make clotted cream, that thick yellow crust which is the *crème de la crème*. It will not be much, and it will not be cheap, but it might be fun, and instructive. A couple of minutes beating it with a wooden spoon will give you a nut of homemade butter.

Cheesemaking is and always has been the most skilled of dairy activities. A whole host of variables go into a cheese; its quality depends on things like the breed of cow, type and abundance of feed, standards of hygiene in the dairy, but above all, it is the long experience of the cheesemaker whose judgment is constantly being tested at every stage of the process which makes the difference between the mass produced rubberized article and a really fine cheese. From the point of view of home cheesemaking this is encouraging – intelligence we may have, judgment and experience we can acquire. Starting with the simple spoon or soft cheeses anyone can make, with ordinary milk and a cloth and bowl, there is no reason, if enough milk is available, why people should not go on to experiment with semi-hard cheeses, of the Brie/Camembert type, and hard cheeses, of the Edam and Cheddar variety. It only needs more confidence, more milk and a bit more equipment.

The fat content determines the cheese; the richer the milk the better the cheese. A hard cheese weighing 2 lb uses about 4 gallons of milk; semi-hard cheeses of the same weight use rather less, as they retain the whey. Using commercial or cartoned milk to make these would be uneconomic.

The next problem with raw milk, is whether to pasteurize it or not? The shortest answer seems to be, yes, if you live in a hot climate, have doubts about the cows, the particular dairy or – if it is your own animal – a particular batch of milk. Maybe the teats were dirty, or there is a bug going the rounds of the family. Bugs thrive in milk. On the other hand, pasteurizing at home is tricky, time consuming and creates its own problems – to make cheese with pasteurized milk a 'starter', which you must buy or make and constantly renew, is essential to get the lactic acid forming bacteria going (all bacteria are killed in pasteurizing, remember) in the 'clean' milk. 'Most people cheesemaking at home will tend to use raw milk,' one commercial cheesemaker told me, 'and provided their hygiene is up to the mark, they can get very good cheese that way – but they should expect some variation and some failures.' Commercial manufacturers always use a starter (and pasteurized milk) because they cannot afford to take any chances. Even so, no two cheeses are alike.

Hygiene is the crux of the matter, and here progress is on our side. Today's kitchen, the domestic equivalent to a dairy for most people, already has hygienic, scrubbable worktops, a refrigerator, stove, surfaces which can be washed down with a mild bleach like the stuff sold to sterilize baby bottles. All equipment used should be washable, and stainless steel in the long run is best value and least bother. The reason for these precautions is that cheeses pick up 'taint' or sour flavors and cleanliness is the best safeguard. Our ancestors, making their 'variable' but often excellent cheeses at home, knew this too, from hard experience, but the difference is they had to work much harder, scouring and scalding, to get the same result.

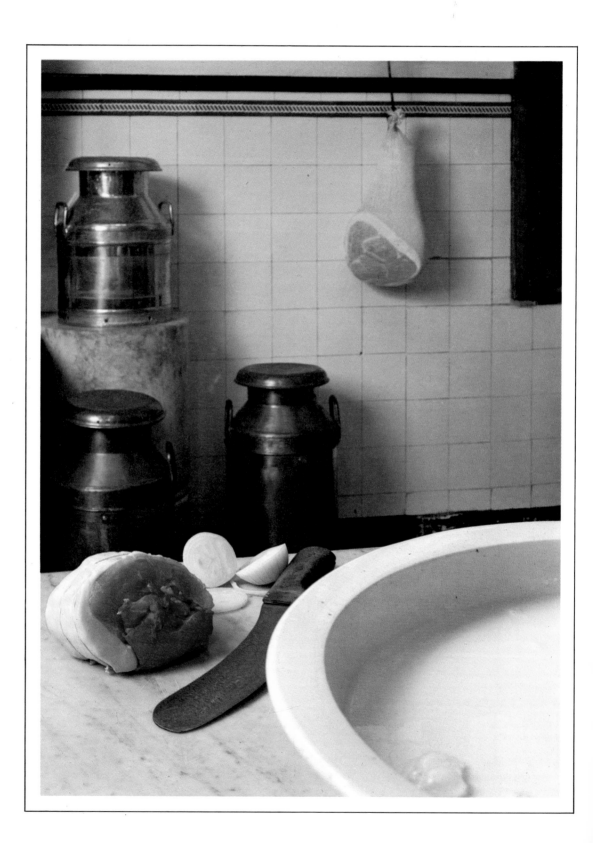

Milk

'Good cows they were and never ailed, and plenty of everything there was in that house,
good milk and butter and cheese and buckets and buckets of skim for the pigs.'

Precious Bane   Mary Webb   1924

Not being scientifically trained, I find it odd that milk which is almost 90% water should be the nearest thing to a complete food capable of sustaining life. But drink a glass of good milk slowly, so the fatness of it clings to your lips, and the statement convinces. When the old writers sought to convey a vision of unimaginable plenty they wrote of a land flowing with milk and honey. Milk *is* the fat of the land made visible, acres of lush herbage churned through the cow's proverbial stomachs and finally transmitted to us through 'large veined udders ponderous as sandbags, the teats sticking out like the legs of a gypsy's crock' to quote Thomas Hardy, always precise about country things.

Cow's milk is only one of many kinds drunk by thirsty humans around the world. All mammals, as we know, ourselves included, secrete milk to feed their young. Of these water buffalo milk is said to be the creamiest of all, and Indians say that *ghee* (clarified butter) and *chenna* (soft cheese) made from it are incomparably rich. Mare's milk is still drunk in Outer Mongolia, camel's and ass's milk in parts of the Middle East, sheep's milk helps support Europe's cheese industry though it is not much drunk, and goat's milk is currently enjoying a revival as more people try their hand at keeping these attractive creatures. Goat's milk, because of its homogenized structure, is easily digested, and makes smooth yogurt and cheeses.

Here, however, cow's milk has no rival for versatility, richness and flavor. A cow's udder is a remarkable processing plant – 55 gallons of blood must pass through it to make 1 pint of milk – which supports a gigantic, complex industry. Milk is high protein food, rich in calcium, and an excellent source of vitamins A, B and some C and D.

Until the last years of the 19th century when a doctor in Glasgow, Scotland, revolutionized dairying with his Thistle pulsator milking machine, all milking was done by hand. Instead of cows being herded into a milking parlor, milkmaids, and men often took pail and stool to where the cows were grazing and milked them on the spot. The early milking might be at 4 a.m. in summer, while the late milking took place some time before dusk, leaving all day for skimming cream, churning butter or cheesemaking in the dairy house itself, a cool and spotless structure, usually of stone, slate roofed and facing north to escape the sun's heat.

White marble and tiles for coolness and cleanliness in the dairy: boned, rolled leg (fresh ham) of pork ready to be cooked to a golden crust in milk, flavored with onions and spices. The lactic acid in milk tenderizes and moistens meat and milk can be used as a marinade.

Cooking with milk

Recipes based on milk are bland, soothing to the stomach, subtle rather than exciting. The 'good for you' tag has left many people with an aversion to milk desserts though they are delicious made with care. Yield: 4 to 6 servings.

White sauce

Hardly original but *the* basic sauce, not always cooked as well as it might be. The butter and flour mixture should be heated for a minute or two before adding the milk, and the sauce simmered for at least 10 minutes to get rid of the raw flour taste and allow it to reduce and thicken a little. A little white sauce enters into recipes as various as quiches, soufflés, and gratins. A few spoonfuls of this and that added to the basic sauce transform it.

2½ cups milk
2 tablespoons butter
1 heaping tablespoon flour
salt and pepper

Heat the milk to just below boiling point. Meanwhile melt the butter in a heavy small pan, stir in the flour, mix and simmer for a minute over a very low heat as the mixture, known as a white roux, should not brown. Then add the hot milk, bit by bit, stirring vigorously to break up any threatening lumps. Rescue a lumpy sauce by straining or blending. Season with a little salt and pepper and simmer for 10 minutes or longer over a very low heat. The secret of a good white sauce is to cook it slowly.

For *Sauce soubise*, add an onion purée. Put two onions, boiled until soft and drained, into the blender, and blend with a little French mustard. Serve with poached eggs, baked fish, sausages or ham.

For *Sauce mornay*, add about ¼ cup grated cheese (Cheddar, Parmesan, Gruyère) to the mixture and stir until melted. At the last minute, add one egg yolk to thicken. Serve with eggs, spinach, fish, chicken and pasta; it is especially tasty when browned quickly under the broiler.

For *Sauce à l'Indienne* stir in 1 teaspoon ground turmeric, 1 teaspoon dry mustard and 2 teaspoons curry powder or paste and leave to simmer for 5 to 10 minutes. Not really Indian in origin, this sauce gives a restrained 'deviled' effect to fish, eggs, chicken, pasta and chops.

Pork cooked in milk

The lactic acid in milk has a markedly tenderizing, moistening effect on meat. There is an old Swedish recipe for lamb marinated for 2 days in milk with a little salt and sugar, then roasted plain. The Italians have a tradition of cooking veal and chicken in milk, which makes for succulent eating. I have chosen a recipe for pork *al latte* because the seasonings make it particularly delicious.

1 onion
⅓ cup chopped ham or bacon
4 tablespoons butter
2 cloves garlic
1 teaspoon coriander seeds
1 sprig fresh (or 1 teaspoon dried) marjoram, fennel or basil
2 lb boned rolled leg of pork (fresh ham)
1 quart milk
salt and pepper

Chop the onion finely and brown with the ham or bacon for a minute or two over a moderate heat in butter. Tuck the garlic cloves, coriander and herbs inside the pork, roll up and tie into a neat sausage with string. Brown in butter with the onion and bacon. Pour the milk over, add a little salt and pepper and set the pan simmering over a gentle heat, *uncovered*. After about 1 hour, when the milk has formed a golden skin, stir and scrape all the delicious gravy stuck to the pan into the bubbling milk, which is by now much thickened. Cook gently for a further 30 to 45 minutes, by which time the milk will have shrunk to a thick gravy. The meat itself should be moist inside its golden crust. Serve sliced hot or cold.

Junkets

Junket is milk curd, set with rennet or, as in Denmark, buttermilk. In Devonshire, England, famous for its junket, milk was used warm from the cow and then left to set in bowls on the stone flags.

English junket

2¼ cups milk
1 tablespoon sugar
1 teaspoon rennet

Warm the milk to blood heat, add the sugar, stir until dissolved, then add the rennet, stir and pour into a dish. Leave to set in a cool place, preferably not the refrigerator. Made in the morning it will be ready the same evening. Pour a thin layer of cream over before serving, and dust with nutmeg.

Danish junket

¼ teaspoon ground cinnamon
½ teaspoon crushed cardamom
1 quart milk
¼ cup buttermilk

Make this junket in four individual bowls. Mix the ground cinnamon and crushed cardamom with the milk. Pour one quarter of the milk into each bowl, then stir 1 tablespoon of buttermilk into each one. Put the bowls in a warm place and leave to thicken overnight. Sprinkle with brown sugar. The Scandinavian partiality for cardamom is understandable; the tiny scented seeds add mystery to a simple milk curd.

A cluster of custards

My dictionary defines custard as 'a composition of milk and eggs, flavored and sweetened'. Custards vary according to how many eggs are used (richer ones use as many as 6 to 2½ cups of milk), whether the whole egg is used, or the yolks only, and whether they are baked in the oven or stirred on top of the stove. Using yolks only gives a creamy, fluid custard – what the French confusingly call *crème* – while adding egg whites and baking sets the mixture. Slow, gentle cooking is the secret of a perfect custard.

Vanilla cream

The texture is creamy, hence the name. It can be used as a sauce with stewed fruit or steamed puddings, but is best eaten on its own, cool and smooth like a sweetened soup.

4 egg yolks
2½ cups milk
1 vanilla bean or 1 teaspoon vanilla extract
2 tablespoons sugar

This must be cooked in a double boiler or in a pan set in another pan containing simmering water, to prevent overheating and curdling. Beat the yolks until frothy. Heat the milk slowly with the vanilla bean or extract and the sugar. When hot, stir about ½ cup into the egg yolks, then return the egg mixture to the pan and cook for about 10 minutes, stirring constantly, until thickened. Remove the vanilla bean. If in doubt *undercook*, as the mixture thickens as it cools. If you stir constantly until cool you will have the world's smoothest custard. A stir from time to time will prevent a skin forming on top. Eat this delectable dish hot or cold.

Frangipani custard tart

Custard tarts have been popular for centuries and they do make a filling dessert from a simple custard. This one gains elegance from crushed macaroons and orange flower water, a combination I find particularly appealing with a smooth custard. Use slightly sweetened pie pastry or a thin layer of crushed graham crackers (add a couple of macaroons to this too) bound with a little softened butter to line the tart pan.

1 egg and 2 additional yolks
¼ cup plain flour
3 tablespoons sugar
2¼ cups milk
2 tablespoons melted unsalted butter
2 crushed macaroons
1 tablespoon orange flower water

Beat the egg with the yolks, then add the flour and sugar and beat until smooth. Add the milk and melted butter and mix, then stir in the crushed macaroons (dry these out for a few minutes in a low oven first) and orange flower water. Pour into the prepared 8 inch tart shell. Bake at 375 degrees for 30 to 40 minutes until the custard filling feels firm and springy. If the top looks like browning, cover with foil for the last few minutes.

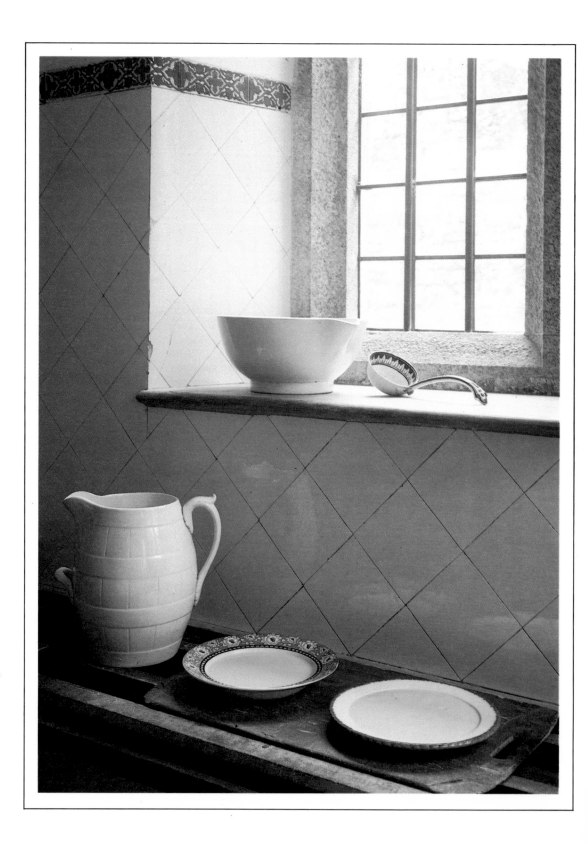

Yogurt

'Mrs Beaver stood with her back to the fire, eating her morning yogurt.
She held the carton close to her chin and gobbled with a spoon . . .
"Heavens, how nasty this stuff is. I wish you'd take to it, John . . .
I don't know how I should get through my day without it."

A Handful of Dust   Evelyn Waugh   1934

There seem to be almost as many countries claiming to have invented yogurt as there are sure-fire ways of making it. Turks, Bulgars, Georgians, Armenians and Indians all have a long tradition of eating, and cooking with, some form of cultured milk. The Bulgars even have an acid forming bacillus named after them. Milk, especially warm milk, is the ideal breeding ground for bacteria of many kinds. If you boil it to kill the noxious variety, cool it to between 100 and 110 degrees and introduce a live culture of fresh, plain, commercial yogurt – the acid forming bacteria contained in this will promptly set about converting the milk sugar into lactic acid. Yogurt is formed by the growth of two different bacterial organisms in fresh milk, *Streptococcus thermophilus* and *Lactobacillus bulgaricus*. Kept at an even warmth for several hours, a soft curd forms which keeps better than milk (one reason for its popularity in torrid climates), is refreshingly uncloying in taste and very easily digested. The health giving properties of yogurt (and the similar *koumiss* and *kefir*) have been long acknowledged. Whether yogurt eating sharpens libido or extends life is unproven as yet; what seems certain is that it encourages the growth of benign intestinal bacteria and these, along with synthesizing vitamins and aiding digestion prey upon less desirable bugs. To keep this internal culture flourishing yogurt should be eaten regularly, especially when one is taking antibiotics because these tend towards overkill, destroying the whole of what medicine prettily refers to as our 'intestinal flora'.

It has taken four centuries for yogurt to gain acceptance in the West as a palatable food rather than a vaguely medicinal substance akin to slippery elm and garlic pearls. Now yogurt has zoomed from the health store shelf to become one of the most widely eaten instant foods of our time.

The smooth, white commercial yogurt is perfectly good for you. It is made from honest milk with (contrary to popular legend) 'live' bacteria, but I doubt that many Indians, Bulgarians, Turks or Georgians would find much resemblance to the yogurt they have been making for centuries. True yogurt is creamy colored, with a voluptuous heavy texture and a taste somewhere between rich and sharp, better plain than flavored.

Fresh plain homemade yogurt ripening in a bowl set on the window sill. In the Middle East, yogurt gives velvety richness to thick soups: the hot chicken soup (left) simmered with mint and yogurt and the cold tomato soup (right), blended with lemon, chives and parsley.

Yogurt making

Whatever equipment or milk you favor, the procedure for making yogurt is the same, and very simple once you have grasped the principles involved.

Always sterilize the milk first by bringing it to a boil to kill off undesirable bacteria. As soon as it threatens to rise up the pan, turn the heat right down, let it simmer for 2 minutes, then remove the pan from the heat and leave the milk to cool until it is lukewarm. Between 100 and 110 degrees is correct if you are using a thermometer. Otherwise dip your finger in it – it should feel warm but not hot. (Homogenized milk is already sterilized, of course, and so you only need to warm this up to 110 degrees.)

At this point you introduce the culture – usually a spoonful of plain commercial yogurt (any brand will do but it must be plain, not fruit flavored). Specific yogurt cultures are available from health stores. For yogurt culture, follow the maker's instructions, but for ordinary commercial yogurt add 1 tablespoon per 1 pint of milk. Stir, breaking up any skin which has formed on the milk, cover and leave undisturbed at a constant temperature for several hours at least. The correct incubating temperature is between 100 and 110 degrees, which is, of course, the same temperature at which you added the culture. The longer you leave it, the thicker, stiffer and sharper tasting the curd will be. Yogurt usually sets lightly in about 3 hours but made at night and left to set overnight it reaches the consistency most people like around breakfast time the next morning. Manufacturers of yogurt making machines, like the one illustrated opposite, that incubate the culture at a low temperature, recommend a minimum of 6 hours in the machine. Yogurt can be kept in a cool pantry or refrigerator.

What milk to use
You can use almost every available sort of milk to make yogurt – milk from animals as different as sheep, goats, water buffalo and cows, and milk processed in different ways (non-pasteurized, pasteurized, homogenized, sterilized, evaporated, powdered, condensed, skimmed milk, fortified with added milk powder or enriched with cream). Some gluttons even make yogurt with light cream. Everyone insists their way is healthier, tastier and simpler. The truth is they all work, with some variation in flavor, texture and creaminess. Homogenized milk gives the most consistent results. Goat's milk fat is naturally homogenized which makes this the most digestible yogurt of all. The consistency and flavor of ordinary milk can be improved by adding some dried milk powder.

Broadly speaking, the richer or stronger tasting the milk, the richer or stronger tasting the yogurt made from it. There is some logic behind the use of evaporated or other concentrated forms of milk because the thicker curd this produces is closer to the old Bulgarian method whereby the milk was simmered until reduced by a third before adding the culture. But of course yogurt made like this works out more expensive. I use non-pasteurized Jersey milk because I find the extra cream it contains makes a particularly delicious yogurt; it is cheaper than evaporated or condensed milk but creamy enough to give delectable, firm curds.

Equipment

There is much controversy about the best way to achieve the ideal environment – steady, milk warmth – for the working bacteria. Solutions range from the basic (bowl, blanket, warm spot), to cosified (pans padded with down pillows), to space age (thermometers and see-through plastic). Once again, they all work, and all have their points, but they are only as infallible as you are. Conscientious cleaning of all equipment (scrub, scald and rinse each time) is most important. The method I use, the thermos, is simple. Get a wide-necked thermos, and a large bottle brush to clean it out with. The thermos automatically keeps the milk at the right temperature. When the yogurt has set in the thermos, transfer it to glass jars for storage in the refrigerator. Traditionally, people used a wide, shallow pottery bowl to set their curd; this is still a simple and attractive method provided you can find a warm corner where the covered bowl can stand undisturbed and out of drafts. Owners of yogurt making gadgets simply fill their containers with prepared milk, add the culture, plug in and switch on.

Things can go wrong

Most people are going to slip up somewhere, sometime. Maybe the milk was insufficiently sterilized, or the culture added when the milk was too hot, or too cool, or not blended in thoroughly, or not left long enough to solidify. Relax, it is not disastrous; buy another carton of commercial yogurt and start again.

Yogurt making equipment can be as simple or as complicated as you like: all you need is a container that keeps the acid-making culture incubating at around 100 degrees till the curd forms. Above, ceramic pots fit into an electric base which maintains that temperature for a recommended 6 hours. A thermos (center) works well for the author who leaves yogurt setting in it overnight, while the commercial version (foreground) is a more convenient shape.

Flavoring yogurt

Fresh natural yogurt can be flavored simply by stirring in honey, jam, fruit, nuts, powdered chocolate, molasses, or maple syrup, after it has set and cooled. After adding the flavoring ingredient, leave the yogurt in the refrigerator for 6 hours to allow the flavor to develop.

Cooking with yogurt

Homemade yogurt is delicious eaten plain, with a little brown sugar, or added to muesli, or stewed or fresh fruit. It has innumerable other uses in the kitchen: as a low-calorie and economical substitute for light cream, it becomes an ingredient in soups, cheese dips, cheesecakes and quiches. To borrow an idea sponsored by the cuisine minceur school, you can fold a little whipped egg white and sugar into yogurt and use it instead of whipped cream – with fresh fruit, fruit salads, compotes. In hot Mediterranean countries yogurt is diluted to make an odd but refreshing salted drink. Or it is beaten with mint, garlic and other flavorings to make an instant sauce for cooked vegetables, and broiled fish. Lactic acid has a tenderizing effect on tough meat, so yogurt is used a great deal to make highly spiced marinades for chicken, meat and kabobs. Indians use yogurt to soften fiery curries, either as an ingredient in the curry or more often as a cool *raita* to eat with it. A spread of different *raitas*, in little brass or pottery bowls, is one of the pleasures of Indian meals, and they only take minutes to make. The simplest consist of chopped vegetables or fruit mixed with a whipped yogurt base then sharpened with salt, a little garlic, lemon or lime juice, a sprinkling of ground spices, or garam masala, cumin seeds or finely chopped fresh herbs. Chopped raw onion, cooked potato, cucumber, banana, grated coconut – all of these are commonly used. In the Middle East yogurt gives velvety richness to braised meat dishes, slowly simmered casseroles, and thick soups. No meal in Turkey is complete without a bowl of yogurt on the table, and they like it with practically everything.

In some dishes yogurt has to be 'stabilized' first to prevent it curdling and separating, which both looks odd and spoils the texture. If yogurt is added at the last minute, to thicken and enrich a dish – as often happens with curries – the danger does not arise so long as the dish is kept at simmering point only. But where it is a major ingredient, and long cooking is part of the process, it is worth spending a few minutes stabilizing it first.

Stabilizing yogurt

To stabilize 1 quart of yogurt, allow 1 tablespoon cornstarch. Mix the cornstarch to a paste with a little milk, stir it into the yogurt and bring the mixture slowly to a boil stirring steadily in one direction, either clockwise or counterclockwise, but not both. Now leave to simmer *uncovered* till the mixture thickens, which takes between 8 to 10 minutes. It is important not to cover the yogurt during this time as a drop of condensed steam falling back into the pan could undo the good work. Once thickened, however, the stabilized yogurt can be cooked without risk of curdling.

Making plain yogurt

1. Sterilize 1 quart milk by bringing it to a boil and simmering for 2 minutes to kill off any undesirable bacteria.

2. When the milk has cooled to lukewarm 100 to 110 degrees. (if you have a thermometer) introduce the culture. This can be a commercial yogurt culture of 1 tablespoonful of plain yogurt. Stir, breaking up any skin which has formed on the milk.

3. Cover with a warmed plate and a small blanket or something similar and leave undisturbed, maintaining the temperature until the curd becomes thick – usually after 6 to 8 hours.

Stabilizing yogurt

1. Mix 1 tablespoon of cornstarch and a little milk to form a paste. Stir it into 1 litre (2 pints) of yogurt, making sure to stir in one direction only, clockwise or counterclockwise, not both. Stir steadily and bring the mixture slowly to a boil.

2. Reduce the heat and leave the mixture to simmer in an uncovered pan until it thickens. This takes between 8 and 10 minutes. The pan is left uncovered because a drop of condensed steam falling back into the yogurt could cause it to separate. Once it has thickened, however, the yogurt can be used in cooking without risk of it curdling.

Note : If you are using yogurt made from goat's milk it does not need stabilizing as it is less fatty than cow's milk.

Cooking with yogurt

Homemade yogurt has a multitude of culinary uses as you will see from the recipes, both hot and cold, which I have included. It can also be mixed with cream for economy. Yield: 4 to 6 servings.

Cold tomato soup

An interesting recipe because no cooking is involved. It requires a blender. If the tomatoes are fresh, and sweet, the flavor is excellent.

1 lb tomatoes
1 cup yogurt
1 teaspoon sugar
a pinch of salt
1 tablespoon Worcestershire sauce
1 tablespoon lemon juice
chives, parsley or basil, finely chopped, to garnish

Blanch the tomatoes in boiling water for 30 seconds, then drain and skin. Put them in a blender with the remaining ingredients (herbs apart) and blend until smooth. If the tomatoes have a lot of seeds, a truly conscientious cook will strain the soup, working it through a strainer. If the soup is too thick, add a little cold milk. Chop the herbs finely and sprinkle on top. Serve cold.

Hot chicken soup with yogurt

A pleasant change from the Greek *avgolemono*, this recipe uses yogurt and mint to thicken and flavor the chicken soup instead of egg yolk and lemon juice.

1½ tablespoons rice
1 quart chicken stock
⅔ cup plain yogurt
1 egg
salt and pepper
1 tablespoon chopped parsley and fresh mint

Simmer the rice in the chicken stock until tender for about 12 minutes. Beat the yogurt with the egg in a bowl, stir in a little hot stock, then gradually add the contents of the bowl to the rest of the chicken stock which is taken off the heat to prevent curdling. Use plenty of salt and pepper to season the soup and very cautiously bring it to simmering point only, stirring the whole time. Serve in bowls, sprinkled with the fresh herbs.

Tandoori chicken

A classic, irresistible Indian dish of spiced, marinated roast chicken. It is the ideal disguise for dull, frozen birds.

1 chicken (3 to 4 lb)
2 medium onions
4 cloves garlic
1 small ginger root or 1 teaspoon ground ginger
1 teaspoon cumin seeds
1 teaspoon coriander seeds
2 dried chili peppers, or ½ teaspoon chili or cayenne
 powder
coarse salt
1½ cups yogurt
1 tablespoon Worcestershire sauce
2 lemons
4 tablespoons melted butter
1 teaspoon garam masala (optional)

If the bird is frozen leave to thaw overnight in the refrigerator, removing the giblets from inside.

In the morning (to eat that night) cut the chicken into serving pieces (wings, legs and breast into four pieces) and remove the skin with a sharp knife. Mince, chop or blend the onions, garlic and ginger to a mush, adding ground cumin, coriander, chili peppers and salt. In a large bowl, beat the yogurt until smooth, adding the Worcestershire sauce, the juice of 1 lemon and the spice paste. Rub this fragrant paste all over the chicken pieces, pour over the remainder and leave all day to marinate and allow the flavors to penetrate. Preheat the oven to 425 degrees, or better still, heat the rotary barbecue spit. Cook the chicken pieces in a roasting pan, with the marinade juices poured over, for 30 to 40 minutes or until the meat is firm and no longer pink in the middle. Baste once or twice if you have time with melted butter. Sprinkle with garam masala, a little coarse salt and the juice of the second lemon.

Serve hot, with hot pittas or chapatis and *salat*, which is the Indian name for an onion, tomato and lettuce or green pepper salad.

Spiced fish in yogurt – Dahi Machi

From India, a hot, spicy dish marinated and cooked in yogurt. As different as can be from our usual ways of cooking fish, and to my mind infinitely kinder to the fish.

1½ lb firm fish (cod, halibut, bass or porgy)
2 medium onions
1 teaspoon ground ginger or 1 small piece fresh ginger
  root
2 teaspoons turmeric
4 green or 3 red dried chili peppers
1 pint yogurt
a pinch of salt
2 tablespoons cooking oil
2 tablespoons ghee (p. 92)
1 tablespoon garam masala or juice of 1 lemon

Cut the fish into chunks, removing the bones and skin. Chop one onion finely. Pound the fresh ginger and mix the chopped onion and ginger, the ground turmeric, chopped fresh or powdered chili peppers, yogurt and salt. Coat the fish chunks with this spiced marinade and leave for at least 30 minutes to absorb the flavors. Now heat the oil and the ghee in a heavy skillet, slice the second onion and fry gently until golden. Then add the fish and marinade and simmer very slowly, covered, for 10 to 15 minutes, or until the fish is firm, white and cooked through. Sprinkle with garam masala (a ready ground spice mixture usually added at the last minute to refresh the spice flavors) or lemon juice and serve with spicy pan juices on plain boiled rice. A cucumber salad – or *raita* – would complement this dish. For this, peel and slice a cucumber and drain with a sprinkling of salt in a colander for 20 minutes. Rinse and dry. Pour over yogurt beaten with crushed garlic, a squeeze of lemon juice and 1 teaspoon of olive oil, chopped mint and seasonings.

Susbarak or meat dumplings cooked in yogurt

This is the sort of dish I imagine Bedouin tribesmen tucking into, hardy, simple and tasty. The meat need not be tender, but it should be lean and preferably ground twice for smoothness. This dish lends itself to flavoring up with whatever herbs and spices you fancy.

Dumplings

1 onion
1 lb ground beef, lamb or pork
a pinch of salt and pepper
¼ teaspoon each of ground cumin and cinnamon
oil
3 cups flour

Sauce or stock

1 cup stabilized yogurt
1 cup milk or stock

Chop the onion finely, mix with the ground meat, salt and pepper and spices and fry in a little oil for 5 minutes or until the onion is transparent and the meat pale brown.

Mix the flour with enough cold water to make a firm dough. Knead for 2 or 3 minutes until smooth. Shape into a sausage sized roll. Roll out the dough to the thickness of a coin, stamp into small circles (2 inches) and place 1 teaspoon of meat stuffing on each. Moisten the edges of the dough, fold over and pinch closed. Heat the stabilized yogurt with milk, or stock, in a deep pan until boiling, then drop in the *susbarak* carefully one at a time and simmer gently with the pan lid half on for 30 minutes.

Serve hot with pittas and a salad of chopped tomatoes, raw onions or salad greens, generously dressed and seasoned.

Orange flavored yogurt sherbet

This is a smashing water ice, with a fine smooth texture and excellent flavor.

1½ cups thick plain yogurt
grated rind of 2 oranges
1 can (approx 6 oz) frozen unsweetened orange juice
3 tablespoons sugar
2 egg whites

Blend the yogurt, orange rind, frozen orange juice and 1 tablespoon of sugar together. Turn into an ice cream maker, or ice tray, and freeze for approximately 30 minutes. Turn into a bowl, beat, then return to the ice cream maker or freezer. Repeat. When mushy, stir in the egg whites which have been beaten with the remaining sugar until stiff and thick. Freeze this time without stirring. Leave to thaw before serving.

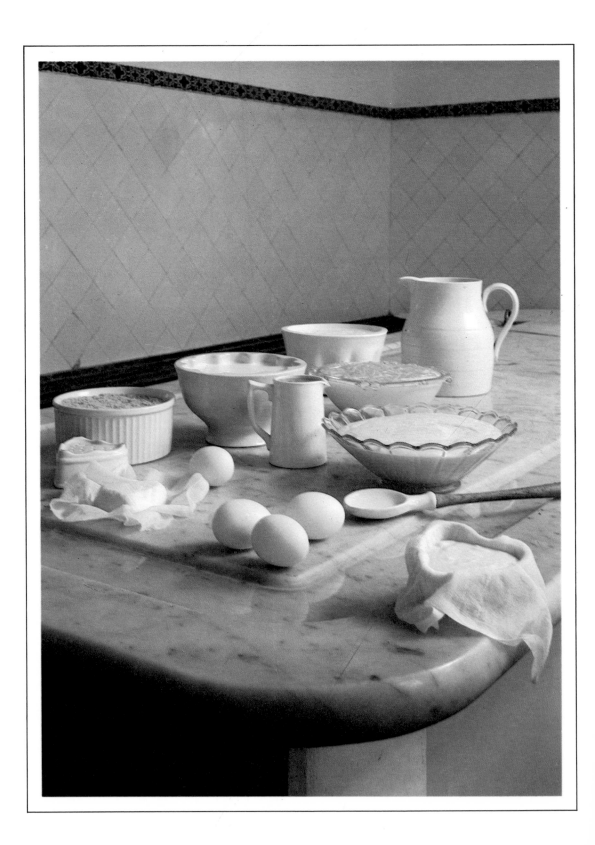

Cream

'"This will be a country supper, girls" said Polly, bustling about.
"There is real cream, brown bread, home-made cake and honey from my beehives.
Butter the toast, Maud, and put that little cover on it."'

An Old Fashioned Girl   Louisa May Alcott   1870

It is cream, that thick, unctuous, yellowish, clinging, incomparable substance which distils, so to speak, the richness of our milk. If a pan of whole milk is left to stand overnight, the fat globules it contains rise to the top, as fat is lighter than water, and the yellow skin of fat is cream. In the old days, before separating machines were invented, it was skimmed off with a perforated disk called a 'fleeter'; a wasteful way of doing things since some fat was always left behind in the skimmed milk, but one which produced delicious cream. As much as 16 gallons of milk would go to make 1 quart of cream. Now the process is carried out commercially with separating machines which spin off the heavier skim milk, with such exactitude that creams of precisely gauged fat content are produced with no trouble at all. Thus we can buy half and half (12% fat content), light cream (18%), whipping cream (35%), heavy cream (48%) and Devonshire clotted cream, richest of all at 55%. As with most commercial processes, such gains in efficiency seem to be balanced by a loss not in quality exactly, but things which can only be measured subjectively like flavor, texture, liveliness. One carton of commercial cream tastes just like the next, which is good insofar as it means a consistent standard is maintained, but seems a far cry from the days when a particular farmer's wife in a certain region could become famous for the glorious flavor of the cream her well-fed cows turned out. Today's pedigree dairy herds are superb milking machines, yet a dairy farmer I know speaks wistfully of the days when cows were fed on what you might call the free range principle, because the milk had so much more flavor to it then.

Devonshire cream is probably the nearest you can get to the 'thicke crayme' of old, which you can well believe was eaten 'more for a sensuall appetyte than for any good nouryshment'. But it is expensive. Anyone living near a dairy farm, however, may well be able to buy milk at wholesale prices to make their own Devonshire cream, and it is not difficult to do provided you can use up all the skimmed milk.

Of all the dairy products, cream contributes most to cooking, or perhaps I should say 'cuisine' since it is the French who have taken this aspect of gastronomy furthest. By this I do not mean that cream is used in greater quantities, but that it contributes a distinctive creaminess to thousands of dishes. There is really no substitute for cream.

Water piped in runnels around a marble slab keeps prepared desserts cool in this old dairy: cremets, thick cream lightened with egg white, in heart molds; burnt cream layered with brown sugar and junkets in molds (left); and lemon soufflé topped with rind, and a syllabub (right).

Cream making

To obtain cream from milk

You need a fair supply, say $\frac{1}{2}$ gallon of fresh, raw milk. Raw milk is untreated, that is non-pasteurized. A wide shallow pan, dish or bowl, preferably with outward sloping sides, and something to use as a skimmer are the only equipment needed. Not so long ago, dairy workers used the flat half of a scallop shell, and it still serves admirably, having a grooved surface for the milk to run off. Otherwise use a slotted spatula, or thin saucer. Proper (stainless steel) skimmers and bowls are obtainable from specialist stores.

Pour the milk into the pan or dish, put in a cool place for 24 hours and you will find a thick, leathery skin of cream has formed on top. If you are making cream from goat's milk you may have to leave it for longer because the fat globules are smaller. Lift this off with your skimmer, turn into a jar and store in the refrigerator. People with a regular supply of raw milk will probably make cream every other day or so, and this can be added to the jar as it is made. It keeps for about a week in the refrigerator. To thin down this cream, simply stir in a little milk. This is the old-fashioned, wasteful way of getting cream – wasteful because some fat always remains in the milk – but it has the advantage that the skimmed milk will be all the richer.

Pasteurizing cream

Cream made from raw milk can be pasteurized to ensure that any contaminating bacteria are destroyd. To pasteurize, heat the cream in the top of a double boiler to 145 degrees and hold it at this temperature for 30 minutes. Stir. Transfer the top part of the boiler to a bowl of iced water and bring the temperature of the cream down to 40 degrees as speedily as possible. Store it in clean, sterilized containers in the refrigerator.

Making cream from butter and milk

This Alice-Through-the-Looking-Glass trick can be accomplished easily with the cream making attachment to an electric blender, and is useful when you need some cream urgently for a recipe and the stores are closed. Some people regularly make cream this way; where butter prices are reasonable, it works out somewhat cheaper than buying straight cream. It makes good thick cream, but the butter *must* be unsalted. If you want a thinner cream use less butter. Melt 1 cup of unsalted butter in $\frac{1}{2}$ cup of milk. Pour into the cream making attachment, whizz away until the butter and milk have combined and leave to cool. Stir before using.

Clotting cream the traditional way

Pour the cream into an earthenware or enameled bowl, or stainless steel milk pan, then heat gently either on top of an old-fashioned range or in a pan of water (*bain marie*) on a gas or electric stove turned down very low. Warm for anything up to 6 hours until the cream has a rich wrinkled crusty look. Never let it boil. Then set the pan to cool and by morning you can lift off a 'clout' to store in jars or lidded pots in the refrigerator.

Clotting cream the quick way

As the cream should not come into direct contact with the hotplate, either use a double boiler or place a pan in a saucepan of water. You also need a thermometer.

Heat until the cream reaches a temperature around 170 to 180 degrees. Check with the thermometer. Keep the cream around this point (not more than 190 degrees) for between 30 minutes and 1 hour, until the cream looks crusty and wrinkled. Early in the proceedings, stir it once, to distribute the heat. Cool the cream pan speedily by putting it in a bowl of cold water, then leave in a cool place overnight to set. Pack into jars and store.

To sour cream

A lot of Russian recipes call for 'smetana' or sour cream. The best is made by letting unpasteurized cream sour naturally at room temperature but this takes a few days. You can hurry it up a little by stirring in a spoonful of yogurt or leftover sour cream. On no account use commercial pasteurized cream past the stamped date as it tastes bitter and can contain undesirable bacteria. All equipment must be kept spotlessly clean and sterilized.

To produce a quick sour cream, stir a spoonful of lemon juice or vinegar into a bought pasteurized light cream and leave in a warm place for an hour or so. Yogurt or sour raw milk will sour bought cream overnight.

To whip cream

Commercial whipping cream produces fluffier whipped cream and costs a bit less than heavy cream. Dilute heavy cream with a couple of spoonfuls of half and half (or light cream) before whipping to give a softer, lighter texture. Single or thin cream does not contain enough fat to whip. Cream for whipping should be left in the refrigerator overnight to 'ripen' and become thicker. Chefs use wire balloon whisks for whipping cream because they beat in more air which makes a lighter cream. Scandinavians swear by whisks made from birch twigs but most of us use a plain old rotary or electric beater. Whichever type you prefer, do not overwhip as the cream should be soft and fluffy, not stiff lest it gives a stodgy taste to dishes which should be light and airy.

In some dishes like fruit fools, or mousses, whipped cream can be bulked by folding in beaten egg whites.

To cook with cream

Half and half and light cream are the best grades to use for most cooking purposes; heavy cream is unnecessarily lavish. Some ice creams and cream desserts are in effect a sort of cream custard; with egg yolks, light cream is adequate since the yolks provide the thickening. When using cream with wine in a sauce for meat, fish or poultry, reduce the wine by boiling hard before adding the cream. This gives more flavor and helps prevent the cream separating. Always draw the pan off the heat before adding cream to a hot sauce, lest it curdles.

Skimming cream

1. For this you need about 2 quarts of fresh raw milk. Pour the milk into a pan or dish with wide sloping sides and leave it in a cool place for a day. You will find a thick leathery skin of cream forms on top. Lift this off with a skimmer – a saucer will do. In South Devon, England, famous for its cream, half a scallop shell was used as the milk ran down the grooves of the shell. Store the cream for up to a week in a covered jar in the refrigerator. The quantity of cream taken from the milk will depend entirely on the fat content of the milk.

Clotting cream

This quick method automatically pasteurizes cream skimmed from fresh milk. Clotted cream can be made from bought heavy cream but it would be ludicrously expensive.

1. Warm the skimmed cream in a double boiler very gently. Use a thermometer and heat until the cream reaches a temperature of around 190 degrees. Hold it at this temperature for about 1 hour until the cream looks crusty and wrinkled. Never let it boil. Stir it once to distribute the heat.

2. Cool the cream pan speedily by placing it in a bowl of cold water and leave overnight to set.

3. By morning you can lift off the great clout of clotted cream that has formed. Store in covered jars or pots in the refrigerator. Serve clotted cream loaded on scones (see recipe on page 38) already spread with sweet butter, and topped with blackcurrant jam.

Cooking with cream : savories

The point to remember when adding cream to soups, sauces or pan juices is that it should not boil, because this tends to curdle it, especially if sharply flavored. The taste is not affected but it does not look good. Yield : 4 to 6 servings.

Likky soup
Likky is Cornish for leek, and their version of leek and potato soup naturally features clotted cream from Cornwall or the neighboring county, Devonshire. Whipped cream is a paltry, but necessary, substitute.

4 slices bacon
1 large potato
2 large leeks
2 tablespoons butter
salt, pepper, chopped parsley
1½ pints beef or chicken stock
¼ cup clotted cream

Cut the bacon into strips, peel and slice the potato, wash the leeks and slice across. Fry all these gently in butter for a few minutes then season with salt, pepper and chopped parsley. Add the stock and simmer for 20 to 30 minutes. Add the cream just before serving.

Eliza Acton's salmon pudding
In her cookbook of 1845 this doyen of Victorian cookbook writers notes tersely, 'A Scotch Receipt – Good'. It is not as extravagant as it sounds since it can be made with leftovers or the cheap tail cuts, and the other ingredients make the fish go further.

1 lb cooked salmon
4 eggs
2½ cups fresh fine white breadcrumbs
⅔ cup light cream
salt and cayenne pepper
2 tablespoons butter

Skin and bone the salmon, and pound, mash or blend until smooth. Beat the eggs until frothy. Mix the fish, eggs, crumbs, light cream and seasonings well together, then press into a well buttered soufflé dish, about 1 quart capacity. Dot with butter and bake at 350 degrees for 1 hour or until firm.

Serve with the following simple but excellent sauce which is also good with fried fish fillets.

⅔ cup whipping cream
¼ teaspoon anchovy paste

Whip the cream until fluffy, adding the paste gradually. Pour over the fish and serve at once.

Pork or veal cooked with apple and cream
Apples, Calvados and cream are characteristic ingredients of cooking in Normandy. Here they turn a simple meat dish into something grander. I make it with pork tenderloin and whiskey and it is just as good. The ideal dish to rustle up at short notice. This amount serves four.

1 lb pork tenderloin or veal scallops
salt, pepper and lemon juice
1 large or 2 small sweet apples
4 tablespoons butter
½ cup Calvados (applejack) or whiskey
1¼ cups heavy cream

The pork tenderloin should be sliced across into miniature steaks, and pounded flat with a cleaver. (Scallops should also be flattened.) Rub salt and pepper into the meat and sprinkle with lemon juice. Peel, core and finely dice the apple. Melt the butter in a heavy skillet. Add the meat and sizzle over a moderate heat until lightly browned on both sides. Add the apple cubes, stir about and cook for a moment longer. Heat the Calvados or whiskey in a small pan, set light to it and pour it over the contents of the pan, shaking them cautiously until the flames subside. Add the cream, reduce the heat and simmer gently for a few minutes, stirring the sauce and scraping the meat juices into it. When thickened, arrange the apple on top of the meat and serve immediately with the sauce poured around. Serve this with just one simply cooked vegetable, such as steamed green beans, peas or broccoli.

Cooking with cream : desserts

Memories of childhood are envoked by delectable desserts made with cream : fools, ices, mousses, trifles, syllabubs, soufflés hot and cold. A cream dessert should be smooth, cool and rich without being oversweetened. Yield : 4 to 6 servings.

Cremets

Starting with the most artless of all cream desserts, and one of the best – thick cream lightened with egg white and left to drain overnight. The result is neither cloying nor sickly. Use heavy, not whipping, cream for cremets, to provide the necessary texture.

1½ cups heavy cream
1 tablespoon half and half
2 egg whites

Some sort of perforated mold is necessary to let the mixture drain. Use a little basket lined with cheesecloth or commercial molds.

To make the cremets, whip the cream with a spoonful of half and half until thick. Beat the egg whites until fluffy and fold in the cream. Turn into the cheesecloth lined mold and set to drain on a cake rack over a pan or dish. Leave the dessert in a cool place. (If you are using the refrigerator make sure no aromatic food is nearby, as cream absorbs smells.) The next day, unmold onto a plate, pour over enough unsweetened light cream to cover and serve with sugar and any fresh soft fruit in season, or alone.

Syllabub

Another uncooked cream, sweetened and flavored with lemon and Marsala.

1 lemon
¼ cup Marsala, Madeira or sweet sherry
2 tablespoons sugar
1½ cups heavy double cream
pinch of grated nutmeg

Grate the lemon rind, squeeze the juice and combine both with the Marsala and sugar. Leave for a few hours, or overnight. Strain (to remove rind) and add to the cream. Then whip until thick, fluffy but not too stiff. Spoon into little glasses, sprinkle with nutmeg and serve cold with cookies.

Sack cream

Sack is a corruption of *vin sec*, which in Elizabethan England was imported from Spain, and seems to have been closer to sherry than wine. Wines were drunk sweeter then; a sweetish sherry gives a better flavor than the white wine usually called for. Sack creams are as old as the syllabub but this cooked version is Victorian.

1 egg yolk
2½ cups light cream
3 tablespoons sugar
½ cup sherry or Madeira
grated lemon rind

Put all the ingredients together, having beaten the egg yolk well first, in the top of a double boiler. Heat gently, stirring, until the mixture is as thick as heavy cream. Remove from the heat and stir until cold. Pour into glasses and serve, traditionally, with bread oven-dried until brittle.

Cold lemon soufflé

Always an acceptable dessert, neither too rich nor too sweet.

1 envelope unflavored gelatin
1 tablespoon milk
3 eggs
3 lemons
⅔ cup sugar
1¼ cups whipping cream
ratafia cookies (optional)

Stir the gelatin in the warmed milk until dissolved. Separate the eggs, combine the egg yolks, the juice of three lemons and grated rind of two, the sugar and the gelatin in the top of a double boiler. Heat, stirring, until thick. Allow to cool. Whip the cream until fluffy. Beat the egg white and then fold both into the lemon custard mixture. Spoon into a soufflé dish and chill until set. Serve cold, with ratafia cookies.

Baked potato pudding

From Italy, a thoroughly unusual hot pudding made from sweetened mashed potatoes baked with raisins and pine nuts. The eggs give it a cake-like consistency.

1 lb hot boiled potatoes
6 tablespoons butter
⅔ cup light cream
a pinch of salt
1 tablespoon flour
3 eggs
3 tablespoons sugar
cinnamon and nutmeg
⅔ cup raisins
3 tablespoons pinenuts

Mash the boiled, peeled potatoes until smooth, then stir in the butter, cream, a tiny pinch of salt, and flour and heat, stirring to mix. Separate the eggs. Stir the egg yolks, sugar, ground spices, raisins (soaked for a few minutes in warm water to soften) and pine nuts into the potato mixture. Fold in the stiffly beaten egg whites and spoon into a buttered floured 8 inch cake square. Bake at 425 degrees for 45 minutes. Serve hot with thin cream.

Vanilla mousse with butterscotch sauce

The combination of hot butterscotch sauce with cold mousse, demurely flavored with vanilla, is the joy of this dish.

3 egg yolks
¼ cup sugar
1 teaspoon vanilla extract or 1 vanilla bean
1 envelope unflavored gelatin
⅔ cup milk
1¼ cup whipping cream, whipped

Butterscotch sauce

4 tablespoons butter
⅔ cup light brown sugar
2 tablespoons light corn syrup
¼ teaspoon vanilla extract

To make the mousse, combine the egg yolks, sugar and vanilla extract or bean in the top of a double boiler and heat, stirring, until thick. Take care it does not boil. Take off the heat. Remove the vanilla bean. Stir in the gelatin dissolved in milk. Stir until cold – this takes less time if you put the pan in a bowl of cold water.

When it shows signs of setting, fold in the whipped cream. Pour into an attractive bowl and leave to set.

For the sauce, merely combine all the ingredients in the top of a double boiler and heat gently, stirring, until smooth. Serve hot in a jug.

Burnt cream

Cambridge University claims to have invented this elegant dish, and it can still be ordered from college butteries (kitchens) for May Ball suppers.

The 'burnt' refers not to the cream but to a sugar layer on top, caramelized to a hard transparent amber disk. This is not the easiest thing to achieve with an ordinary broiler (a salamander – metal disk heated red hot – was used) but it is spectacular if you succeed.

4 egg yolks
2½ cups light cream
2 tablespoons sugar
small piece orange rind
small piece stick cinnamon
1 teaspoon cornstarch mixed with 1 teaspoon milk
⅔ cup light brown sugar

Beat the egg yolks and combine with the cream, sugar, orange rind and cinnamon in the top of a double boiler. Mix the cornstarch with the milk, as a precaution against curdling, and add to the mixture. Heat slowly, stirring, until thick. Remove the cinnamon and the rind and leave to cool, stirring now and then. Pour into a dish, and chill until firm. Now sift the brown sugar evenly over the top, making sure the sugar continues right up to the rim. Heat the broiler and set the dish on a baking sheet under the broiler until the sugar turns to caramel – you may have to turn the dish carefully to reach every bit but do not cook too long or the caramel will blacken. Remove and cool. Serve cold.

Note : use a flameproof soufflé dish, such as Pyrex. Cambridge chefs set the cream dish inside another bowl of crushed ice while browning the top. This helps prevent curdling.

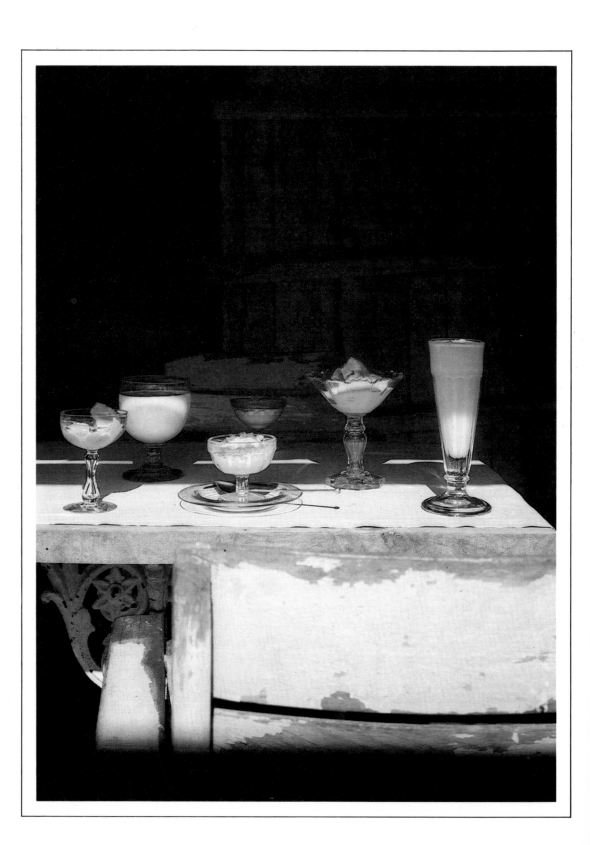

Ice Cream

*'HOT ICE CREAMS FOR COLD DAYS, it said on the next door.
"Extremely useful in the winter," said Mr Wonka, rushing on. "Hot ice
cream warms you up no end in freezing weather."'*

Charlie and the Chocolate Factory   Roald Dahl   1968

It is quite amazing how resourceful and clever people can be when it comes to gratifying an appetite. How those egregious gluttons, the patricians of old Rome, managed to transport ice from the nearest glacier to make ice-caves where frozen creams and other dainties could be made and stored in the Roman summer heat, is a mystery. Italy seems to have held the lead in the ice cream department, for the frozen confections Marie de Médicis introduced via her Italian chef to the French court were so elaborate they put to shame the childish mess of sweetened snow which Chaucer mentions.

Making ices today is no problem, as every house has its own ice-cave in the shape of the freezing compartment of the refrigerator. Some own freezers too. A perfectly good ice cream can be made in a refrigerator or freezer provided you remember to take it out from time to time and beat it well, to inhibit the formation of crystals. Some people, however, prefer the crunchy texture of crystals, in which case do not beat the mixture when it is partly frozen. To produce an ice cream of velvety smoothness, the ingredients need to be kept moving as they are cooling. The old fashioned hand-cranked ice cream churns fulfilled this requirement by churning a little metal tub of ice cream round and round in a bed of cracked ice and salt. These are still the best ice cream makers around but it is sometimes difficult to get enough cracked ice and people are reluctant to sit turning handles for 20 minutes at a time. Technology has come up with the solution – an electric ice cream making gadget which you put into the ice compartment of the freezer, switch on and leave paddling away quietly like an Arctic troll. Various models are obtainable. The ice compartment must be defrosted first and you need to make sure the gadget's cord has not been pinched too tight in the refrigerator or freezer door. To remove the ice cream from the molds, dip them in hot water for a moment. Prizing out the ice with a knife would wreck the mold. The pan and paddles can be immersed in hot water to clean, but the casing should only be wiped over with a damp cloth as it is electrical. Some brands stop paddling automatically once the ice cream has reached the proper consistency, and the paddles lift out of the ice. With others you need to keep an eye on proceedings otherwise the ice cream simply sets around the paddles.

Icy cold ices, creamy smooth, served on a summer's day: raspberry-flavored frozen fruit mousse, then sack cream served in a giant goblet, an orange-flavored yogurt sherbet in a tall sundae glass and simple vanilla ice cream topped with crunchy almond praline.

Ice cream making

Points about ice cream making

Use the ice tray or a plastic box in the freezing compartment of a refrigerator. Stir the mix at 30 minute intervals, then when it is beginning to set firm all the way through, turn into a chilled bowl and beat hard to stop any crystals forming. This is also the best time to add liqueurs, nuts, bits of chocolate or fruit. If you are using a machine, add these extras when the paddles stop.

Ice cream can be too cold: this annuls the flavor and it is agony to eat. Take an ice out of the freezing compartment or freezer and let it ripen, or mellow, in the center of the refrigerator for between 15 minutes and 1 hour depending on how hard it is. Ice cream keeps well for about a month in the freezer but needs considerable thawing before use.

Ingredients

Ice cream can be made from various mixtures, ranging from pure cream flavored and frozen solid, to custards of varying degrees of richness according to the ratio of cream to eggs. Rich ice cream results from richer, more expensive mixtures but a thinner mix, using twice as much milk as cream, gives excellent results in an electric ice maker.

The right amount of sugar is important – too little gives too solid an ice, too much prevents it freezing properly. All the ingredients must be chilled before use. If you make the custard base and leave it to chill overnight before adding the cream, it takes only 1 hour to finish in the gadget and a little longer in the ice compartment.

Ices are cruel to filled teeth unless they are smooth enough to swallow without chewing. So if you are adding nuts, it might be kinder to add them only on top – chewing frozen nuts or crunchy praline straight from the freezer – has been known to make guests scream aloud.

Budget ice creams

For cheaper ice cream, popular with children though not perhaps with gourmets, you can substitute evaporated or condensed milk for fresh light or heavy cream. Both these milk concentrates have a powerful flavor of their own, quite different from that of the fresh products, which the purist might object to, so the usual advice is to use these only when making strongly flavored ices, such as coffee, chocolate or strawberry. In both cases look for the unsweetened variety, otherwise you will upset the sugar balance in the recipe concerned. A useful rule of thumb when making a basic vanilla ice cream is that 3 to 4 tablespoons of sugar per $2\frac{1}{2}$ cups of cream or custard ice cream base, is the maximum quantity needed. When making fruit ices, the proportion of sugar to base mixture is increased. The evaporated milk is usually scalded, chilled, then whipped before the remaining ingredients are added. The cheapest ices are the water ices, usually a frozen fruit purée into which some beaten egg white is incorporated for lightness. See the yogurt section for a refreshing orange ice with a smooth texture based on plain yogurt (orange flavored yogurt sherbet, page 73), photographed on page 82 with the ice creams.

Ice creams

Ice cream can be made from various mixtures, ranging from pure cream flavored and frozen solid to custard mixes. I have included both simple and rich recipes for you to experiment with. Yield: 6 servings.

Simple vanilla ice cream

2 eggs and 2 additional yolks
6 tablespoons sugar
1¾ cups milk
1 teaspoon vanilla extract
1 cup heavy cream

Beat the eggs and extra yolks with the sugar until smooth and thick. Heat the milk to scalding point, then pour it into the eggs, beating all the time. Strain into the top of a double boiler and stir over a gentle heat until thickened. Chill. Add the vanilla extract and fold in the lightly whipped cream. Turn into an ice cream paddler or ice trays – in the latter case, beat three times at 30 minute intervals during freezing. The ice cream will set in 2 hours.

Use this plain vanilla ice cream as the base for the following 3 recipes:

Ginger ice cream

Add ⅓ cup chopped preserved ginger and 1 tablespoon syrup to vanilla ice cream, after the final beating.

Caramel ice cream

Spread ¾ cup sugar in a thick bottomed pan and put over a medium heat to caramelize, watching it all the time. Boil for a short time, stirring with a metal spoon, until evenly golden brown. Quickly pour a thin layer onto a greased baking sheet. When cold, pound to a powder in a mortar or blend. Follow the vanilla ice recipe using 6 tablespoons of the caramel powder instead of sugar. The remainder can be folded into the ice cream at the final beating, or sprinkled on top.

Praline ice cream

Praline is a candy made with chopped almonds and sugar, ground finely as for caramel.
Put ½ cup unblanched almonds and 5 tablespoons sugar into a heavy pan and heat gently, stirring with a metal spoon, until the sugar melts. Raise the heat a little and cook until nutbrown. Pour quickly into a well greased pan. When cold, pulverize coarsely.

Add the praline powder to the vanilla ice cream after the final beating.

Brown bread ice cream

An arresting and delicious combination of slightly crunchy crumbs and smooth ice cream.

1¼ cups whipping cream
1 tablespoon vanilla sugar or sugar plus vanilla extract
2 tablespoons half and half or light cream
1½ cups fresh brown breadcrumbs
½ cup light brown sugar

Whip the cream lightly with the vanilla sugar, add the half and half and freeze, beating three times once every 30 minutes – or churn in an ice cream maker. Meanwhile combine the breadcrumbs with the brown sugar, spread on a baking sheet and bake at 400 degrees until the sugar is just caramelized. Cool quickly, crush then chill. Fold the crumbs into the frozen mixture. Freeze for a further 30 minutes and serve.

Frozen fruit mousse

Any fruit can be used for this – from canned guavas to fresh blueberries. A mousse base is a little different from a custard base, rather easier and quicker to make. A good family ice cream.

1¼ cups chilled heavy cream
1 pint fruit purée made from fresh, canned or cooked
  dried fruit, sweetened to taste and chilled
3 egg whites

In a large bowl, fold the lightly whipped cream into the fruit purée, then fold in the softly beaten egg whites. Pour into containers and freeze without stirring. For an elegant touch, put a paper collar around the inside of a soufflé dish and overfill so that on removing the paper, before serving, the mousse appears to have 'risen'.

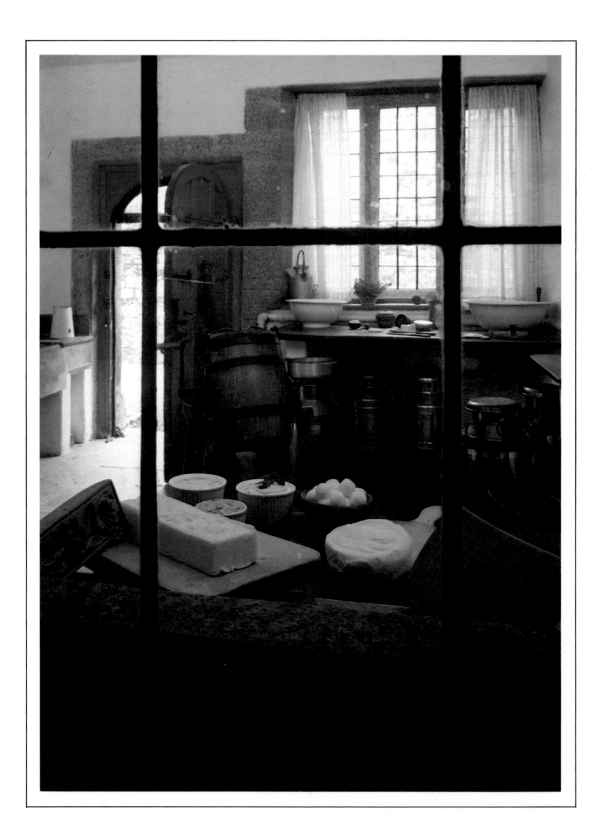

Butter

*'Ellen put in the dasher and the cover and began to churn.
It was tiresome work: the cream was rich and cold,
and at the end of half an hour grew very stiff.
It splattered up on Ellen's face and hand and apron,
and over the flour; legs and arms were both weary;
but still the dasher must go up and down; she must not stop.'*
The Wide, Wide World   Elizabeth Wetherall   1893

If milk is largely water with a little fat in it, butter, conversely, is largely fat with a little water in it. It is made by agitating (rocking, spinning, shaking) fresh or sour cream steadily until the fat globules in the cream clump together and separate from the cloudy, slightly acid liquid called buttermilk. The butter, churned from good rich cream, and eaten fresh, or very lightly salted, has a purity of flavor which beats anything commercial.

Making butter is neither complicated nor difficult. It is most economic for those people who keep cows or can buy suitable milk at wholesale prices. In earliest times it was made by simply shaking cream vigorously in a skin pouch. Today scientific know-how and mechanization has the whole process firmly under control, but traditionally butter making was reckoned to be a temperamental business. Some days, for no apparent reason, the butter 'went to sleep' and refused to 'come'. Women, who did so much of the dairy work, came in for some of the blame, and fairies were thought likely culprits, as Shakespeare acknowledges when he earmarks Robin Goodfellow as the saboteur who 'bootless makes the breathless housewife churn'. Pastures were regularly inspected for weeds (ivy, wild garlic, buttercups were all suspect) which might 'taint' the milk, and thus the butter.

In the days before refrigeration, much trouble went into keeping the dairy, or wherever the milk and its by-products were stored, cool and airy. Roofs were thatch or stone-tiled to keep out the summer sun's heat, surfaces inside were of smooth slate or stone and windows faced north. All equipment was scalded to keep it sweet, and left to bleach in the sun and wind. A dairymaid's hands were supposed to be as white as milk, smooth as butter and cool as spring water, though it was a matter for pride (and hygiene) that the butter was handled as little as possible between churn and table. A skilled worker used wooden butter 'hands' to press out whey and shape the pats, which might then be further embellished with the farm's individual butter stamp formed in a hand carved wooden mold.

Butter is churned, then worked with butter 'hands' on the cool slate table beneath the dairy window: three savory butters in pots: black olive butter (left), anchovy butter (center) and mint butter. Carved molds add an individual touch to the plain butters. So do butter curls.

Butter making

Equipment

A standard electric mixer with adjustable speed settings may not be as aesthetically rewarding as the old fashioned plunge or rocker churns which still turn up occasionally in country junk stores and sales, but it efficiently turns cream into butter. Small glass jar churns, with hand turned wooden paddles, can still be bought, though an electrically operated churn seems the obvious choice for regular butter making. Wooden spoons or butter making 'hands' are required for squeezing and shaping the finished butter.

Cream

Fresh or sour cream may be used for butter making but do not use any pasteurized cream which has been allowed to go 'off'. Pasteurized cream does not sour naturally like the non-pasteurized variety, and the bitter taste it develops would spoil your butter. Fresh cream may be used pasteurized or non-pasteurized, according to whatever is available and your preferences in the matter – non-pasteurized cream from a reputable tuberculin tested herd is quite safe. The thicker the cream the more fat it contains and thus the more butter it will make. So it is false economy to buy more of a cheaper, thinner cream. Butter made from fresh cream tastes delicately sweet, and ineffably 'buttery', best eaten right away unsalted. Butter made from sour cream has a richer, stronger flavor – it does *not* taste 'sour' by the way – and is best for salting and storing. Also sour cream takes about a third of the time to churn.

Churning

Churning adequately describes the whole range of ways of keeping cream on the move; hand or electric beater, hand cranked churn, power churn. Everything for butter making (*vide* the old dairies) should be cool, between 50 and 65 degrees is ideal. Keep the ripened cream in the refrigerator for an hour or so beforehand to harden the fat and help it turn to butter. If you are beating in a bowl use a big one as the cream will splatter. A guideline is that 1 quart of heavy cream makes approximately 1 lb butter, but it depends entirely on the fat content of the cream.

The method for making butter is the same whether you use fresh or sour cream. Tip the cream into a bowl, mixer or churn. If you are using the mixer, set it at a slow speed and keep your eye on it. Otherwise just start slowly and steadily churning away. The cream will get thicker, and thicker, and suddenly 'break', the vivid term for the moment when the stuff separates out into solids and liquid. At this point a splash of *cold* water – 'breaking water' – helps, but do not overdo it, no more than a quarter of the total amount of cream. Churn on until the butter granules are about the size of barley grains, then pour off the buttermilk into a bowl – it is excellent for mixing bread, biscuits, soda bread. Add a cup of *cold* water to the churn (or the mixer) and churn on for a few seconds. This is to wash out the traces of buttermilk (if left in they can turn butter rancid) and should be repeated until the rinsing water runs off clear. Now turn the butter into a fine strainer or cheesecloth and leave in a cool place to firm and drain.

If you are in a hurry, the butter can be eaten but ideally, it should be worked further to expel the last dregs of water. To do this put it on a wet board, and with a pair of wet wooden spoons, spatulas, or butter 'hands' pat it out flat, squeezing it at the same time and tilting the board to help the water to run off. When you think you have worked out all the water, you can salt the butter. Use 1 or 2 teaspoons of coarse salt per 1 lb butter for the keenest flavor. Simply sprinkle salt over the butter and pat it in, pressing and squeezing with your wooden implement.

For storing, shape into pats (carved molds are not expensive and add an appropriately individual touch), wrap in wax paper or foil and store in a refrigerator or a cool pantry. Alternatively store butter in the freezer, where it will keep for months.

To wash salt out

I frequently find some of the cheaper commercial butters are oversalted. By reversing the above procedure it is quite simple to remove excess salt. Chop up the butter, pat into smallish chunks, put them into a bowl of cold water, squeeze with the hands for a moment or two, then rinse under cold running water. Press out most of the water as described above, shape and chill.

Carved molds for shaping butter pats add a decorative and individual touch to butters. Traditionally, dairy farms had their own wooden butter stamp – a carved swan indicated the farm stood among watermeadows, a myrtle spray that it was a hill farm with richer milk, a cornsheaf that it was a mixed arable and dairy farm. Butter curlers come in a variety of shapes and materials: the elegant Parisien butter curler is made of boxwood and the modern butter curler of stainless steel and wood has a distinctive spade shape. Use them to print out the pattern on commercial or homemade butters.

Making salted butter

1. To make 1 lb of butter, leave 1 quart heavy cream in an earthenware bowl or panshon to 'ripen' at room temperature for anything up to 48 hours.

2. Tip the cream into a bowl, mixer or churn. If you are using a mixer, do not fill it more than half-full as the mixture will splatter, and set it at a low speed. Otherwise, churn slowly and steadily until the cream separates into butterfat and buttermilk.

3. Add a splash of cold water – no more than $1\frac{1}{4}$ cups – at the point when the mixture separates into solids and liquid. Then churn on until the butter granules are about the size of barley grains.

4. Pour off the buttermilk into a bowl. It is excellent for making bread, biscuits and soda bread.

5. Add 1 cup of cold water to the butter and churn on for a few seconds, to wash out any traces of buttermilk that can turn butter rancid if left.

6. Turn the butter into a fine sieve or cheesecloth and leave in a cool place to firm and drain. The butter could be eaten now but ideally it should be worked further to expel the last dregs of water.

7. Turn the drained butter onto a wet board and, using a wet wooden spoon, spatula or wooden hands, pat it flat, squeezing it at the same time and tilting the board to help the water drain off.

8. Sprinkle 1 or 2 teaspoons of coarse dairy or kosher salt over the butter and pat it in, pressing and squeezing with your wooden implement, or butter 'hands'.

9. Shape into pats, wrap in wax paper or foil and store in the refrigerator or cool pantry. Before freezing, I usually make up a few interesting flavored butters to be used as spreads on broiled meats and fish as a substitute for a sauce. Butter will keep for months in a freezer.

When molding butter, first place the softened butter in the carved wooden mold, making sure that the corners of the mold, spikes of the thistle, or whatever are filled, then freeze overnight. Leave the butter to thaw the next morning for about 30 minutes, then quickly run it under warm water, and ease it out of the mold with a round edged knife blade. Freeze the butter immediately, before the edges begin to soften, to keep the imprint of the mold sharp.

9

8

6

7

Butters

Here are a few interesting flavored butters which can be used as spreads on toast and crackers, or on broiled meat and fish where they substitute for a more elaborate sauce, and the recipe for clarified butter to seal cooked dishes.

Clarified butter or ghee

Ghee, or clarified butter, is a mainstay of Indian cooking and deserves to be more widely used in the West; it tastes rich and nutty, keeps up to a year in a cool place without going rancid, and can be heated to a higher temperature than any other frying medium (oil, lard, margarine) without catching and burning. One snag though – it is a butter concentrate and therefore expensive. I make a large jar and reserve it for frying rice for risotto or pulao, frying fritters and doughnuts. The classic English use for clarified butter is as an edible airtight seal for the more elegant potted shellfish. Do not use it to cover a large pâté, or terrine, where melted lard is cheaper and as effective a seal. In India, tiny bowls of *ghee* and salt accompany every meal.

2 lb of butter, preferably unsalted, yields a medium sized jar of *ghee*. A heavy, thick bottomed pan is essential to prevent the melted butter sticking during the long cooking. What happens during the cooking is that any moisture left in the butter evaporates, and any of the impurities that cause butter to burn, sink to the bottom of the pan.

To make *ghee*, put the butter in a heavy pan and melt it over a gentle heat. Keep it just below the simmering point for between 40 minutes and 1 hour, or until you can see the sediment settling on the bottom. The *ghee* should be crystal clear. Line a conical strainer with cheesecloth and pour through the *ghee* into a warmed jar (I use a canning jar with its lid) leaving the sediment behind. *Ghee* is quite soft so you can scoop out what you need with a spoon. For a clarified butter seal, melt 1 or 2 tablespoons of *ghee* over a low heat and pour over your shrimp or whatever. Cover completely, excluding any air. Cool, then cover with a lid or foil and store in the fridge.

Green or Snail butter

Do not keep this garlic delight for the rare snail, but use it on broiled meat, or steamed carrots and lima beans, or mushrooms on toast.

3 to 4 cloves garlic
2½ tablespoons finely chopped parsley
2 tablespoons finely chopped chives, chervil or tarragon
8 tablespoons butter
2½ teaspoons olive oil
salt and pepper to taste

Pound the garlic and herbs to a paste, or chop to a mush. Work into softened butter (not melted, but with the chill off), adding olive oil, herbs and seasonings to taste. Roll in foil and chill.

Anchovy butter

A basic fish and butter paste.

a handful fresh parsley
6 anchovy fillets
¼ clove garlic or 1 shallot
8 tablespoons unsalted butter
salt and black pepper
juice of ¼ lemon

Simmer the parsley in a little water until limp. Squeeze out the water. Pound to a paste with the anchovy fillets (wipe these first) and the finely chopped garlic or shallot. Mix the paste into the softened butter. Season to taste with salt, black pepper and lemon juice and chill before using.

Excellent with meat, potatoes, or as a spread.

Mushroom butter

A sumptuous and unusual sandwich spread.

¼ lb mushrooms
8 tablespoons butter
lemon juice, salt, pepper or cayenne

Cut off the dusty ends of the mushroom stalks but do not peel. Chop the mushrooms roughly, then simmer in 2 tablespoons butter until just tender, about 3 or 4 minutes. Blend until smooth or pound in a mortar with the remaining butter and seasonings to taste. Chill until just workable.

Tarragon butter

A way of storing fresh herbs throughout the winter to use with meat, fish and to glaze vegetables.

2 heaping tablespoons finely chopped fresh tarragon
* leaves*
½ lb (1 cup) butter
juice of 1 lemon
salt and cayenne pepper

Work the tarragon into the softened butter with the lemon juice, salt, pepper and a little cayenne. Either roll in foil or pack into jars, and freeze.

Mint butter

Mint butter is good with lamb, white fish, kippers, peas, carrots and new potatoes.

2 tablespoons finely chopped mint
8 tablespoons butter
a pinch of salt, pepper and sugar

Work the chopped mint into the butter, mix well, with sugar and seasonings, wrap and freeze.

Black olive butter

Black olives are best bought loose from a Greek grocer or delicatessen. If you have to use the sort packed in brine, wash them in a couple of changes of cold water to get rid of excess salt. Anyone who likes black olives will find this butter delicious with roast lamb, steak, plain pasta, toast or green beans past their prime. I use olives and butter in roughly half and half proportions but this can be altered to suit your preferences and purse.

¾ cup black olives
a little finely chopped onion, garlic or shallot (optional)
8 tablespoons butter (unsalted if possible)
black pepper
juice of ½ lemon

Pit the olives. Chop them coarsely with the onion, then either put them through the blender with the butter until smooth, or pound the mixture in a mortar. Add seasonings and the lemon juice.

Curry butter

Add an instant touch of exoticism to broiled meat, sausages, fried fish and ham sandwiches with this butter.

2 teaspoons curry powder or paste
8 tablespoons butter
juice of ½ lemon
a pinch of salt

Mix the powder or paste into the softened butter, add the lemon juice (a little more may be needed) and salt, to taste. Chill or freeze.

Cinnamon butter

The best and classic use for this is to make hot cinnamon toast. Nothing is easier, or more welcome on a cold winter morning. If you *can* use the whole stick ground, do, because cinnamon is a subtle spice and loses strength quickly when exposed to air.

6 tablespoons unsalted butter
1 tablespoon soft brown sugar
1 tablespoon ground cinnamon

Soften the butter and work in the sugar and spice. Spread on hot toast, remove the crusts and stack in a pile to keep warm (this lets the spicy butter drip through). Cut into fingers just before serving.

Rum butter

This probably needs no introduction as it is the traditional accessory to British Christmas pudding. You might like to try it, less conventionally, with steamed puddings, mince and apple pies. The pudding should be hot, the butter cool but not rock hard.

½ lb (1 cup) unsalted butter
2⅔ cups light brown sugar
¼ cup rum
½ teaspoon each grated nutmeg and ground cinnamon

Blend or beat the butter until soft, then add the sugar and blend or beat until non-gritty. Add the rum and spices, mix well, spoon into small dishes and smooth the top. Chill slightly.

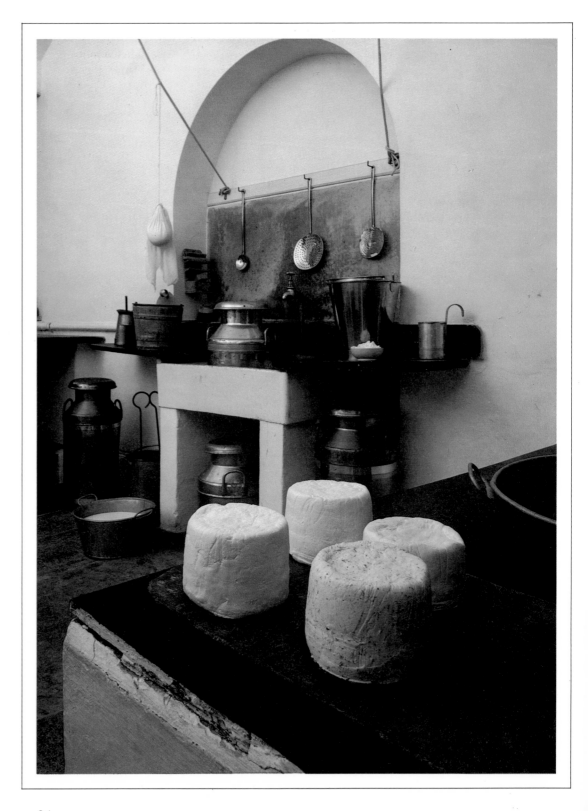

Cheese

'Half the white milk he curdled, and gathered it with speed
In baskets of woven wicker; and half in pails he stood,
Leaving it waiting ready to be his evening's food.'

The Odyssey   Homer

A noble cheese, like a fine wine, is an aristocrat and an individual. Both are made from the simplest ingredients, elaborated upon by man, time and nature, and the result is unique. A good cheese may be pungent, yet subtle, substantial but melting, rich but cleansing to the palate. Commercial ingenuity, backed up by technology, has reduced most of the mysteries of cheesemaking to a set of formulae, yet even now one element in the process – the effect of time – escapes analysis. Even cheese made according to a time tested recipe, salted, pressed and cured exactly as before, will, after a certain period of time, take on a character all its own.

Cheese is the best way to store perishable milk for any length of time; indeed, until refrigeration, the only way. In the days when most families kept a 'milch cow' cheesemaking was a regular part of the household routine and an excellent way of turning surplus milk into a compact, nourishing food which not only lasted through the winter months but actually improved with keeping. Working from instinct and commonsense, our ancestors came up with a concentrated food which contains more protein than meat, twice as much calcium as milk and vitamins A and B.

Cheesemaking is, and always was, by far the most challenging aspect of dairying. Women handed on family recipes to their daughters and the best regional cheeses became classic. An outstandingly successful cheese could make your name and fortune. The celebrated Stilton, for example, is said to have first been made by a farmer's wife for her brother-in-law to serve to travelers stopping at his inn in the small market town of Stilton, England.

Cheese can be roughly classifed as soft, or spoon cheeses, which is usefully vivid, semi-hard and hard. Cheesemaking is based on the principle that certain enzymes and acids can cause milk to coagulate, forming solid curds and liquid whey. The natural lactic acid producing bacteria in milk works on the protein 'casein' causing the milk to clot. Broadly, curds (clotted casein) provide the body of a cheese while acidity gives it flavor and helps to preserve it. The other element is moisture, or whey. Most soft cheeses should be eaten within a few days, semi-hard ones after a couple of months, while a really hard cheese – Parmesan leads the field – is matured for 2 years and more.

In the dairy, fresh raw milk in pails ready to be stirred with rennet and allowed to drip through a cheesecloth bag for curd cheese, the small, shallow bowl of 'crowdie' or cottage cheese, and, foreground, 4 cream cheeses, including a herb cheese flavored with parsley, chives and tarragon.

Soft cheese making

Making soft cheese is the process most likely to interest people who live miles from the nearest dairy farm. Master the terminology and it is childishly simple. It can be made from a range of commercial dairy products in a matter of hours and costs rather less homemade than the commercial equivalent. It is the obvious way to use up sour (but it must be non-pasteurized) milk or skimmed milk, from cream making. Eat it straight, or flavored with herbs and spices to make dips or use as a basis for lots of interesting and tasty dishes.

I am using the term 'soft cheese' to include all the quickly made, perishable mushy sorts of cheeses made from drained curds: curd cheese, cottage cheese, cream cheese, lactic cheese, acid or immature cheese and so on and so forth. To a purist these distinctions are important but apart from slight variations in the making (dealt with in the recipes) and slight differences in flavor and texture, most of these soft cheeses are virtually interchangeable. The real criterion is expense and convenience, and few people would go to the extra trouble and expense of buying buttermilk or yogurt to make curd cheese, when ordinary milk will do just as well. If you must have cream cheese for cheesecake, and can afford the cream to make it, well and good. I have made cheesecake for years using cottage or sour milk cheese, and it is as tasty and cheaper though less rich.

Equipment
Most kitchens already have the necessary equipment except possibly for cheesecloth squares in which to drain the curds (a clean napkin will do instead, or squares of well boiled old sheets) and rennet to set the milk. You also need a strainer or colander to turn the curds into, somewhere to hang the bundle up while draining and something in the way of a small mold, perforated in most cases, to shape the cheese in if you are not eating it with a spoon. These can be bought from the classier sort of kitchenware stores, or improvised from little baskets, cartons with holes punched, or even made up at home from wheat or rye straw, or rushes roughly woven together as for the traditional 'rush cheese'. Straw mats are required for some of the recipes. All cheesemaking equipment must be kept scrupulously clean and sterilized lest the milk becomes tainted.

Ingredients
Soft cheese can be made from fresh or sour raw milk, fresh pasteurized milk, light or heavy cream, yogurt, buttermilk and skimmed milk. Raw milk and its by-products will sour and separate naturally, but slowly, to make curds. Pasteurized milk and its pasteurized products need help, from rennet or acid (lemon juice) and sometimes a 'starter' too. Pasteurized milk which is on the point of souring can be used – tasting will soon tell if it has reached the bitter stage and should be poured down the drain. The Indian method of producing a firm curd cheese, using lemon juice to curdle the milk, is used in many vegetarian Indian dishes which are among the best in the world. Panir, as it is called, has no special taste of its own but it absorbs spices and seasonings wonderfully, like all soft cheeses.

Making a sour raw milk soft cheese

1. For $\frac{1}{2}$lb soft cheese, allow 1 quart fresh full cream milk to stand in a shallow earthenware pan or saucepan until a thick clout forms on top. To speed this process you can add a starter, such as rennet or 1 tablespoon of yogurt, or buttermilk or sour milk.

2. Heat the soured milk gently in the top of a double boiler to separate the curds from the whey.

3. Turn the curds into a cheesecloth-lined strainer or colander and hang the bundle up over a sink or bowl to allow the whey to drain off. Curds made by souring the milk naturally without heating it take longer to drain.

4. When the curd reaches the consistency you want, it can be turned out and eaten straight or mixed with a little cream or butter to make it richer. It can be salted and blended with chopped herbs to make a soft spreading cheese, and eaten within a few days.

To 'ripen' and flavor a soft cheese like crowdie that keeps in the refrigerator for 3 or 4 days, wrap it in various leaves – dock or vine leaves, or spring's early nettle leaves before they become bitter and prickly.

Soft cheeses

There are quickly made but perishable cheeses made from drained curds that should be eaten within a few days of making. Both 'raw' milk and pasteurized milk will make a perfect curded cheese without inconvenience or expense.

Crowdie

Crowdie is the Scottish term for cottage cheese. Still the best way of using up skimmed milk, but pasteurized whole milk can be used.

1 quart milk
1 rennet tablet

Heat the milk until tepid, add 1 rennet tablet dissolved in water. Stir well, then leave in a warm place until set to a firm curd. This takes about 2 hours. With a long bladed knife, slice the curd across one way, then the other to make inch sized cubes, spoon the cut curd over and cut the long pieces up into more cubes. Now heat the curd in its whey gently until warm, stirring. Leave to settle for a few minutes, then turn into a cheesecloth bag and drain for a few hours. (The curd cutting is routine in hard cheesemaking and enables whey to drain freely off the curd.) Salt the crowdie lightly and mix in a little half and half to make it spread better. It will keep for several days in the refrigerator.

Note: if crowdie is mixed with butter in a ratio of 2:1, you have Cruddy butter which my old Scots cookbook tells me will keep for months in wooden molds 'when it becomes very highly flavored though mellow'.

Panir

An Indian firm curd cheese using lemon juice to curdle the milk.

1 quart whole milk
2 lemons (or 1 teaspoon powdered alum)

Bring the milk to a boil, remove from heat, stir in the lemon juice or alum, then return to the heat and stir until the curd separates cleanly from the whey. Turn into a cheesecloth bag and drain for 1 to 2 hours. It can be cooked in its crumbly state, with spices, or for some dishes, made firm enough to cut and fry, by pressing, in its cheesecloth, under a weighted board overnight.

Cream cheese

Two recipes for cream cheese, one old and one modern. It is amusing to compare the casual authority of the old 'receipt' with the fussy detail of the modern one. Both work – but the old one needs non-pasteurized cream which has been left to ripen.

Old receipt

'Put a wet damask napkin on a marble or stone slab and pour on a mutchkin ($2\frac{1}{2}$ cups) of thick cream. Spread it out and leave to dry until next morning. Now put it into a small form in which a wet cloth has been laid and place a weight above – it will be ready by dinner time.'

Modern recipe

$2\frac{1}{4}$ cups heavy cream
1 rennet tablet (or 1 teaspoon of rennet liquid)

Heat the cream in the top of a double boiler until warm, then add rennet liquid or a rennet tablet dissolved in cold milk. Stir and set aside in a warm place to curdle. Drain for 24 hours. Open the bag a few times to scrape the curd off the cheesecloth and mix into the softer stuff inside. Changing the cloth once or twice will drain the cheese quicker. Add a little salt, mix and shape into a pat. This cream cheese will taste sweeter and last a little longer than the old recipe because it uses rennet.

Labna

A Middle Eastern soft cheese made with yogurt, inexpensive if you make your own. This is very simple to make, with a light, creamy texture.

$2\frac{1}{4}$ cups plain yogurt
$\frac{1}{4}$ teaspoon salt
paprika

Mix the yogurt with the salt, pour into cheesecloth and drain overnight. Shape into little balls and roll in paprika.

Soft cheese dishes

Recipes that make use of the soft curd cheeses which, delicious though they are, cannot mature. Flavored with herbs and spices, roasted with seeds, sweetened with honey, soft cheeses are the basis for many tasty dishes.

Herb cheese in sesame seeds
Easy to make, impressive to serve at a party.

½ lb soft cheese
2 tablespoons top of milk or half and half
1 clove garlic
2 tablespoons chopped chives
2 tablespoons chopped parsley
1 tablespoon chopped tarragon or fresh basil or mint
salt and pepper
¼ cup toasted sesame seeds

Blend or pound the cheese with the top of the milk until smooth. Add crushed garlic, very finely chopped herbs and salt and pepper to taste. Shape into a little cushion and chill until firm. Then roll in sesame seeds, toasted until aromatic over a gentle heat.

Cheese flan with eggs and mint
A surprising combination of cheese, cucumber, baked eggs and mint, to be eaten cold. Refreshing, but substantial enough to make a main lunch course with a tomato salad.

pie pastry made with 1¼ cups flour
½ lb crowdie
5 eggs
salt and pepper
a bunch of fresh mint
½ cucumber
butter

Line an 8 inch tart pan with the pie pastry, pricking it here and there. Beat the cheese until smooth with one whole egg. Season with salt, pepper and a little finely chopped mint. Pour this into the prepared pastry shell. Cover with overlapping rings of very thinly sliced cucumber. On top of this, gently break four eggs, one in each quarter. Dot with butter, sprinkle with more chopped mint and cover with a piece of buttered paper. Bake at 375 degrees for 30 to 40 minutes until the eggs are set and the pastry is golden.

Cheese dip
Make a large bowl for children's parties and give them potato chips and carrot and celery sticks to dip.

1 lb crowdie or cottage cheese
¼ cup plain yogurt
¼ cup light cream
a small bunch of scallions
parsley and chives
½ cucumber
2 tablespoons horseradish sauce
salt and pepper

Blend the crowdie, the yogurt and the cream until smooth. Clean the scallions, removing only the tough green tip, then chop finely with the herbs. Peel and finely dice the cucumber. Stir the scallions, horseradish sauce, herbs and cucumber into the cheese dip and season. Serve cold.

Soft cheese quiche with bacon
A richer version of the standard bacon quiche and rather quicker to make.

¼ lb bacon slices
pie pastry made with 1¼ cups flour
2 eggs and 1 additional yolk
½ lb crowdie, curd or cream cheese
¼ cup cream or yogurt
salt and pepper

Fry the bacon until it is just crisp, then cut into small pieces. Line an 8 inch quiche or tart pan with the pie pastry, prick all over and dot with the bacon. Break the eggs into a bowl, reserving one white, and beat until smooth with the cheese and the cream. Salt and pepper well. Beat the remaining egg white until fluffy, fold into the cheese mixture, and pour into the prepared pastry shell. Bake at 400 degrees for 15 minutes, then lower to 350 degrees and bake for a further 15 to 20 minutes, or until the top is puffed and golden brown.

The dairy

Spiced cheese loaf

A quite different approach from cheesecake, though using similar ingredients, the spiced sweetened soft cheese mixture is bulked out with breadcrumbs and has no pastry base.

½ lb crowdie or curd cheese
3 egg yolks
2 tablespoons butter
¼ cup sugar
tiny pinch each ground cloves, nutmeg, cinnamon
½ teaspoon vanilla extract
1 thick slice of stale white bread

Sieve or blend the cheese until smooth, and mix with beaten egg yolks, softened butter, sugar, spices and vanilla. Grate or grind the bread (minus crust) in an electric grinder into fine crumbs, then mix well with the cheese mixture. Pour into a well buttered glass or pottery baking or soufflé dish. Grate a little nutmeg over the top and bake at 375 degrees for 45 minutes. The loaf should be well risen and browned on top. Eat hot from the dish, or unmold when warm.

Peas and panir with tomatoes

Typical of the brilliant Indian vegetarian dishes, so spicy, tasty and colorful that you never regret the absence of meat.

½ lb fresh panir
4 tablespoons ghee or margarine
1 medium onion
1 teaspoon each ground turmeric and cumin
½ teaspoon ground dry chili peppers
½ lb (1½ cups) frozen peas
5 fresh tomatoes
a pinch of salt
chopped fresh coriander or basil

Make panir from 1 quart of full cream milk, drain but do not press. It should be crumbly, like dry scrambled egg. Melt the ghee or the margarine (less apt to burn than butter) in a heavy pan, fry the chopped onion until soft, then add the spices and fry until the spice smell is warm and rich – 3 minutes. Stir in the panir and cook gently, stirring for another 2 minutes. Add the peas (thawed and heated until tender, then drained) and chopped, skinned tomatoes. Salt to

taste. Cover the pan and simmer until the juice from the tomatoes is absorbed – this is a 'dry' dish. Sprinkle with chopped herbs and serve with rice or chapatis.

Moroccan egg and cheese turnovers

Imjibinah, as these are called, are savory egg and cheese stuffed turnovers, fried or baked, then for the daring – dipped into a spiced syrup. These savory-sweet mixtures are typically Middle Eastern and very good.

Use the Indian panir cheese as a base for this unusual dish.

Cheese filling

1 onion
a small bunch of parsley
6 oz panir cheese
4 hard-cooked eggs
salt and pepper
2 teaspoons ground cinnamon

Pastry

8 tablespoons butter or margarine
2 cups sifted plain flour
a pinch of salt

For the filling, finely chop the onion and parsley together. Cut the panir (pressed overnight until firm) into small cubes. Chop the eggs roughly, then mix the cheese cubes, egg, chopped onion and parsley together with salt, pepper and ground cinnamon.

For the pastry, work the chilled fat into the flour and salt, adding enough water to make a firm paste. Roll out to make a thin – but not paper thin – sheet. Cut out rounds approximately 5 inches across (or cut into roughly equivalent squares), put a dollop of stuffing on each half, then fold over the other half and pinch shut. The *imjibinah* can either be fried in hot oil until golden brown (not all Moroccan households have ovens) or baked at 400 degrees until the pastry is firm and golden brown.

Make a syrup by heating together 1 cup sugar, $\frac{2}{3}$ cup water and 1 stick cinnamon, and simmering for a few minutes. Use tongs to dip the turnovers into the boiling syrup for just long enough to soak them, then arrange on a plate. Eat hot, warm or cold.

Pashka

The traditional centerpiece to a Russian Easter time celebration, this is a rich, sweetened cream cheese mixture – like an uncooked cheesecake filling. Uncooked pashka is finer and more delicate than cooked.

1 lb homemade unsalted cream cheese
½ lb (1 cup) unsalted butter
1 cup sugar
4 egg yolks
1 teaspoon vanilla extract
1 cup chopped lightly toasted almonds
⅔ cup seedless white raisins soaked in sherry

Strain the cream cheese into a bowl. Cream the butter, sugar and egg yolks together until smooth, adding the vanilla extract. Now mix carefully and lightly with the cream cheese and fold in nuts and fruit. Pashka should be pyramid shaped – line a scalded flowerpot with cheese-cloth, pour in the cheese mixture and top with a small plate or saucer and a 2 lb weight. Leave for 24 hours to drain. Turn out and surround with garlands of tiny spring flowers.

Cheesecake with honey and crumb base

A scented honey flavors soft cheese most delicately. This is a richer, creamier filling than the first, with a closer texture. A crumb base is quicker and easier to make than pastry, and it does combine particularly well with cheesecake. Serve it unadorned – covering a cheesecake with cream cannot improve on what is a perfect formula.

Crumb base

3 cups crushed graham crackers
¼ teaspoon ground cinnamon
4 tablespoons butter or margarine

Filling

½ lb cream cheese
2 eggs
¼ cup light cream, yogurt or half and half
2 tablespoons sugar
1 teaspoon grated lemon rind
⅓ cup raisins
2 tablespoons honey

Add the crushed graham crackers to the melted butter and cinnamon, mix well, then press into the bottom of an 8 inch round springform cake pan. To make the filling, sieve the cream cheese into a bowl and beat in eggs, yogurt (or cream), sugar, grated lemon rind, raisins and honey. Pour into the pan over the crumb base. Bake at 375 degrees for 40 minutes. Leave stand for 10 minutes in the oven with the heat off. The flavors improve with time – eat it 24 hours later if you can wait that long.

Classic sweet cheesecake

There are countless minor variations on the theme of sweetened, soft cheese bound with egg and studded with dried fruit, baked in a pastry shell. Some recipes call for a richer mix – cream cheese with added cream. It is all according to taste and your pocket. This is an old English recipe laced with a little optional liqueur.

½ lb soft cream cheese or crowdie
2 eggs
pie pastry made with 1½ cups flour
4 tablespoons butter
½ cup sugar
½ cup ground almonds
1 lemon
½ cup currants or raisins
2 tablespoons brandy, rum or whiskey
grated nutmeg

The soft cheese should be well drained, squeezed to remove as much moisture as possible then sieved, or blended, until smooth. Line an 8 inch tart or pie pan with the pie pastry, pricking it here and there. Separate the eggs. Cream the butter with the sugar until soft, then beat in egg yolks, ground almonds and the cheese. Add grated rind and juice of the lemon and the dried fruit, soaked for a few minutes in the brandy, if you have time, to soften it. Beat the egg whites until fluffy, fold in the cheese mixture, then pour the lot into the pastry shell. Bake at 375 degrees for 40 minutes, or until well risen and firm to the touch. Look at it after 20 minutes – if it already looks golden brown, turn the heat down a notch for the rest of the cooking time. Sprinkle with grated nutmeg before serving – it adds zest to the cake.

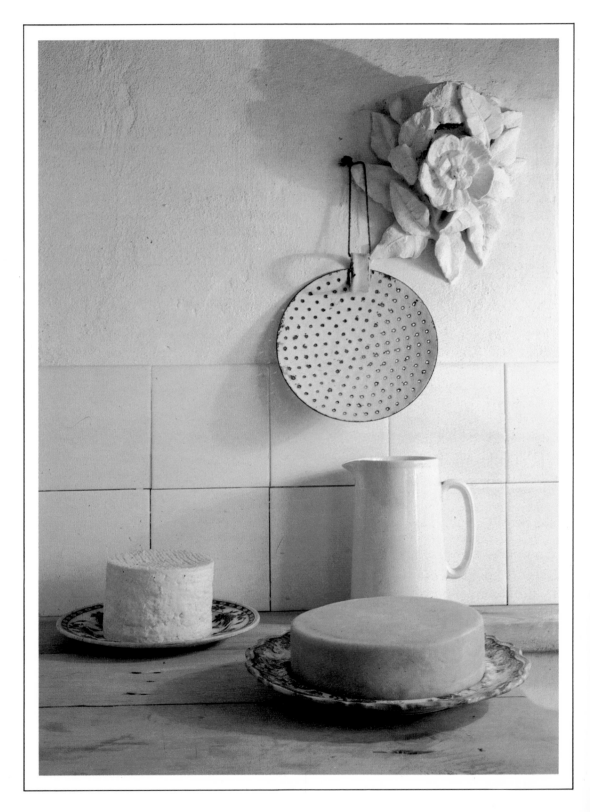

Hard cheese

The making of semi-hard and hard cheese, once undertaken routinely in every household which kept a cow or goat, is obviously not beyond the capabilities of any sensible person. A sensible person, however, is not going to consider seriously investing time and money making something, however interesting and delicious, if it is cheaper to go out and buy a good commercial product. It takes 9 quarts of milk to make a small $1\frac{1}{2}$ lb semi-hard cheese and proportionately more to make a hard cheese. If you are buying your milk through the usual commercial channels that makes it rather expensive. I should hate to discourage enthusiasm and enterprise, but I am sure cheesemaking on any serious scale only makes economic sense if you keep cows or goats, and must use up the surplus milk, or know a dairy farmer who will let you have milk at wholesale prices. If you burn to try your hand at cheesemaking, and have to use commercial milk, experiment modestly with a simple curd cheese like mozzarella. These give more cheese per pint of milk, are not complicated to make (no expensive equipment is needed) and make a mild cheese of delicate flavor if kept for a few days. Making a true hard cheese, of the caliber of Cheddar, Double Gloucester or Parmesan, is probably beyond the scope of most non-specialists, even those with a dairy herd, because it really requires expensive equipment and a lot of attention.

Cheesemaking is a pleasant, sensuous process, right through from the cutting of the curd, white, shiny and sweet smelling, to the rather proud moment when the enticingly bouncy cushion of cheese is coated with paraffin wax and set on a cool shelf to cure. Having tried my hand at making a few cheeses for the purposes of this book I am now addicted, and making cheese regularly is going to become a part of my life. I hope readers will follow suit, because there is a great deal of forgotten expertise waiting to be rediscovered, and the more people are involved in sampling and experimenting, the more information will sift back, and the better cheeses we shall all be making.

The instructions may appear complicated, but once you have made your first cheese the unfamiliar terms will soon make good sense. If in doubt at any point, trust your instinct – people once made superb cheese without the help of thermometers, special 'starter' cultures, or stainless steel presses, and I am sure instinct, which I will define as intuition plus commonsense, was their most useful piece of equipment.

All cheesemaking equipment should be clean, not hospital sterile maybe but super clean. The wrong bacteria, traces of detergent, smell of bleach can all taint a young cheese as ripening curd is extraordinarily absorbent. Wash all equipment first in cool water, then scald, then rinse in hot and set it in the sun or wind if you can to dry. This applies to shelves where cheeses sit, as well as the things you make them with. Do not make bread, beer or wine in the same room simultaneously. Having said that, relax – cheesemaking should not be intimidating.

Two of the author's cheeses made at home: a Coulommier semi-hard cheese molded until firm, rubbed with salt and ripened for 2 weeks in a cool dark room (left) and a mild simple cheese wrapped in cheesecloth, pressed until smooth and solid, then sealed with melted lard (right).

Hard cheese making

Equipment
For the simpler, semi-hard cheeses equipment can be improvised. The most important item is some sort of arrangement for pressing the cheese. Pressure on the moist curds needs to be steady, all around and adjustable, so it can be increased to force out more and more whey. I use a meat press, a simple kitchen gadget. A homemade press can be improvised with a couple of thick boards (non-resinous hardwood is best) and 2 lengths of dowel. The upper board slides down the dowel uprights, securely bedded down in holes drilled through the base. Pressure is supplied by bricks piled on the top board.

The next requirement is molds to contain the curd during pressing. A cake tin with detachable bottom is a good improvised mold but a coffee tin with the bottom cut out can make a mold for a smaller cheese. Each mold needs a 'follower' i.e. a rigid disk of wood, metal, even stout plastic, cut to the inside diameter of the mold and deep enough to be driven down inside the mold onto the curds by whatever type of pressure you are using. The cake tin base illustrates the principle perfectly. Also needed is a spare tin or other cylindrical object to stand on top of the follower and supply necessary pressure.

Other equipment needed: a large enough container to hold the milk, and an even bigger one to put the milk container in for scalding. A 2 to 3 gallon plastic bucket and big preserving kettle or old fashioned boiler will serve. A thermometer. Cheesecloth squares, for draining, wrapping and storing. A long, sharp, stainless steel knife for cutting the curd, a slotted spatula or thin saucer for skimming, a wooden spoon for stirring and a ladle for ladling.
Note: All cheesemaking equipment should be kept as clean as possible. The wrong bacteria, traces of detergent or the smell of bleach can all taint a young cheese if you are not careful.

Rennet and starter cultures
Diluted rennet is added to the milk to coagulate the curd. Rennet is available from drug, grocery or dairy supply stores in liquid or tablet form. Buy the smallest size bottles as liquid rennet loses strength gradually.

For some recipes a 'starter' is required. A starter is not essential in cheese made from raw milk, and can make it too acid, but it is essential with cheese made from pasteurized milk. Briefly, what it does is encourage lactic acid production in the milk – this compares with using a yeast nutrient to get a healthy ferment started in wine or beer. A commercial powdered cheese starter is available. Or substitute a homemade starter of a spoonful of yogurt, sour raw milk, or buttermilk. Add it to the fresh milk a few hours before cheesemaking or as stated in the recipe. Raw milk is unpasteurized. If you are in any doubt about the cleanliness of your milk, pasteurize it. To do this, stand the milk bucket in a bath of boiling water. Raise the temperature of the milk as quickly as possible to 163 degrees stirring constantly. Maintain this temperature for 15 seconds, then cool the milk as quickly as possible to 40 degrees by putting the milk bucket in iced water.

Ripening

The milk, bought fresh from a farm, or brought in straight from the evening milking needs ripening first. This means warming the milk slightly, and leaving it to sit for a while to encourage lactic acid bacteria. Before doing this, however, skim off any cream which may have risen to the top, warm it to around 85 degrees and stir it back into the milk. This is important, otherwise it may not set with the rest of the milk and the cheese will lack valuable fat. Leave for 1 hour. Now set the milk bucket in a large pan of hot water, set that on the stove and gently raise the temperature to 90 degrees (or 85 degrees for goat's milk). If you are adding a starter, put it in now. Remove the bucket from the hot water and leave the milk covered for an hour.

Renneting

Use rennet in a ratio of 1 teaspoon to 9 quarts of milk. Dilute it in three or four parts cold, boiled water, add to the milk and stir with a long handled spoon which reaches the bottom of the bucket, for 1 minute. Then top-stir (stir just the top $\frac{1}{2}$ inch or so) until the milk begins to form a curd. Top stirring stops the cream from rising to the top which makes a 'thin' cheese. Or stir the milk around with your hand, keeping the milk moving until it begins to set and cling to your fingers. Then 'top stir' or stroke the emerging curd gently for a few minutes to send the cream down. As the renneted curd turns the milk stiffens dramatically.

Now leave the curd to set solid in 10 minutes or less. If it takes much longer you may have to scald longer so note the time taken. Cover the curd and leave. When the back of a finger pressed into it causes a clean split, with no curd sticking to the finger, it is ready – after 45 minutes. Do not hurry this part – too short a time means the rennet has not coagulated all the solids in the milk which means a smaller cheese.

How to cut the curd

When you do this you will find it by no means easy – the curd spins around in its curd bath while you cut. Remember, however, that you are simply trying to reduce the curd to small even fragments, and relax. Spoon the curd over gently when you have done your best with the old slashing technique, and cut any large lumps.

Scalding

To scald means simply warming (not usually to much beyond 100 degrees) the cut curd very gradually, meanwhile stirring it by hand or with a spoon. Keeping the bucket in a pan of hot water on the stove is one method, but difficult to control. Otherwise put the bucket in the sink filled with hot water. The third method is to ladle out whey into a pan, heat that, tip it back and stir. Check repeatedly with the thermometer. The effect of this scalding is to firm and separate the curds. Instead of the voluptuously yielding texture of renneted curd the milk has become rubbery.

Pitching

Pitching means that the scalded curd is left to settle and soak. The time for this varies.

Milling

Break up the sturdy fragments of curd into little bits by hand. This is not difficult, indeed rather delightful, but it takes longer than you might expect. Ladle the morsels with a slotted spoon or spatula (to let the whey drip off) into the cheesecloth-lined mold which is standing ready. Now salt it.

Salting

Use flake or coarse salt if possible. Add salt at the specified rate and mix in thoroughly with both hands. Now wrap the bundle of curds tenderly in its cheesecloth square, squeezing a little with both hands to help any excess whey drain and smoothing the cheesecloth as much as is feasible. Put the cheese into the press.

Pressing

For the first press tighten the screw, or pile on bricks, until a good bit of whey can be seen oozing up around the sides of the mold. The mold should stand on something which helps the whey drain freely: a clean, scalded straw mat, or grooved bread board. Stand the whole press over something to catch the overflowing whey. Do not squeeze so hard the soft curd starts being forced up around the rim of the follower. Leave under this pressure for the prescribed time. Then remove the cheese – by now firm enough to handle – change the cloth, replace and increase the pressure. This process can be repeated many times, but for the average semi-hard cheese, two or three turns of the screw, plus changes of the wrapper should be enough. Scald your mat or board as often as you can, to prevent them smelling sour. When sufficiently pressed for your purposes, unwrap the cheese and seal it for storing.

Sealing or covering

The simplest method of sealing is to dip the cheese in hot whey or water for just long enough to cook the outer skin and form an airtight rind, about 1 minute is usual. Alternatively brush it with melted paraffin or lard. Some cheeses do not need to be sealed, but if they are to be matured for any length of time it is a useful protection. In country districts, leaves (nettle, dock, vine, nut tree) were tied on with string and changed regularly. Alternatively, cover the cheese with a cheesecloth wrapper and paint over this with melted paraffin or lard.

Storing or maturing

A young cheese fresh from the press tastes of nothing much, though it has a pleasant clean texture. After a few days you will begin to notice a faintly cheesy odor. The longer this goes on, the more powerful and yet richly complex your cheese will taste. Store cheeses in cool dry places. Turn them frequently to begin with, two or three times a day in summer, once a day in winter – not to air them so much as to prevent the fat content settling to one side. Brush off any mold that forms. After some time the cheese wrapping will feel dry and taut, and the cheese will have a distinct though delicate 'bouquet'. Eat it when you cannot wait any longer.

The dairy

Making a simple semi-hard cheese

1. Take 13 quarts of fresh raw milk. First skim off the cream and warm this to 85 degrees, then stir it into the milk in a bucket. Leave for 1 hour.

2. Set the milk bucket in a large pan of hot water on a cooker and gently raise the heat to 100 degrees. Then add $\frac{1}{4}$ cup of plain yogurt, stirring it by hand.

3. Remove the bucket from the hot water and leave the milk, covered, for 1 hour.

4. Stir in 2 teaspoons of rennet diluted in 8 teaspoons of boiled water. Stir thoroughly for 2 minutes. Leave for 1 hour until the curd forms a solid mass from top to bottom.

5. Top stir the mix (just the top $\frac{1}{2}$ inch) until the milk forms curd. Cover and leave for 45 minutes until a finger pressed into it causes a clean split, with no curd sticking to the finger.

6. Cut the mass from left to right, top to bottom then diagonally both ways into small even fragments. Spoon the curd over, cutting any long piece into dice.

7. Warm the curd to 100 degrees – check with a thermometer – by standing in a sink of hot water. This drives out more whey.

8. After the scalded curd has pitched (settled and soaked) for 30 minutes, break up the sturdy curds by hand into small pieces.

9. Ladle the morsels with a slotted spoon into a cheesecloth-lined mold to let the whey drip.

10. Mix in 1 tablespoon salt.

11. Wrap up the bundle of curds in the cheesecloth square, squeezing out the whey a little. Smooth the cheesecloth and stand the mold on a scalded straw mat to allow the whey to drain.

12. Press the cheese under a weight, not so hard that the soft curd is forced up round the follower rim. Turn the cheese, changing the cloths 2 or 3 times. Gradually increase the pressure every day until the cheese looks smooth and feels solid. Then lower the cheese in its cheesecloth bag into water heated to 160 degrees for 1 minute to form a skin.

13. Cut two rounds of cheesecloth to fit top and bottom and bandage the side. Stitch round to hold the shape, brush with melted lard and turn daily until the cover is dry. Store in a cool place and turn twice daily. It can be eaten after 1 month but gains flavor if kept longer.

Semi-hard and hard cheeses

Now that you have familiarized yourself with the technical terms, try your hand at one or all of the following semi-hard cheeses. Basically, the more whey that is pressed out, the harder the cheese and the longer it keeps.

Pressed and cured crowdie

This is a good cheese to try first as it is the next step on from cottage cheese or crowdie. Make a large batch from skimmed milk if you are taking the cream off your own milk.

3 tablespoons coarse salt
3 lb crowdie or cottage cheese

Mix the salt with the cottage cheese, wrap in cheesecloth and fit into a small mold. Put the follower in place on top and press until the whey oozes out visibly. Leave under pressure until the next day, then replace the cloth, and increase the pressure slightly. Repeat daily until the cheese coheres, and feels solid, with a smooth outer surface. Then lower the cheese, in its cheesecloth bag, into water heated to 160 degrees for 1 minute. This forms a thin skin, the basis for a healthy protective rind. Cut two circles of cheesecloth to fit top and bottom and bandage the side. Now brush the whole cheese with melted paraffin or lard. Store on a cool shelf, and turn daily until the outer cover feels quite dry. Then turn once a week, and eat after a month.

Coulommier

The most interesting thing about Coulommier – a semi-hard cheese – is that the renneted or 'set' curd is not heated but ladled straight into the special two part mold. Make your mold with two identical sized cans – about 6 inches across and 4 inches deep. Cut out bottoms, put together and tape.

1 gallon milk
½ teaspoon cheese starter
1 teaspoon rennet liquid

Heat the milk to 90 degrees. Add the starter and leave for 10 minutes, covered. Add the rennet (diluted in 8 teaspoons of boiled water) to the mixture and stir well. Top stir the mixture for 10 minutes to prevent the cream from rising. As soon as the milk starts to clot you should cover it and keep it in a warm place for 1 to $2\frac{1}{2}$ hours or until the curd breaks evenly over your knife. Take care not to hurry this stage.

When the curd has sunk to the lower half of the mold (in a few hours) remove the top. Place a mat and board on top of the mold and carefully invert. Gently take away the straw mat, which may stick a little. Scrub the board and mat. Turn the cheese twice a day for the next 2 days. Keep the cheese in a room with a constant temperature, preferably 65 to 70 degrees.

When the cheese is firm, rub the surface with salt. Keep in the refrigerator until the next day when it will be ready to eat.

If you wish to ripen the cheese, keep it in an airy, dry room for a few days. Then leave it to ripen in a cool, dark room for 2 to 3 weeks, turning it daily. If any light mold develops, wipe it off with a cloth.

A stronger, mellow cheese will result.

Cantal

A hard, sharp-flavored cheese. It is worth the long wait for the cheese to mature.

13 quarts fresh raw milk
¼ cup plain yogurt as a starter
2 teaspoons rennet liquid
3 tablespoons coarse salt

Make the cheese exactly as for the semi-hard cheese on pages 107 and 109 until you have pressed the curd under 30 lb of pressure until firm. Now remove it, unwrap and leave at room temperature for a day. Break it into small pieces by hand and work in 2 tablespoons of coarse salt. Knead well, put back into cheesecloth and press for another 2 days. Now unwrap, wipe with a clean cloth and wash in hot water for a firm rind. Keep in a dry place, turn and wipe daily until a rind starts to form. Cure for at least 3 months, washing every 4 days by dipping into salt water – $\frac{1}{4}$ cup of salt to 1 quart water.

Mozzarella

Easy to make, it can be eaten at once or used as a layer on pizzas because it melts well.

9 quarts fresh raw milk
¼ cup plain yogurt as a starter
1 teaspoon rennet liquid
1 tablespoon coarse salt

Heat the milk to 86 degrees, add the yogurt and leave in a warm place overnight. Add the rennet (already diluted in 4 teaspoons of cooled, boiled water) and stir hard for 2 minutes. Cover the bucket and leave for 45 minutes until the curds are well set. Now, instead of cutting the curd, break it up into small pieces by hand. Heat slowly until the mixture is as hot as you can bear, then stir continuously, crumbling the curds until they 'squeak'. Tip the curds and all into a cheesecloth-lined colander over a bowl and drain until fairly dry. Keep the whey. Now whip away the cheesecloth and shake and tilt to remove dry excess whey. Work with wooden paddles until cool – about 90 degrees then add 1 tablespoon of coarse salt and mix it in thoroughly. Cool further then ladle into a cheesecloth-lined mold and press. Increase the pressure over the next hour or two to 30 lb starting with a 10 lb weight. It should now be solid enough to handle. Put the cheese into whey pre-heated to 180 degrees. Remove from the heat and leave the mozzarella in the whey until cool. Then drain, on a straw mat, for 24 hours.

Feta

Feta is a slightly salty, fresh tasting, crumbly, Greek goat's milk cheese.

9 quarts goat's milk
¼ cup plain yogurt as a starter
2 teaspoons rennet liquid
2 tablespoons salt

Warm the milk to 86 degrees, add the yogurt and stir well. Cover and set in a warm place for several hours or overnight. Now add 2 teaspoons of rennet (already diluted in 8 teaspoons of cooled, boiled water). Stir for 2 minutes to mix in the rennet. Let it stand undisturbed for 30 to 45 minutes, until the milk has coagulated. If the curd splits evenly over the finger it is ready to be cut. Make 1 inch sized cubes by slicing the curd every way with a long bladed knife. Break up any oversized lumps by hand. Heat the curd, in the whey, slowly and gradually bringing the temperature up to 95 degrees (this will take about 30 minutes). Hold at this temperature and stir gently until the curd firms. Pour the curds and whey into a cheesecloth bag and hang for 48 hours to drip until the cheese is firm. Feta is not pressed. Remove the cheesecloth, slice the curd, sprinkle with 2 tablespoons of salt and work in well by hand. Return the curd to the remaining whey. Leave for 24 hours. Pat the cheese with a clean cloth and put it on a scrubbed board to form a rind. It is ready to eat in 3 or 4 days.

Caerphilly

A fine sharp-but-mild cheese.

13 quarts fresh milk
¾ cup cheese starter
1¼ teaspoons rennet liquid
coarse salt

Heat the milk to lukewarm, add the starter, then cover and leave to ripen for 1 hour. Add the rennet (already diluted in 6 teaspoons of water), stir hard for 1 minute then top stir until the curds start to form. Cut the curd as before. Heat quickly to 92 degrees and keep the curd at this heat for 40 minutes, stirring constantly. To test if the curd is firm enough, press your hand onto the top – the impression should linger. If not stir on. Leave the curd to 'pitch' in the whey for 5 minutes, then tip the bucket and pour off as much whey as you can. Leave the bucket on its side, and after 5 minutes pour off any more whey if possible. Cut the curd into cubes and again tilt off any free whey. Keep turning the curd. After 10 minutes break it up small and add 1½ tablespoons coarse salt per 4 lb curd. Pack the curd into a mold lined with a damp cloth and press lightly with a 4 lb weight. Remove after 10 minutes, turn and double the weight. Repeat twice more, stepping up the pressure each time, then leave under 20 lb pressure for a day. Take out, unwrap, dry with a clean cloth, bandage and brush with paraffin. Ripen for 2 weeks, or more, turning daily.

Cooking with hard cheese

Hard cheese is so concentrated in flavor that a little goes a long way. Cheese is best cooked either with a little starch – mustard, flour, potato – to stop the fat separating and hardening, or with something acid to cut the richness, like wine or shallots.

Gougère

Cooked cheese dishes seem to be either tricky or absurdly easy. This is a tricky one, a great golden puffy ring of choux paste studded with cheese, which is a smashing accompaniment to red wine and so no surprise that it should be a Burgundian specialty. The choux paste is no problem but the oven heat must be just right. However, the combination is so delicious that I am happy to eat a gougère which has gone flat.

1¼ cups water
4 tablespoons butter
salt and pepper
1 cup sifted flour
4 eggs
¼ lb Gruyère or homemade semi-hard cheese
1 tablespoon milk

Do not be alarmed at the prospect of making a choux paste, it requires chiefly a strong right arm.

In a heavy pan bring water, butter and salt to a boil and stir to melt the butter. Remove from the heat, and beat the sifted flour in all at once, to make a sticky yellow lump. Return to a very gentle heat and beat your paste hard for as long as you can bear – 5 to 15 minutes. Remove from the heat. Beat in the eggs one at a time, incorporating each one thoroughly before adding the next. By now the paste should be smooth, shiny and fluid enough to stir. Cut the cheese into tiny dice, reserve one spoonful and stir the remainder into the paste. Grease a baking sheet. Preheat the oven to 400 degrees. Spoon the paste onto your sheet to make a ring shape, building it as high as need be to use up the paste. Brush with milk, sprinkle the remaining spoonful of cheese on top and bake for 45 minutes. Resist peering in during that time or the gougère – sensitive to temperature changes – may collapse. A very gentle and cautious look after 40 minutes is allowable – it is ready when firm to the touch. Rush to the table, shielded from drafts and eat immediately.

Aligot

An interesting, easily made regional French dish, combining mashed potatoes, cheese, cream and butter, scented with a little garlic. The French use a local semi-soft white cheese which melts easily but I use a homemade Caerphilly or a pressed crowdie cheese. This is very filling.

2 lb floury white potatoes
4 tablespoons butter
1 large clove garlic
⅔ cup light cream
1 lb Caerphilly or crowdie
salt and pepper

Boil the potatoes in their skins, peel and sieve to make a dry purée or mash. Melt the butter in a large heavy pan, heat the crushed garlic in it for 1 minute (uncooked garlic spoils these dishes) then add the purée and cream and stir until mixed. Chop or grate the cheese, then add. Stir until the cheese melts and the mixture becomes thick and smooth, season to taste, and serve at once.

Zucchini au gratin

A vegetable gratin is a mixture of lightly pre-cooked vegetables, usually chopped fairly small and baked in a cheesy custard mixture until firm.

½ lb small zucchini
¾ cup grated cheese
salt, pepper and grated nutmeg
1¼ cups white sauce
2 eggs

Steam the zucchini until just tender, then chop them finely, skins as well. Mix the grated cheese and seasonings into the hot white sauce, stir for 1 to 2 minutes, then add the well-beaten eggs and chopped zucchini. Mix, pour into a butter dish and strew the top with a little more grated cheese. Place the dish in a roasting pan of hot water and bake at 350 degrees for 45 minutes, or until set.

Fondue

One of the best cooked dishes, and best kept simple. The most superior fondue is nothing but plenty of Gruyère melted with Riesling and Kirsch and bound with a pinch of cornstarch (note: acid plus starch) and maybe a nut of butter.

Classic Swiss fondue

Allow approximately $\frac{1}{4}$ lb Gruyère, $\frac{1}{4}$ cup Riesling and 2 tablespoons of Kirsch per person. One tablespoon cornstarch and 2 tablespoons butter are stirred in to thicken. Fondue should be cooked in a special dish – shallow earthenware – over a small alcohol burner at the table, and everyone dips their French bread or squares of toast into the communal dish, washing it down with more Riesling.

Rub the dish with a cut garlic clove. Set grated cheese and wine to heat slowly over alcohol burner, stirring until they combine to make a thick mixture. Mix the cornstarch separately with the Kirsch, stir it in, and continue stirring until it thickens. Add the butter, stir until melted and eat at once.

Note: Add more wine if too thick.

Poor man's fondue

A tasty, if coarser, fondue can be concocted with various odds and ends of cheese, soft as well as hard, stretched with a few eggs. Use any dryish white wine and skip the Kirsch.

1 clove garlic
$\frac{1}{2}$ cup white wine
1 cup grated cheese
1 teaspoon dry mustard
salt and pepper
4 eggs
4 tablespoons butter

This is best made in a double boiler, so the eggs do not set, but it must be stirred constantly. Crush the garlic and place with the wine in the top half of the pan. Heat, add grated cheese, mustard, salt and pepper and stir until thick. Add well beaten eggs, and butter and go on stirring for 7 or 8 minutes until smooth and thick. Eat at once.

Potted cheese

A delicious spread for crackers, sandwiches and savory toasts (that nice Edwardian bachelor indulgence) which can be made from stale odds and ends of cheese. Use a pungent cheese for preference. It will keep for ages, sealed with clarified butter or lard.

1 lb cheese
8 tablespoons butter
$\frac{1}{4}$ cup sherry, port or brandy
$\frac{1}{2}$ teaspoon grated nutmeg
a pinch of mustard powder or curry powder (optional)

Pound the cheese (remove hard rinds), butter, sherry and seasonings in a mortar, or beat together in a mixer. When smooth pack down into little jars or pots, seal the tops with melted clarified butter or lard and cover with wax paper and string. Store in a cool place.

Cheese soufflé

A well made cheese soufflé manages to be light and firm yet slightly creamy all at once. With garlic bread and a good salad you have a quick, cheap and attractive lunch.

2 tablespoons butter
1 tablespoon flour
$\frac{2}{3}$ cup milk
3 eggs plus 1 additional egg white
mustard, salt, pepper and cayenne
1 cup grated cheese (Cheddar will do)

Butter the soufflé dish or ramekins. Melt the butter in a pan, stir in the flour, add hot milk and stir until smooth and thick. Separate the eggs. Stir in the well beaten egg yolks, mustard, grated cheese, salt and pepper and keep stirring over a gentle heat until smooth. Beat the eggs until fluffy and firm, but not 'rocky', and fold into the soufflé base. Turn into the dish or dishes and bake at 400 degrees until well risen, firm and golden brown on top. This will take 8 minutes for small, individual soufflés and 20 minutes for a large one. Reassure yourself with a squint into the oven towards the end of the cooking time; but open and close the door as stealthily as a burglar. Eat at once, with a dusting of cayenne pepper on top. Soufflés collapse very quickly.

Fish

Keeping the catch

The sea is generally held to be the cradle of life on this planet. Covering as it does three-quarters of the earth's surface, it offers by far the largest reservoir of wild food at our disposal, though as the declining whales sadly illustrate, its riches are not inexhaustible. While overfishing is a real danger, other and stranger phenomena can affect fish distribution – submarine waves, shifting currents, climatic changes – and these can redirect marine traffic with disastrous consequences, as was the case with the Baltic herring fisheries in the Middle Ages. However, give or take the odd tidal wave or cod war, the source has always been pretty reliable.

Fish is an excellent food for man, rich in high grade protein, vitamins (A, D, and E especially) and in minerals, as one would expect in sea creatures. Fatty fish – like herring, or mackerel – are also rich in polyunsaturates which inhibit cholesterol formation. Pound for pound, fish offers more meat and less waste than animal meat. Easily digested, it is a classic item in an invalid diet. Best of all, from the cook's point of view, fish in prime condition is delicious eating. It is as good quickly broiled and served with a pat of herb butter as when treated with all the pomp and ceremony of *haute cuisine*.

The bulk of fish eaten throughout the world comes from three main groups: the herring group, including pilchards or Pacific sardines, and American and hickory shads; the cod fishes, including Atlantic and Pacific cod, pollack, hake, haddock and whiting (four million tons of cod are taken annually); and the mackerel and tuna family. Thanks to advanced equipment which allows fish to be kept frozen, or chilled on ice, from capture to point of sale, more fresh fish is eaten today than ever before – in some parts of the world fish accounts for a fifth of people's annual animal protein intake. To replace this with land animal protein would require half as much land again as is now under cultivation, an impossibility which gives some idea of the importance of fish as a food.

Early man looked to the sea for some of his first instant meals, finding mollusks on the shore and, it seems, even venturing out to sea to fish, as he has continued to do, at some risk and much profit, throughout history. In the days before refrigeration and rapid transport, fresh fish must have been a rare item of diet unless you lived on or near the coast, or had access to inland waters. Big houses and monasteries went to the lengths of creating fish ponds, stocked with freshwater fish, which were netted periodically and the fish transferred to 'stews' – similar to the tanks used in some fish restaurants – where they were kept alive until required. However most people would have eaten their Friday and fast-day fish preserved by one or other of the traditional methods – dried, dried and salted, pickle-cured (in brine, not vinegar by the way) in barrels, or pickle-cured and then smoked for as long as 3 weeks. Pickle-cured and smoked red herrings, mahogany colored and dry as a chip, would be far too salty for modern tastes but they kept safely for years.

All these methods seem to have been in use since earliest times. The method chosen would probably have been determined by the type of fish – lean fish, such as cod and whiting, were most efficiently and cheaply preserved simply by drying, or salting and drying. Salt cod or stockfish (dried cod) was a staple food for centuries, despite the fact that it needed lengthy soaking and careful cooking to make it palatable. Since harmful micro-organisms require moisture to multiply, thoroughly drying fish – or anything else – is a sure way of preserving it. Salt, by extracting the natural fluid in the fish, helps speed up the process, as well as acting as a powerful preservative in itself. Fatty fish such as herrings, however, are turned rancid by drying, unless the fish are heavily smoked as well. Traditionally the way to preserve oily fish such as herring was to pack them in brine in airtight barrels; they kept well enough this way to be exported overseas.

Smoking, unless prolonged and intense, as it was with the red herrings where it acted as an anti-oxidant to prevent the herring going rancid, is a mild preservative, allowing fish to be kept for only a few days. If you own a freezer, the most practical proposition is to store the bulk of your fish there, smoking only for immediate use. And it is important to remember that cool smoked fish must always be cooked before eating, since cool smoking itself is not enough to kill harmful bacteria present in the fish.

However, the success then, as now, of the final preserved product stemmed to an enormous extent from the freshness of the original articles, for freshness with fish is everything. Perfectly fresh fish, as any fisherman knows, is sweet tasting with a firm, flaky texture, and no 'fishy' smell. Though eating fish straight from the water is a rare treat for most people, there is no good reason – given today's refrigeration techniques – why we should not all be able to buy the next best thing, which is fish held at temperatures low enough to prevent deterioration throughout its journey from fishing ground to fish market.

Where fish have been rapidly and conscientiously 'processed' (chilled or frozen immediately, gutted in some cases, packed and transported in cold storage), the results, say the experts, are virtually indistinguishable from the fish which leapt straight from the water into your skillet – a point you might like to raise with your fish merchant next time you are offered the flaccid, bleary-eyed specimens too often displayed for sale.

If everyone knew exactly how to tell fresh fish from stale, fish merchants would be prevented from offering the latter up for sale. Look fish in the eyes: these should be clear, bright and bulging – sunken, bloodshot eyes are a giveaway. Gills should be bright red – bleached or brownish gills denote staleness. The flesh should be firm, tight-skinned and springy – a fresh mackerel, as one authority vividly puts it, should be 'cool and firm as a cucumber'.

Stale fish tend to be limp, the skin loose and slimy. Stale fillets – usually cod or haddock – can be spotted by brownish red discoloration along the fillet in line with the backbone; in steaks this radiates out from the center bone. Really fresh fish has no unpleasant smell.

Fish caught in local waters, however unfamiliar, are often more rewarding than those which may have spent days *en route* to your store or market. Eel or lamprey, for example, has dense, sweet white meat. Both porgy and mullet are excellent eating when fresh.

Preparing fish

Fish merchants will of course clean and fillet fish for you, but it is sensible to know how to go about it yourself. Provided you have sharp knives and plenty of newspaper, cleaning and filleting is not the gory ordeal pictured by squeamish souls. I suggest you wear rubber gloves, not just to make you feel braver, but because fish scales can be surprisingly sharp.

Equipment

A short, sharp, pointed knife for gutting, removing the gills and head, and a bluntish blade for scaling are both essential. A small stiff brush is useful for cleaning out the gut cavity thoroughly. Professionals, dealing with masses of fish, keep a trough of clean water handy to rinse fish and knife as they proceed. For domestic purposes a bowl of cold water should be adequate, or the sink, but make sure you do not block up the outlet with scales. Paper towels are handy for a final wipe over, and newspaper for wrapping up the guts (burn these where possible).

Scaling

1. This is the first step in preparing a fish. Holding the fish firmly by the tail and using your blunt blade, scrape vigorously up towards the head – against the grain as it were – trying not to break the skin. With most fish this dislodges the scales quite easily. Some, like grey mullet, have tougher scales which need really energetic scraping. Wipe and rinse both the knife and fish as needed. When the skin is sleek, the fish is done. Don't ever be tempted to skimp scaling. Loose scales will get inextricably mingled with the fish or sauce in cooking, and they are not nice to eat.

Gutting and cleaning

2. Leave the head on, to use as a handhold. Grip the fish by the head, insert the knife just below the gills and slit down to the vent before the tail.
3. Then stick the blade into the cavity and scoop out the gut on to your newspaper. Rinse the cavity under cold running water. This should not, in fresh fish, smell too unpleasant, except in the case of the grey mullet, which being vegetarian, has a particularly large and offensive gut. Be careful to brush out all the gut, including the kidney which is situated just below the backbone. Cod, and similar species, have a thick white swimbladder which must be removed to

expose the kidney. Where the fish head is to be left on, the gills should be cut out cleanly with a sharp blade. To remove the head, slice off with a slanting cut to avoid wasting good edible fish meat. Cut along the line of the gills, then diagonally out of the top of the head.

Skinning
4. Where recipes allow it, leave the skin on during cooking and remove before serving. Otherwise for round fish, split the skin down the back and across the tail (the belly is already open), hold the tail firmly and cut the flesh away from the skin underneath in one movement, keeping the knife blade on a slant. To skin flat fish run the point of your knife around the fins, make an incision at the tail, tip thumb and finger in salt and strip off dark skin (the white skin is usually left on) in one sweep. The tension between skin and blade makes this easier than it sounds, but the knife must be sharp.

Splitting
5. To split fish for broiling, simply extend the ventral cut as far as the head or gills one way and the tail in the other. Open the fish out flat like a book. Head and tail may be left on or not, according to what you want to do with the fish. For kippering, split the herring (or mackerel) down the *back*, leaving the belly wall intact. Cut off the head and remove the gut from the dorsal rather than the ventral side. The backbone remains, lying to one side and lending strength while smoking (see page 127).

Filleting
Most round and small flat fish are best separated into two fillets, one each side. For round fish, first slit the stomach from head to tail and scoop out the gut as shown for gutting, left.
6. Cut cleanly along the spine.
7. Keeping the knife flat, prise and loosen the fish from the backbone and cut away in one piece as cleanly as possible, gripping the fish firmly with your free hand. Turn over and repeat.
8. The method is similar for flat fish. Cut off the side fins which surround the body with a sharp pair of kitchen scissors. Make an incision by the head and begin filleting. In the case of a large flat fish, slit it down the backbone and separate into four fillets, in smaller fish take off in two.

Preserving fish

All the traditional methods of preserving and preparing fish – drying, salting, pickle curing, smoking and potting – can successfully be applied, in some cases in a somewhat modified form, by people today, faced with a sudden glut of fish to dispose of, or make the best of. While the bulk of a catch is probably best stored in the freezer, if you want to keep it for long, there comes a time when choosy eaters rebel at plain unvarnished fish, and then it is a great asset to be able to choose from a variety of techniques which give results as different as, say, a kipper and a rollmop.

For straight preservation purposes, where keeping qualities count for more than sheer deliciousness, drying or drying and salting, suggest themselves as first choice for lean white fish. A fair bit of space is needed, and the process is fairly lengthy and needs watching, but provided you get your fish bone dry you can rest assured that it will keep perfectly for months, even years.

In the case of fatty fish, such as mackerel or herring, a modified form of the old pickled-in-the-barrel treatment is quite a neat and compact solution, and if you add spices to the brine the fish will emerge tastier as well. The same applies to the various vinegar and/or brine pickles and souses of which the Dutch and Scandinavians make such a feature in their cold spreads.

For short term keeping, fish pâtés and potted fish dishes generally are an easily made delicacy accompanied by toast, or salads. These have a long history in the English kitchen, probably because housewives found them useful for 'putting by' leftover fish for later in the week. However it would be unwise to lean too heavily on the preservative aspects of these methods. Soused, pickled or marinated fish dishes, however, have a longer safe life expectancy, since the acidity of the marinade is a more effective safeguard.

I am quite certain that smoking, particularly cool smoking, is the technique which will come as a revelation to most people. Once upon a time the notion of producing kippers, smoked haddock and so forth in your own backyard would have seemed far fetched, but today there is a growing number of home smoking enthusiasts who have cut their teeth on miniature smoke boxes of the type sold in most large stores and are raring to try something bigger and better, which gives greater control over the end results. A light, cool smoke gives fish a rich but subtle smoky flavor, without appreciably drying it, so the texture – especially with prime fat fish – remains succulent.

Apartment dwellers, or people who simply want to give an intriguing smoky taste to a few fish for supper without too much hassle, will find the small Scandinavian-type smoke box the best choice, as the whole operation takes hardly longer than putting the fish under the broiler and they emerge cooked as well as smoked – this is the technique known as hot-smoked. Most people are probably familiar with commercial hot-smoked products such as smoked trout, mackerel and eel, with their wrinkled amber skin. All these, like the fish (or sausages) cooked in your smoke box, are cooked and should be eaten within a few days, as for any cooked meat or fish.

With the cool smoker, which any reasonably handy person with enough space can make out of scrap materials, the possibilities are greatly increased. Provided you can get 1. prime fat fish and 2. suitable hardwood sawdust, it is not difficult to cool smoke your own kippers, haddock, mackerel, or any other suitable fish (oily or fatty ones seem to smoke most successfully), not to mention much larger items such as turkey and goose (p. 176), with results which compare very well with anything you could buy and which will certainly be vastly cheaper.

It takes a little practice to get a cool smoker working smoothly unless you are one of those lucky people with a natural flair for building and controlling fires, but it really is worth persevering because there can be few cheaper ways of raising simple materials into the luxury food class. Even if your homemade kippers look a bit rougher than the commercial ones, they will have a far superior freshness of flavor.

One last word about food poisoning. Various types of bacteria can grow in foods, causing illness ranging from minor stomach upsets to the dreaded, though fortunately rare, botulism. Fish in its raw state is one of the safest protein foods, but cooking kills the numerous and competing harmless bacteria and, if conditions are right, allows food poisoning bacteria, which may accidentally be introduced, to grow unchecked.

There are certain simple rules that should be observed, and if carefully followed will prevent the risk of illness from this cause. All equipment must be kept scrupulously clean, to reduce the risk of infection. Bacteria grow more rapidly as temperature rises, and many grow most rapidly at about blood heat. As soon as food is cooked, and this includes hot smoked fish from the kiln, allow it to cool and put it in the refrigerator. Do not leave it out in a warm kitchen. Remember also that cool pantries may not be as cool as they feel and a marble slab is no cooler than the air surrounding it. Food poisoning bacteria will not grow at temperatures around 32 degrees and even if your refrigerator is a bit warmer than this, the growth will be very slow.

Where cool smoked products are concerned, fish are safe as long as you cook them before eating them after only a day or two in the refrigerator (they may also be frozen). This is common practice, except in the case of smoked salmon. The makers of commercially smoked salmon naturally impose the most rigorous checks and precautions but since it would be difficult to follow their safety code at home, on balance I think home smokers might be better off avoiding smoked salmon.

Where a product is hot-smoked, the risk of poisoning is eliminated provided you eat the food within a day or two, as you would normally do with cooked food in any case. Any leftovers should be kept in the refrigerator, and if in any doubt, you can always cook them up again before eating them, in kedgeree, or fish pie.

Finally, pâtés and potted fish. These present a special problem, since bacteria may breed more rapidly in airless – that is sealed – conditions, especially where the basic materials have been previously cooked, thus destroying all competing organisms. Here the rule is store the product in the refrigerator and eat within 48 hours. Or, for longer keeping, store in the freezer and eat as soon as thawed.

Provided you observe these precautions, and maintain scrupulous hygiene as a matter of routine you should not have anything to worry about.

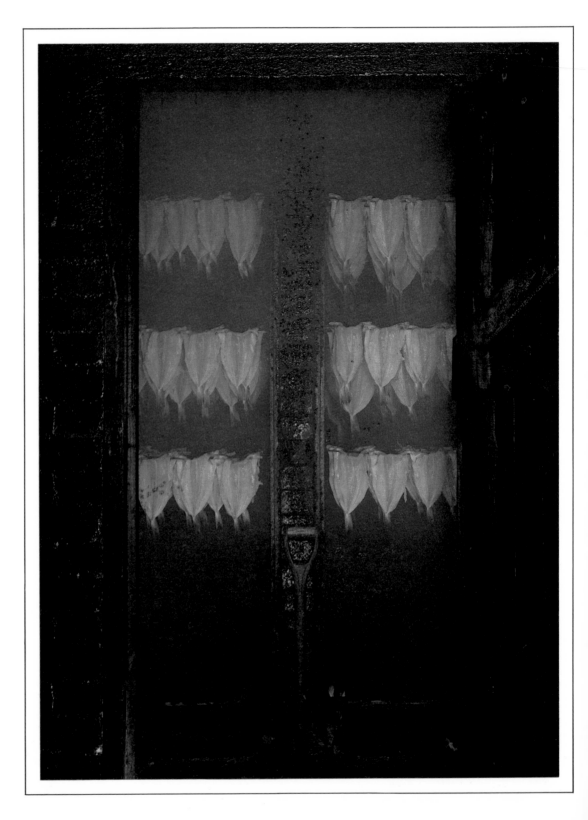

Smoked Fish

*'A Finnan haddock dried over the smoke of the seaweed
and sprinkled with salt water during the process
acquires a relish of a very peculiar and delicate flavour.'*

Notes to Boswell's 'Tour of the Hebrides'   *Sir Walter Scott*

Smoke plus fish is one of those ideally harmonious blends, like Earl Grey tea, producing a substance of suave texture and mellow flavor which really can claim to be a whole new food, quite different from the untreated fish.

Originally, back in the Middle Ages, smoking seems to have been used chiefly for its preservative effect, which increased the longer the fish hung smoking and drying in the old brick smoke towers – three whole weeks for red herring. The results would have been hard, bone dry and indescribably pungent – a little like Bombay Duck. Today, with cold storage taking care of the preservative side of things, smoking is used to enhance fish flavor and texture. A short spell in the smoke kiln produces fish which has a distinctively smoked taste without being unpleasantly dried out.

You will not need me to tell you that fish smoking, essentially, involves suspending raw fish in a continuous stream of smoke for a prescribed length of time. But not everyone realizes that there are two types of smoking which produce rather different results. Cold, or cool smoking, which gives you smoked salmon, kippers and smoked haddock for instance, is done at a temperature of around 80 degrees, well below blood heat, so the product is saturated with smoke but remains raw. Cool-smoked fish (except for salmon) are invariably cooked before eating. In hot smoking, which produces smoked trout and herring for instance, the fish are usually cool-smoked to begin with to give the desired flavor but the kiln temperature is raised gradually towards the end of the smoking time. The product emerges cooked, and ready to eat.

I have found with our own homemade smoker (p. 125) that cool smoking gives the best results for the time and effort involved, and if you want a hot-smoked effect you can simply pop the cool smoked product into your domestic oven, wrapped in foil, for 5 or 10 minutes until cooked. Or, alternatively, buy one of the small tin smoke boxes (or make one out of cookie tins for a fraction of the cost, p. 129), which will hot smoke anything fairly small – half a dozen small herrings, a pound of smelts, a fillet of cisco (making it into poor man's Finnan haddie) – in a few minutes.

Curing in the silvery haze of an oak sawdust fire, split haddocks skewered on rods. The fish are split, brined in a salt solution, then hung on rods to drain and put into the smoke hole. Haddock are cured higher, smelts and mackerel brought closer to the heat.

Building a smoke house

The homemade smoker

There are various possibilities to consider, from an *ad hoc* arrangement of ground sheets propped on sticks over a small camp fire of green twigs (the angler's or camper's version) to a permanent bricks and mortar job like my own backyard smoker, which looks for all the world like a surrealist brick refrigerator with a small stovepipe chimney. If you are planning to smoke food regularly, it is worth building a permanent structure, in my experience. It need not be any bigger than a refrigerator, but site it far enough away from house windows, patio and washing line to prevent everything reeking of hardwood smoke – delicious in the right place, but overpowering to live with.

Basically what is required is some sort of airtight, or potentially airtight, container, through which you can channel your smoke stream from a separate firebox via an inlet pipe and out through a chimney. A galvanized water tank, old stove or office safe are all possibilities but although these have the charm of all *objets trouvés*, I would plump for the bricks – or breeze blocks – and mortar structure as being more attractive, more efficient and purpose built.

Points to observe when building your smoker: the separate firebox should be set at least a foot below the level of the smoker floor, to encourage the smoke to rise up through the pipe and thence through the smoker and out through the chimney. You can achieve this either by raising the smoker up on a brick platform with the firebox at ground level (the advantage of this is that you could fix it so a second fire can be lit directly below the smoker itself, for hot smoking), or by siting the smoker on the ground but digging a pit below ground level for the firebox. A slope facilitates the second system. Either way the smoker and its satellite firebox should be linked by a clay drainage pipe of about 6 inches in diameter, both ends of which need to be cemented in. 100 per cent smoke-tightness is not vital to success, but nor do you want precious smoke rushing out all over the place.

Roof the smoker with overlapping roofing slates and then spread a 1 inch layer of mortar over the top. Leave to harden. A small chimney pipe should be set into the roof too, roughly diagonally opposite the clay pipe funneling the smoke in from below, plus a tile as damper to adjust the amount of smoke coming out of the smoker chimney. Once put into use, more roof slates, or a metal sheet, or something similar, will be needed to cover the firebox. The firebox cover needs to be easily removable as you may have to inspect your fire fairly often, until you gain experience.

As far as furnishing the smoker goes, provide it with a door, even if it's only a sheet of ply, and some way of suspending your 'tenters' (poles with hooks for hanging the fish) while smoking. Grooved bricks can be incorporated in the smoker walls to provide good supports for tenters or mesh trays. Alternatively use shelf bracketing cemented in, or screwed in place, or soldered if the smoker is metal. But do not make the positioning of your tenters and fish too awkward. In a smoky atmosphere you will not enjoy groping about for a minuscule bracket on which to rest your load of fish. The ideal, I think, would be sliding mesh trays similar to oven shelves which are easily manageable.

The fire

No smoke without fire, and getting the right sort of fire – basically hardwood sawdust brought to a pitch where it gently and constantly smolders and smokes – is the secret of successful cool smoking. The professionals are up to all sorts of dodges – some keep the sawdust in a can with a small open fire burning below, others stick glowing logs or coals into the can of sawdust itself. The way we find works best (my husband is the fire maker in our home) is to get a hearty blaze going in the firebox with a heap of dry kindling wood before you load the fish into the smoker. When this has burned down to a hot red heap, rake a mound of *dry* sawdust over and leave until the smoke is flowing well. It takes about 15 minutes to get a constant stream of smoke billowing through the smoker. When you see it spiraling through the chimney, block the chimney off partially with a tile, and the smoker is ready to use.

Then it is in with the fish, all prepared, brined, dried and impaled or netted and apart from periodic checks, every 30 minutes or so, to see if more sawdust is needed or an occasional booster of kindling, that is it. To rescue a burnt out heap, try shoving in a hot coal or glowing red log with fire tongs. If necessary – it may be at first – to get the fire started over again, clear a little pit in the middle of the extinct ashes. If the fire goes out for a short period during smoking, interrupting the smoke flow, do not panic as it will not be disastrous, but it is better not to make a practice of it.

Sawdust

Commercial fish smokers sometimes use softwood sawdust only when smoking white fish, or perhaps a blend of softwood and hardwood sawdusts to give their products a resinous flavor, but hardwood sawdust used alone gives fish the most delicate and appealing taste. Almost any hardwood sawdust may be used – elm, beech, oak, juniper, apple or hickory – depending what sort of trees grow where you live. But it is important that the sawdust comes from trees which have not been sprayed and treated with fungicides or insecticides as these could leave harmful deposits on the smoked food.

People who saw up their own firewood will be well placed for sawdust – if you do not, however, you may have a friend or neighbor who would help out in return for a sample of your smoked products. Otherwise contact lumber yards or builders' supply houses. However, you must be confident in your source, not only with regard to fungicides, but also alert to the possible infiltration of plastics into your sawdust supply. Few builders nowadays can entirely avoid laminated and plastic faced materials, and to use sawdust containing anything but untreated wood could be a little risky. If you live in the country, or near it, and you ask around, it is surprising how many people may be able to help, or think of someone who could. For city folks, a kind friend living in the country is the best bet. It is impossible to give accurate estimates of how much sawdust it takes to operate a given smoker, but roughly speaking, half a sackful seems to provide enough for 6 hours' smoking. Over rather than underestimate, however, as you do not want to run out of sawdust in the middle of smoking.

Preparing fish for the smoker

1. Split the fish head to tail along the spine.

2. Cleanly slice off the head, spread the fish open like a book, and scrape the gut out from the back, leaving the belly wall intact.

3. Brining fish prior to smoking firms the flesh, improves the flavor and adds an attractive salt-gloss to the finished product. Use a large white plastic bucket, glazed sink or wooden cask, well scalded and aired, as the brining vessel. For a strong solution, add 4 cups pickling salt, never table salt, to 4 quarts of cold water. Don't overcrowd fish in the brine bath, and stir now and again to make sure the ones on top get a good soak. Small fish should be well enough salted in 10 to 15 minutes, larger ones take up to 30 minutes. On removing the fish from the bath, hang them immediately for 1 to 2 hours to drip and dry, before going into the kiln.

4. When preparing fish for the kiln, remember that the entire surface should be exposed to the smoke throughout the process. The simplest way to achieve this is to impale fish on sharpened nails studded along wooden poles or tenters made from a 1 × 1 inch section cut to fit across the smoker. If the nails are slightly curved upwards with pliers, there is little risk of the fish becoming dislodged. Alternatively, two fish may be tied by their tails back to back, and looped over sticks, but care must be taken not to knock them off when loading and unloading the smoker. Threading fish on wire passed through their eye sockets, as well as being a grisly business, can also result in unevenly smoked fish as they tend to hang folded like clothes on hangers.

Smoking techniques

Cool smoking

The fish should be prepared as described on the previous page and loaded onto the tenters – a rather laborious process – while you start the fire going in your firebox. Commercially, a thermometer would be used to check that the temperature inside the smoker is around the 80 degree mark, but in practice – using the separate firebox type of smoker – there is little likelihood of overheating, since it is only smoke, and not heat that you are channeling through.

You might find wearing goggles or a skin diving mask is a help when loading the fish, as the smoke makes your eyes water copiously. Fix the fish with sufficient space between each fish and between tenters to let smoke circulate freely, then shut off or block the smoker door. Incidentally, if you want to smoke small fry such as smelts or sardines, which are delicious treated this way, you will have to contrive some sort of mesh tray on which to spread them out so the smoke envelops each fish. This should be positioned near the top of the smoker.

In commercial smoke kilns it is usual to shift the fish around once or twice during the smoking process, since the intensity of smoke in the kiln varies somewhat with the position of the fish, but it is rarely necessary to do this if you are only smoking a dozen or so fish.

The length of time needed for thorough smoking varies with the size and type of fish, but again, for domestic purposes, I do not think this is critical. Three or 4 hours will give small fish, such as herring, a distinct kippered flavor, though 6 to 12 is the professionals' allowance. Between 6 and 10 hours might be needed for a large fat haddock or cod fillet, but this is really a matter of personal taste. A little experience will confirm your preference as to degree of smokiness. Keep a log in which to note briefly times of brining, drying and smoking, and the results, to guide you. Do not expect your cool-smoked fish to have the deep tan of the commercial variety – this is achieved by dyeing. If the fire peters out during the smoking period, re-light it at once. Do not aim for billowing clouds of smoke; a light haze will soon build up in the smoker.

When smoking is complete, leave the fish in a cool place for 1 to 2 hours. Fish you do not want to eat immediately can be stored in the refrigerator or a cool place, protected by flycovers. I find flies avoid smoked fish on the whole, but there is always a risk with amateur smoking that one or two fish are not evenly smoked and the flies will go for any untreated flesh. Smoked fish can be frozen, if you want to keep them longer than a couple of days, but the flavor and texture are not as fine.

Recipes using smoked fish are given overleaf but first, one tip from the experts – the best way to cook kippers made from spent (ie spawned and lean) herring is the simple old way of steeping them for 3 minutes in a jug of boiling water. Any other way dries them out too much.

Note: There is a vogue for treating uncooked kipper as poor man's smoked salmon, and eating it raw, thinly sliced or made into pâté. I have done so in the past. Alas, expert advice recommends we drop this practice since cooking is necessary to destroy any harmful organisms naturally present in the fish.

Hot smoking

Your cool smoking kiln can be converted into a hot smoker if it is designed so that you can introduce an added source of heat. If built up on stilts, a second fire may be lit directly below the kiln. Alternatively you could insert into the smoker itself an electric hot plate.

The fish are prepared in exactly the same way as for cool smoking, and indeed start life in the smoker just as they would for a cool smoke. However, to achieve the cooked, wrinkled characteristics of hot-smoked fish (smoked trout or herring for example) the temperature inside the smoker will need to be raised gradually to about 200 to 230 degrees for the last 1 to 2 hours of the smoking time. The time necessary will vary, depending on the size and fatness of the fish. A thermometer is essential, and you must take frequent temperature readings, since there is the risk of the fish disintegrating as they cook and dropping off their tenters. Too much heat and the fish may become dried out, 'case-hardened' as they say in the trade, too little and they are undercooked, less pleasant to eat, and a possible health risk. Undercooked fish can of course be rescued by a short spell in the domestic oven or a minute under the broiler.

Alternatively you can improvise a 'one off' hot smoker, perhaps not as efficient or tidy as the commercial smoke box, but *free*. This can produce some delicious results, if a little crude in comparison with the kiln-smoked variety. One example is illustrated and described below, using a pair of cookie tins. If you can get hold of one, a large, sturdy, solidly made can of approximately 4 quart capacity will also make a good home smoker following the same principles. Don't waste hours measuring and perfecting such equipment – the idea is to make it quickly, use it and throw it away. And don't forget always to use oven gloves when handling this type of smoker – at its best used out of doors.

The fisherman's answer to the hot smoker (left) can easily be copied by even the least practical among us. All you need is two identical cookie tins, two canes or straight sticks and a handful of sawdust.

Puncture holes on opposite sides of one cookie tin near the base, and suspend canes to which your fish are secured. This tin is to be placed upside down on top of its twin (which is the right way up) and the sawdust is heaped on the floor of the lower tin.

To raise the necessary smoke, place the tins on either a camp fire out in the open or a small camping gas ring or over a domestic gas ring, adjusting the flame so the sawdust just smoulders without catching fire. Leave for 8 to 10 minutes until the sawdust is consumed and the fish cooked.

Cooking with smoked fish

Home smoked fish is an inspiring food to experiment with. It has endless versatility – delicious plain; hot or cold; it can also be dressed up for parties or down for economy, pounded into pâtés, whizzed into a mousse or baked in a flan. Yield: 4–6 servings.

Ways of cooking whole smoked fish
Three recipe suggestions for smoked fish, such as mackerel, herring, small haddock, whiting, buckling, bloaters:

Broiled with cream
Cook the fish under the broiler until done, rubbing them with a little butter if necessary. Serve with a large blob of whipped cream melting on top.

Flamed in whiskey à la Rob Roy
Cisco or lake herring or bloaters are best for this dashing 19th-century dish.

Split the fish and remove the heads and as many bones as possible. Lay them in a skillet and heat a ladleful of whiskey over a low flame for a moment. Pour over the fish, tilting the pan, set light to the whiskey and when it stops blazing the fish will be done.

Fried with bacon and mushrooms
The smoked fish should be divided into fillets. To make the dish fry two or three slices of bacon per person, until the fat runs, then add the fish fillets and fry for a further 3 or 4 minutes. Lastly add the mushrooms, and cook until just tender. Serve.

Smoked fish mousse
Urbane food for summer lunch parties, expecially when served with cucumber and cream sauce. The swankiest version uses smoked salmon, but hot-smoked mackerel or trout or cooked kippers may be substituted.

½ lb smoked fish
¼ cup homemade mayonnaise
½ lemon
salt, pepper
Tabasco sauce or anchovy paste
a pinch of cayenne
2 envelopes unflavored gelatin and water to mix
⅔ cup heavy cream
3 egg whites

Put the smoked fish and mayonnaise into a blender, and whizz smooth. Add the juice of half a lemon, salt, pepper, a dash of Tabasco and a small pinch of cayenne. Dissolve the gelatin in a few tablespoons of warm water, then blend with the fish mixture. Put in a decorative mold in the refrigerator until it just begins to set, then fold in the egg whites, beaten until fluffy and the cream, whipped until thick. Return to the refrigerator and chill for 3 hours, until firmly set. To unmold, dip the mold very briefly into hot water (just the mold, not the contents), then reverse carefully onto a dish.

Smoked fish bolster
Flaky pastry makes the bolster cover, and the stuffing consists of smoked fish and hard-cooked eggs in a creamy white sauce speckled with parsley. Using frozen commercial pastry, this is a quick dish to make, and attractive enough for a supper party.

1 pint white sauce flavored with 1 tablespoon grated cheese, grated nutmeg and chopped parsley
1 package frozen flaky or puff pastry
¼ lb cooked smoked fish
2 hard-cooked eggs

To make the bolster roll out the dough into a rectangle roughly 12 × 8 inches. Flake the fish, removing any skin or bones and mix gently with the sauce. Slice the hard-cooked eggs and spread them over the middle of the pastry. Spoon the fish mixture on top – it should be thick enough to stay put. Moisten the edges of the pastry rectangle, fold the side flaps up over the fish to meet in the middle and pinch all the seams shut. Lift the bolster tenderly onto a baking sheet, and put in the oven preheated to 425 degrees and bake for 10 minutes, then lower the heat to 375 degrees and bake for a further 25 minutes, or until the pastry is crisp, risen and golden. Buttered sprouts are good with this.

Kedgeree

Khichri, the Indian ancestor of this dish, is a spicy mixture of rice and lentils. The only thing Indian about our kedgeree is the light seasoning of curry powder.

2 cups patna or long grain rice
salt
4 large onions
8 tablespoons butter
1 tablespoon oil
½ lb cooked smoked fish
1 sliced hard-cooked egg
1 teaspoon curry powder or garam masala
black pepper
¼ cup light cream (optional)
juice of ½ lemon

Bring a large pan of water to a boil and throw in the rice and a little salt. Cook for 12 minutes, then drain in a strainer, running hot water through the rice. Put it into a large shallow baking dish and into a low oven to dry. Meanwhile peel and roughly chop the onions and fry gently in a little of the butter and the oil. When the onions are softening add the smoked fish, which has been flaked and the skin and bones removed. Cook for 1 minute. Add the hot rice to the pan and mix lightly with a fork. Add the sliced hard-cooked egg, curry powder or garam masala, and salt and pepper to taste. When hot put in the rest of the butter and fork it about until the rice is buttery. Spoon the cream over, add a squeeze of lemon juice and serve on hot plates.

Zapekanka

Russians make this with salt herring, but smoked fish is just as good and more commonly available.

1 onion
chopped fresh dill (optional)
3 cups hot mashed potatoes
3 eggs
1 thick slice white bread soaked in milk
½ lb smoked fish, flaked
salt, pepper
2 tablespoons butter
dry breadcrumbs
½ cup sour cream

Finely chop the onion and mix with the dill into the mashed potatoes, which should be smooth and rather thick. Separate two of the eggs, beat the yolks and add to the potatoes. Stir in the soaked bread, which has been squeezed out. Mix well, then add the fish and seasoning to taste. Beat the two egg whites until firm, and fold into the mixture. Generously butter a baking dish, sprinkle with the crumbs, then fill with the fish mixture. Beat the third egg with the sour cream and spread over the top. Bake at 375 degrees for 30 minutes, or until golden. Serve cut in squares with a sauce made of sour cream, chopped dill (or parsley) and a little lemon juice.

Quiche surprise

Smoked fish quiches are deservedly popular, the smoky fish taste contrasting nicely with the bland custard filling. This is a grand and partified version. A few spoonfuls of lumpfish roe can be added to the filling, for a richer effect.

pie pastry made with 1½ cups flour
choux paste for topping made with ¾ cup flour

Filling

5–6 oz smoked fish – mackerel, kipper
4 teaspoons lumpfish roe (optional)
3 egg yolks and 2 egg whites
½ cup light single cream
½ cup grated cheese
salt, pepper, grated nutmeg

Grease an 8 inch quiche or tart pan. Roll out the pie pastry and line the pan, pricking here and there with a fork. Arrange the flaked fish (skin and bones removed) evenly in the pastry shell, with blobs of roe in between. Beat the two whole eggs and one yolk, plus the cream and grated cheese. Season with salt, pepper and nutmeg. Pour this over the fish. With a large spoon cover the quiche filling with large blobs of choux paste, leaving no filling showing. Then slide into the oven preheated to 400 degrees and bake for 30 minutes. *Do not* open the oven door before the time is up, as choux paste hates drafts. On the half hour mark open the door a crack, to check the choux cover is firm and golden. If not cook a further 5 minutes. Serve at once.

Drying and salting

The pungent flavor of dried and salt fish is the making of certain traditional and hearty peasant dishes, and has a particular charm for those who enjoy it – by no means everyone – so it might be best to buy some and try it on your family first.

To follow these efficient traditional methods of preserving fish you will need quantities of suitable lean white fish like cod (stockfish). Herrings were never salted and dried because the salt encourages oxidation of the fat. So oily fish are pickle cured in brine. The best time to dry fish is when the weather is blowy and cold, and after a week or two of hanging in the breeze, they should be dry as a bone and stiff as a board and ready to keep for a year.

Equipment

You will need knives for scaling and cleaning (p. 118), and a large clean container. White (not colored) plastic buckets as used for wine making are suitable, as are earthenware crocks and glazed sinks, but scour, bleach and scald them carefully. For drying and draining the fish, a washing line or wooden clothes rack will serve to support small fish tied together by the tails in pairs. For large fish, like cod, slatted racks or plastic netting trays are needed for stacking and eventually drying the fish, spread out. Salt, if you are using it, should be pure pickling salt since fine salt can cause the outer layers of fish to become altered too quickly thus preventing the salt from 'striking through', and the fish would then be liable to go off.

Method

In the right weather conditions the fish may simply be dried outdoors after cleaning and splitting, leaving on heads and tails and stringing them up on a line, or impaling them on nails or hooks driven into a long piece of 1×1 inch section. Protect all drying and salted fish against cats and birds and at night take them into a cool shed or cellar. After a week or so most of the fluid will have drained out and the fish will be acquiring the proper hard dryness of texture. Leave them until they are stiff and no moisture can be felt when you pinch them. These may be fried or grilled and served with butter and parsley.

To speed the process of drying by encouraging the fluids to drain out (as well as giving a stronger flavor) fish may first be salted. A brine is the easiest method with small fish. Make a brine by mixing salt with really cold water in proportions of 1 lb ($1\frac{1}{2}$ cups) salt to 3 quarts of water – there should be enough to cover all the fish. Clean, scale, remove the heads and split open, then pack them – not too tightly – into the brine and leave for 1 hour if small, 2 if large. Remove and hang up to dry.

Large fish such as cod are generally dry salted. Use approximately 1 lb ($1\frac{1}{2}$ cups) salt to 3 lb of fish. Rub the salt in well all over both sides of the cleaned, split fish, then stack the salted fish in piles on your slatted racks, fleshy side up (with an extra sprinkle of salt between) until you have a stack ten deep. Now put the top one on skin side up and salt the top. After a couple of weeks of dry salting, spread the fish out so the air can get at them and leave to dry out completely, which is when they are hard, stiff and resist an enquiring pinch. Store in a cool dry place.

Dried and salt fish

Countries all over the world relish their own particular dried and salt fish recipe, some plain, some offset with sweet root vegetables, some hotted up with garlic and herbs, and some simply 'wind dried'. Yield: 4–6 servings.

Salt cod, parsnips and egg sauce

A favorite medieval dish, which nicely balances sweet mashed parsnips with salty fish. The sauce is a classic English one.

2 lb salt cod
2¼ cups milk
2¼ cups parsnips
10 tablespoons butter
salt, pepper
coriander (optional)
1 tablespoon flour
3 egg yolks

Soak the cod in several changes of cold water (they used to peg it down in a stream bed) to extract most of the salt. Put it into a pan with cold water, bring to a boil, then throw this water away. Repeat two or three times (depending on how salt the fish is), then cover the fish with milk and water (50–50) to cover. Add the peeled parsnips cut in strips. Simmer, covered, for 45 minutes or until the fish and parsnips are tender. Lift the fish out carefully and place it on a serving platter. Leave in a low oven to dry. Drain the stock into a jug. Mash the parsnips well, with about 8 tablespoons of the butter, salt, pepper (possibly a little crushed coriander) and a little of the stock, until creamy. Make the sauce by melting the remaining butter, stirring in the flour, and slowly adding about 1 pint of the stock stirring until smooth. To serve, surround the cod with the mashed parsnips. Remove the sauce from the heat and stir in the well beaten egg yolks. Stir until thick and golden and serve with the fish.

Bacalao

In the classic Basque recipe which is much more drawn out, the fish and sauce are cooked separately, and only combined at the end. This is a simpler, rustic and tasty fish stew.

If the tomatoes are not very juicy, add a little juice from canned tomatoes.

1 lb salt cod
3 onions
4 potatoes
1 large green pepper
6 large tomatoes (or canned tomatoes)
parsley
cooking oil (preferably olive oil)

Soak the salt cod in several changes of cold water, then drain. Pick off the skin and bones, and break into small pieces. Peel the onions and potatoes, remove the seeds from the pepper and slice all thinly into separate heaps. Slice the tomatoes, and chop the parsley. Put a layer of oil in the bottom of a deep thick saucepan, then make alternate layers of vegetables, parsley and fish, starting with tomatoes (for their juice) and ending with a potato lid. Cook very gently, covered, on the lowest flame (use asbestos mat over gas) or heat, for about 1 hour, or until the potatoes are tender. Shake the pan now and then to prevent sticking.

Salt cod with scrambled eggs

An unexpected, sophisticated mixture of flaked salt cod and scrambled eggs.

1 lb salt cod
2¼ cups milk
8 tablespoons butter
6 eggs
salt, black pepper
juice of ¼ lemon
4 slices bread

Soak the cod for 8 hours, changing the water twice. Cover with equal quantities of milk and water and simmer for about 30 minutes until tender. Drain, flake and dry in a warm oven. Melt the butter in a heavy skillet, stir in the beaten eggs, add salt and pepper, and cook slowly, stirring, until thick egg flakes are formed. Add the fish flakes, mix gently, squeeze the lemon juice over and serve with fried bread triangles.

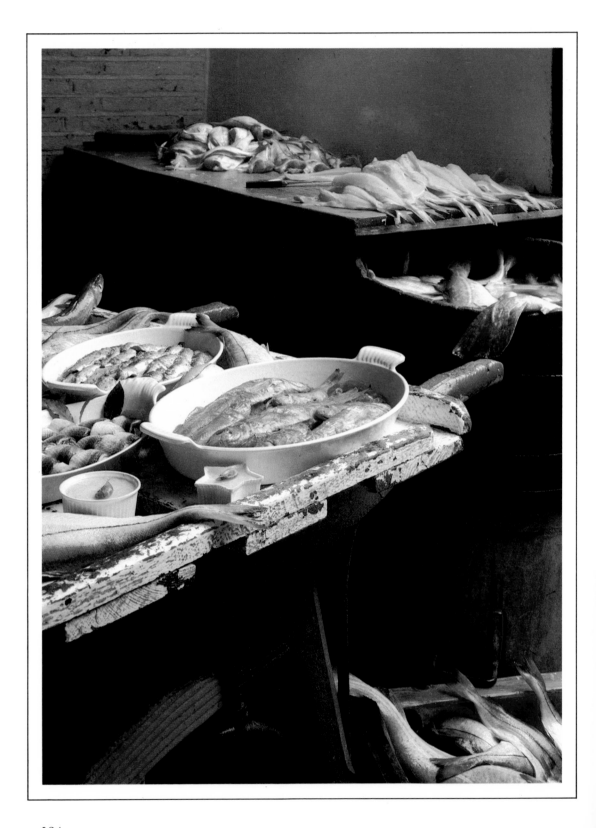

Pickled & Potted Fish

'The breakfast is the prosopon of the great work of the day.
Chocolate, coffee, tea, cream, eggs, ham, tongue, cold fowl – all these are good
and bespeak good knowledge in him who sets them forth: but the touchstone is fish:
anchovy is the first step, prawns and shrimps the second;
and I laud him who reaches even these: potted char and lampreys are the third . . .
but lobster is, indeed, matter for a May morning and demands
a rare combination of knowledge and virtue in him who sets it forth.'

Crotchet Castle   Thomas Love Peacock   1831

These succulent ways of preparing fish, formerly (erroneously) favored for their preservative qualities, are now enjoyed on their own highly individual, often spicy merit alone.

Traditionally herring, mackerel and salmon are the fish used for pickling and sousing, probably because their oiliness consorts well with the sharp spicy pickle. Use ovenproof casseroles of any shape and size, preferably with lids. The finer the vinegar the more subtle the pickle. I add a little sugar which I think improves all fish dishes. The fish are cleaned and filleted, but the skin – with herrings anyway – is often left on. The fish are packed into a suitable dish, the pickle poured over and the dish then baked in a low oven, for an hour or so. Cooked like this the bones are softened enough to be eaten – you do not have to, but they are rich in calcium. Despite the long cooking, the vinegar keeps the fish surprisingly firm in its texture. Alternatively, the fish may just be left for longer to marinate to obviate the need for cooking.

Most fish can be potted, including smoked fish, shellfish, and leftovers but fish of strong flavors – shrimp, bloater or cisco, mackerel, herring, crab – give the most interesting results. Small pottery dishes make the most attractive containers. An electric blender is useful for making fish pastes. Unsalted or lightly salted butter is the best for the purpose, and the spices, as usual, are more aromatic bought whole and ground in a mortar or food mill. Nutmeg, mace, allspice and pepper are traditional. Usually the fish are gently baked in the oven with spices and seasoning until tender, then mashed, flaked or blended – depending how smooth a consistency you want – pressed into pots, and covered with clarified butter (see ghee). Shrimp are left whole. Eat within 48 hours if kept in the refrigerator, or freeze for longer and eat as soon as thawed.

Fresh fish for filleting in barrels, freshly cooked fish dishes on the barrow: potted shrimp sealed with butter, rollmop herrings soused in brine, Arabic *Shtoon Fufarran* with sardines marinated in a spice paste and Chinese crispy mullet flavored with garlic and ginger.

Pickled and potted fish dishes

The common link between pickled and potted fish is that they have both been previously cooked. From there on, they differ entirely, potted fish offering a delicious convenience, pickled, an unexpected piquancy. Yield: 4–8 servings.

Rollmops
The classic soused herring dish.

8 herrings
3 tablespoons pickling salt
2¼ cups water
1 quart white wine vinegar
2 shallots or 1 onion
2 bay leaves
4 small pickles, sliced
1 tablespoon pickling spices

Clean the fish, split down the back and remove the backbones. Fillet if large. Mix the salt with the water, and soak the fish in this brine for about 3 hours, then drain and dip them in the vinegar. Roll each fish or fillet around a little chopped shallot or onion and pack into a jar with the broken bay leaves and pickles. Boil the vinegar with the pickling spices. When cold pour over the herring. Store in a cool place and eat after 48 hour infusion. Will keep 3 weeks, or longer.

Chinese crispy red fish
The Chinese are marvelously skillful at bringing out the best in fish, using a combination of flavorings – especially the garlic ginger sherry mixture as here – which makes the flesh sweet and tasty, or as the Chinese say 'de-fished'. The redness comes from the addition of red food coloring. The distinctive feature of this recipe is that while the fish bones are soft and edible, the skin becomes delectably crisp.

2 lb herrings or fresh sardines or mullet
3 medium onions
3 cloves garlic
1 inch piece of ginger root
¼ cup sugar
¼ cup soy sauce
6 tablespoons wine or cider vinegar
6 tablespoons sherry
1 quart fish or chicken stock
½ teaspoon red food coloring

Scale and clean the fish. The Chinese leave the heads and tails for elegance, but to economize you could remove these and simmer them with a little soy sauce, sherry and chopped onion to make stock. To cook the fish slice the onions, crush the garlic and finely chop the ginger and spread over the bottom of a large shallow casserole or cast iron dish which can go on top of the stove. Then arrange the fish on top, head to tail, in layers if necessary. Mix the sugar, soy sauce, vinegar and sherry with the stock and pour over fish. Bring to a boil, add the food coloring and simmer gently, uncovered, until the liquid has completely evaporated about 1 hour. Or transfer to a 325 degree oven and cook until the liquid is gone, but check after 30 minutes to see that the fish is not scorching.

Arabic pickled pilchards Shtoon Fufarran
Make this dish with any small fish – pilchards, smelts. It is splendid for a cocktail party.

3 lb small fish
1 head garlic
2 large handfuls parsley
¼ teaspoon cayenne
1 tablespoon cumin
juice of 3 lemons
6 tablespoons olive oil
4 tablespoons water
1 tablespoon salt

Soak the fish in cool salty water for a few minutes. Snap or cut off the heads, pulling out the guts. Pour boiling water over the fish, and leave for 2 minutes until they have split open. Then remove the backbones, so you have 2 tiny fillets. Pound the garlic, parsley, cayenne and cumin together to a paste. Mix the liquid ingredients together with the salt and spicy paste. Arrange the fish and spice mixture in layers in a shallow dish, ending with the paste. Cover and refrigerate. Eat after 24 hours. It will keep for 1 week.

Marinated anchovies

Anchovies, sardines, smelts, even whitebait would be good for this. The quantities given here would be enough to fuel a small party – for domestic purposes half is enough.

6 small onions
7 tablespoons olive oil
½ cup dry white wine
chopped fresh herbs, fennel, parsley, 1 bay leaf, pinch
  of thyme (about 2 tablespoons in all)
1 clove garlic
1 teaspoon coriander
juice of 1 lemon
salt and pepper
2 lb fresh anchovies or other small fry

Make the marinade by frying the sliced onions in half the oil, and when golden adding the wine, herbs, garlic, coriander and lemon juice. Season with salt and pepper and simmer for 10 minutes. Clean and fillet the fish as described for Arabic pickled pilchards. Spread the fillets in a large flat baking dish, sprinkle with the remaining oil, plus a little salt and pepper and bake at 425 degrees for 12 minutes or until golden and crisp. Cool, pour over the cooled marinade and keep in the refrigerator for 48 hours to develop flavor before serving.

Scandinavian pickled herring

2 lb fat fresh herrings
2 medium onions or shallots
3 heaping tablespoons sugar
1 tablespoon allspice
2½ cups white wine or cider vinegar

Use a large sterilized glass jar to pack the fish in. First clean and remove heads from the fish, rinse under cold water, then leave overnight in lightly salted water in the refrigerator. Next day fillet the fish neatly and remove fins, but do not remove the skin. Cut fillets across into ½ inch strips. Peel and thinly slice onions. Mix sugar and spice together. Put the fish strips in the glass jar with a good sprinkle of sugar/spice and sliced onions between each layer, then pour over vinegar to cover the fish completely. Chill in the refrigerator for 48 hours.

Potted mackerel or herring

6 mackerel or herrings, filleted
¼ teaspoon each of grated nutmeg, ground cloves and
  ground ginger
2 tablespoons salt
6 bay leaves
lemon rind
¼ lb (1 cup) butter

The fish fillets need not be skinned. Mix the spices together with the salt, then rub into the fish fillets. Lay these in a ovenproof dish, interspersed with the bay leaves, strips of lemon rind and pats of butter. Dot with the remaining butter, then cover the dish with foil and a lid and bake at 300 degrees for 3 hours. Remove any skin and bones, as well as the bay leaves and rind, then break up the fish roughly with a fork and leave to cool. When cold, top with a layer of clarified butter (see page 92).

Potted shrimps

Made with fresh shrimp and creamy butter, this is the apotheosis of potted fish. Best eaten with dry toast or thin brown bread. It looks as beautiful, with the whole shrimp merged in a rosy paste, as it tastes.

¼ lb fresh shrimp (unshelled)
¼ lb whiting, dab, flounder or other delicate
  white fish
tiny pinch each of cayenne, ground mace or grated
  nutmeg
12 tablespoons unsalted butter
¼ teaspoon anchovy paste or ½ anchovy fillet (optional)

Shell the shrimp. Put the shells and heads in just enough water to cover and simmer for 5 to 10 minutes, with the pan lid on. Strain the liquid and use it to poach the white fish until tender – about 10 minutes over a low heat. When cool pick out any skin or bone and pound or blend the white fish until smooth with the spices, butter and anchovy. Put the mixture back into a pan, cook over a moderate heat until thoroughly hot, then stir in the whole shrimp. Ladle the contents into small china pots or dishes, leaving ½ inch head room. When cold cover with a thin layer of clarified butter.

Meat

Meat: its cuts and cures

Meat is not only good eating but an outstandingly nutritious food. A mere $3\frac{1}{2}$ oz of cooked meat – or about 10 per cent of an adult male's daily calorie intake – provides him with 45 per cent of his day's protein requirements, 36 per cent of his iron, plus significant amounts of the essential B complex vitamins. Cooked meat also has what nutrition manuals prosaically describe as 'satiety value'; it leaves you feeling warmed, nourished and pleasantly full. You can easily work out a nutritious non-meat meal, but even when nicely cooked and satisfying it somehow fails to restore and comfort the inner man in quite the same way.

Meat is defined as the 'muscular flesh of edible animals' and broadly classified by color – dark, red, pale – as well as type. Muscle itself is especially nourishing, which makes the meat of older, muscular animals good value, provided it is slowly and carefully cooked to make it tender. Freshly killed meat is tough and indigestible; all meat sold commercially is hung in a cool place for at least a day or two to make it tender and improve its flavor. Tastes in meat change slowly but profoundly. Today's preference is universally for meat with the minimum of fat, and stock breeders naturally take note of this, producing lean pigs and trim steers which would appear undersized compared with the fatted-up animals of a century or more ago. In breeding out fatness, however, we may have bred out a fair bit of flavor too – fat, as it cooks, automatically bastes the lean, which adds to the flavor as well as succulence. I find that much of the meat sold today looks better than it tastes. Whether this is due to selective breeding, standardized foodstuffs, or over-use of steroids or other artificial meat-builders is debatable. What is certain, happily, is that many of the old, traditional ways of preserving meat – salting, brining, drying, smoking – have a new relevance today, whether or not you are interested in their preservative value. They add flavor and interest to almost any type or cut of meat, and this includes the whole range of poultry, and lamb and beef, as well as the traditional favorite, pork.

A spell in the brine tub, for instance, transforms any cut of pork, giving it a flavor and texture akin to the finest ham, which is particularly valuable in the case of fatty cuts. Overnight dry curing with spices, salt and sugar, followed by a few hours cool smoking is the answer for anyone who finds turkey meat, especially frozen turkey meat, insipid eating. It makes the dark meat every bit as appetizing as the white, and is at its best eaten cold, the carcass making an exceptionally delicious soup. Dry spicing a fine roast of beef for a week or two produces a cold cut of uniquely rich and racy flavor. At the other end of the price scale, there are all the time honored ways of making the best of cheap, fatty cuts, scraps and trimmings and variety meat, ranging from the familiar pâtés and terrines to homemade sausage fillings, which can be bland and subtle, or ablaze with spice and garlic. These are pleasant and satisfying to make and can be stored in the freezer, or in many cases, dried and hung from the kitchen ceiling to be added to stews, paellas and thick soup as need arises. Larding fried sausages in stoneware or glass jars is another simple old method of storing sausages. Tastier than when frozen, these sausages need to be heated for just 3 minutes at 158 degrees before eating.

I will not pretend that any of these traditional ruses are as simple as stashing stuff away in the freezer, but they greatly extend a cook's scope and many people will think the time and effort amply rewarded if it results in superb eating at very little extra cost – make one batch of homemade sausages and you will find yourself doing it for life.

The cheapest way to buy meat, as many freezer owners now do, is in bulk, a half of lamb or pork, or a quarter of beef at a time. Instead of freezing the lot, I would suggest that a more enlightened approach might be to reserve precious freezer space for choice roasting or broiling cuts, and use traditional preservation methods to deal with the remainder of the carcass, which might include along with such lesser cuts as heads, feet and tail, a selection of variety meats, including tongue, brains, heart and spleen. Most of these are the basis of excellent traditional recipes – pickled tongue, smoked heart, liver pâté, head cheese or brawn, faggots, salt feet, smoked chap. If you have a cool smoker, or a suitable woodburning fireplace, it would be a pity not to try your hand at curing and smoking your own ham, since this is one of the most expensive meats to buy, and the techniques involved are quite simple if lengthy – after all home-cured hams were commonplace until electricity and gas heating did away with the old, roomy wood-burning hearth. A leg of lamb, incidentally, can be made into 'lamb ham', a delicacy little known outside Norway today but once made in all the sheep farming areas.

Having decided on your plan of campaign, draw up a list of what you hope to get from your half of lamb, pork, or quarter of beef, and then consult your butcher, or whoever is supplying the meat. It is a bit cheaper to cut up your carcass yourself, but this is such a skillful operation that it would be false economy for most people to try it. If you *must*, my butcher's advice is to start on something small like a half of lamb. Take it apart as if you were cutting up an outsize rabbit, remembering – as with sawing wood – to cut across the grain, not along it. Otherwise leave it to the butcher, but let him know what cuts you want – hams for instance are cut quite differently from the conventional leg (fresh ham) roasts.

More people keep poultry than raise livestock, so the possibility of a glut at certain times of year does arise here. Domestic fowl are plucked immediately after killing, then drawn. Hanging in a cold pantry or cellar for a few days improves the flavor, but only when the the weather is suitably crisp and cold and no flies are about. One of the most attractive traditional methods of dealing with surplus poultry is the celebrated *confit d'oie*, from the Périgord region of France, in which lightly salted and spiced goose pieces are gently cooked and stored in their own rendered down fat, copious in the case of a goose. The method can be applied successfully to other birds, if their own fat is supplemented with clarified lard or drippings, and the result is meat of exceptional tenderness and flavor – miles away from the watery defrozen stuff – plus bowlfuls of delicious fat for cooking and frying. But make quite sure you do as the French always have: cook the jars of *confit* every few months for the prescribed time – a few minutes in a low oven – to destroy any harmful toxins, and repeat this before finally eating the meat concerned. Poultry meat, home-raised or not, makes delicate and delicious terrines and galantines which will keep for months in a freezer.

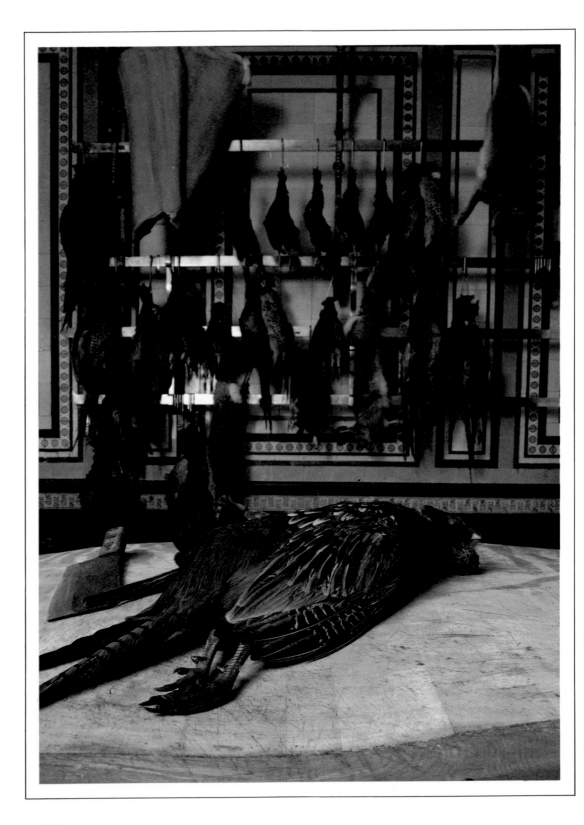

Game

*'If there is one month worse than another for the amusement of shooting,
I should be apt to consider that it is November.
The warmer weather of September and October is then gone by,
and the birds become wild and cunning. The fall of the leaf,
with the sports of rabbit, woodcock, snipe and wildfowl shooting,
are not in general to be fully enjoyed till December and January.'*

Instructions to Young Sportsmen   Lt. Col. P. Hawker   1814

The meat which seems most in harmony with country living, vivid to taste and eye with all the concentrated essences of its wild habitats, is game, or the flesh of wild animals, such as venison, wild boar and hare, and the many varieties of game birds and wild fowl. A license, or permission of some sort, is usually required to shoot any of these, and in most countries, a closed season is observed in order to protect the animals and birds during their breeding times, and ensure that they are not hunted to extinction. Some wild creatures, like rabbits and pigeons, are classified as vermin in many countries, and can be shot at any time of the year, and not so long ago deer were considered vermin in some places.

For most people, their first taste of game is positively startling, so richly colored and strongly flavored is it compared with butcher's meat, but carefully cooked and served with appropriate trimmings, game meat is noble fare and the basis for many superb, classic dishes. If you have never tasted game I suggest you begin with one of the milder flavored meats – pheasant is a safe choice, or a fat rabbit – and ask the butcher to prepare it for cooking. Having once acquired a taste for this sort of meat, you can move on to the more robustly flavored dark meats such as venison. Of the game sold in butchers' shops, hare is exceptional value for money, with enough meat to feed ten, or stretch to three meals – roast saddle, say, plus a pâté, turnover or jugged dish. When buying game, look for signs of youth and health – bright plumage, sleek fur, supple uncallused paws or claws. Or trust your butcher. Old game is usually cheaper, stronger flavored and meatier but needs long slow simmering *en casserole* to make it tender, as in those two classic dishes, jugged hare and *perdrix au choux*. All game meat is extraordinarily rich, and needs an astringent contrast to be enjoyed fully; a sharp fruit jelly, a squeeze of orange juice, a dash of herb vinegar or a wine marinade are all traditional solutions. Most game meat, beast or bird, is dryish, since few wild creatures run to fat, so compensate when cooking – plain roasts should be basted with butter frequently, or larded with fat back, and game birds wrapped in bacon.

A brace of pheasants on the butcher's block for plucking and drawing before cooking; hanging on butchers' hooks to ripen the meat, still furred and feathered, are hare, quail and grouse. For first-time game cooks, pheasant is milder flavored, hare robust dark meat.

Hanging

How long you do this depends on the weather (cold weather allows game to hang without spoiling for 1 to 3 weeks, while warm muggy weather means you should not leave it more than a few days), your tastes, and to some degree the age and size of the animal or bird. Old game is hung longer to tenderize it; large game like deer keep better longer than small birds. Note these rules. Except for rabbits, cleaned or disembowelled immediately they are killed, all game, furred or feathered, is hung with the guts and the fur or feathers on. They keep better that way, oddly enough, and it is after they are made ready for cooking that they should not hang too long. My butcher hangs venison for 2 weeks before cleaning and skinning, and for a week after; game birds, on the other hand, are plucked and drawn the day before the customer wants to eat them. Game that is 'high' – smelly, in plain English – is quite safe to eat, provided you cook it thoroughly, but some claim it is indigestible.

Plucking and drawing

I do plucking sitting down, with the bird on my lap, and a large bucket for the feathers between my feet – even a small bird carries a mass of feathers. Take the bird in the left hand and begin pulling out the feathers from under the wing. Large feathers can generally be pulled out a few at a time, with a firm tug – pull the way the feather points – but breast feathers should be extracted one at a time to avoid tearing the delicate skin over the breast, so wasting valuable juice when it cooks. Obstinate feathers can be dealt with by singeing carefully over a gas flame. Wing tips are generally cut off before cooking, so do not bother plucking these. The same goes for head and neck. But the rest of your bird should be plucked smooth and bare as a bald pate. Where possible, extract any stray shot while plucking and drawing as these can be injurious to teeth if inadvertently chewed. Game birds and wild fowl are drawn like chickens, except for woodcock, which are cooked with the guts in. Cut off the head, feet and wingtips, and pull out the guts, retaining the liver to spread on toast under the bird.

Skinning and cleaning

Skin first, then clean, except for rabbit (see above). Professionals leave the head on, but you will find it is easier to cut the head off with the first joint of the legs, both fore and hind, which is the first step. Then slit the skin up the stomach and from there it is a bit like taking off a jacket. Using a sharp knife, cut and pull the legs clear of skin, then peel the skin back over the body of the animal, and give a good tug to release. To clean, make a cut up the stomach, in the same direction as the skin was cut, and take out all the guts. Wipe out the cavity, or rinse out with clean cold water. Rabbit is often soaked in lightly salted water before cooking to whiten the meat and soak off any blood clots; hare's blood on the other hand is carefully saved, where possible, and added to the gravy or stock. If you are eating hare, rabbit or venison (or other game animals) regularly, and doing the skinning yourself it might be an idea to try your hand at curing and stretching the skins.

Plucking, drawing and trussing a pheasant

1. Hold the bird firmly in one hand to support its weight as you begin taking out the feathers. Always pull the way the feathers point. You can tug handfuls at a time, except over the delicate breastbone where the skin is likely to tear. Obstinate feathers can always be singed off over a gas flame. Leave on the feathers at the wingtip as you will trim these later.

2. Pull a fold of skin down the neck towards the body to give yourself a flap of skin once the head is removed. Then cut the head off, but before severing it, ease the knife blade round the inside of the neck passage to loosen the windpipe and the grain sack at the base. The whole matter should come away with the head.

3. To remove the entrails, heart, liver and guts, run your finger round the inside of the bird to loosen any matter from the bones. Then gradually ease the organs out of the bird. Do not hurry this process and peer inside later to see that everything has come away. The bits and pieces can be used for the stock, except for the liver which embitters any stock. Cook it separately while the bird is roasting and spread it on toast to serve underneath the bird, the way the French chefs do. Cut off the wingtips and the feet, above the knobbly socket.

4. Pull the flaps of skin both top and bottom over the openings. The bird is now ready for roasting. Once you have made a stuffing and placed it in the cavities, skewer the skin flaps in place and place larding strips of bacon over the bird as pheasant dries out when cooking.

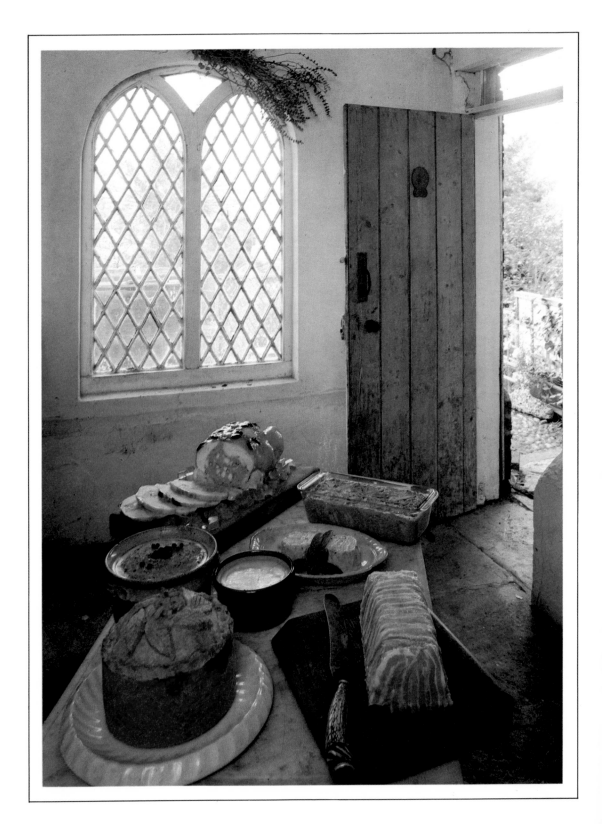

Pâtés, Pies & Galantines

'"There's cold chicken inside it," replied the Rat briefly;
"coldtonguecoldhamcoldbeefpickledgherkinssaladfrenchrollscress
sandwichespottedmeatgingerbeerlemonadesodawater –"
"Oh stop, stop," cried the Mole in ecstasies: "This is too much!"'

The Wind in the Willows   Kenneth Grahame   1908

I think of these made-up meat dishes as a sort of meat cake in which you can alter the texture by grinding everything several times, for smoothness, or inserting a layer of meat slivers, or stirring in a proportion of diced meat, or simply roughly chopping everything, for a coarse homespun effect. The main difference nowadays between a pâté and terrine would seem to be the frequent inclusion in terrines of slices or chunks of contrasting and different meats. A galantine, also a layered structure of meat, consists of either a boned, forcemeat-stuffed cut (a fresh pork picnic shoulder or breast of veal), or a whole bird (chicken, turkey, pheasant), also boned and packed with forcemeat and good things like truffles or pistachio nuts, before being stitched up and rolled in a floured piece of linen or cheesecloth. When cold and pressed, a galantine cuts as easily as a loaf of bread and looks spectacular.

Finally, a good meaty mix can be enclosed in a sturdy edible container which makes a substantial and attractive pie. It is the surprise element in a pie that fascinates: the medieval banqueting showpiece piecrust held a whole aviary of birds boned and fitted inside each other. Today, there are many much simpler pies that can be made with a raised crust and the meat filling of your choice.

Ingredients can be cheap and basic, or as recherché and expensive as you like or can afford. I make a cheap, simple pâté regularly, using the least expensive liver and that most adaptable cheap cut, fresh pork sides – varying the seasonings according to what is growing, or how I feel. It is one of my most reliable stopgaps. All the cheaper, fatty, gristly, or strongly flavored meats are potentially suited to pâtés and terrines because grinding refines the texture (always pick out stringy bits of gristle and chunks of fat as nasty surprises are another matter), prevents meat being tough, and a judicious use of bland flavored meat like pork sides softens the most powerful tasting liver. I find the idea of a French pâté of lark's tongue unedifying, but there is a place for the lavish set piece and the galantine fits the bill beautifully.

Cold meat dishes: Melton Mowbray raised pork pie and a veal and ham terrine larded with bacon (foreground); rabbit pâté, pork rillettes covered with butter and game pâté sprigged with sage (center); and at the back, chicken galantine and simple daily pâté.

Pâtés and terrines

Pack a well seasoned forcemeat base of various meats, ground together with herbs or spices, juniper berries, maybe alcohol, garlic or onions, into a dish lined with bacon or strips of fat (speck or hard fat back is best), cover it and bake gently. When making a terrine, a *salpicon*, or mixture of meat in strips or chunks, is sometimes added to the basic mixture to vary the texture. Stir it into the forcemeat, or keep it in a separate layer halfway up the dish. When cooked and pressed, it shows as a vein of marbling in a fine textured setting.

Take care to pick over the meats before and after grinding – cut off the gristle, membrane and any fibrous stuff which will not grind down properly and will not cook nicely either. A balance of flavor in the meat used helps both pâtés and terrines. Thus, some well flavored lean meat, some bland fat meat and some meat of smooth texture with concentrated flavor, like liver, is a good combination. If you add a little bacon or ham to line the dish, go easy on the salt.

You can add a little flour or beaten egg to the mixture before cooking to bind it. Do not overdo it or the mixture can become stodgy. Dishes to be unmolded can have a decorative spray of bay leaves laid on the bottom underneath the fat strips.

Equipment
An electric blender or food processor does make preparing ground meat mixtures very much easier and quicker, and some will deal with chopping onions, garlic and herbs finely as well. However, chopping by hand with a sharp *demi-lune* or cleaver is still the slow but sure way to the juiciest and freshest tasting pâtés and terrines. Electric gadgets do bash some of the natural springiness out of meat and the juice tends to get lost. Make several small pâtés rather than one large one so that you can seal some with lard to keep in the pantry. They are best made in traditional earthenware dishes, round or oval, the simpler the better. Lidded dishes are the most useful.

Cooking pâtés and terrines
All pâtés and terrines should be cooked slowly and evenly, the dish placed in a pan of hot water. Remove the lid to brown the top for the last half hour if they are not to be unmolded. They are done when the meat shrinks away from the sides of the dish – do not be misled by a pinky tinge to the meat as any bacon colors the contents like that. To press out the fat, lay a plate with a small board on top, and weight with cans overnight. Next day loosen around the edges with a knife, and unmold onto a dish. Pâtés and terrines will cut better when pressed.

For keeping longer (up to a few days) leave the dish to get cold then pour a good layer of pure lard – $\frac{3}{4}$ inch deep – over the top to seal it well, making sure it adheres to the dish all around. Keep in the refrigerator. Or you could unmold the pâté when cold, scrape off all the fat on the outside, return to the dish and pour in hot lard, enough to float it in. When cold pour a sealing layer on top. Or, lastly, pack the pâté into a canning jar up to the level indicated, put on the lid and sterilize by putting into a pan with cold water to cover, bringing slowly to a boil and simmering for 2 hours.

Pies and galantines

Pies

The most handsome traditional pies are meaty fillings enclosed by hand-shaped raised crust pastry. The stock is poured in after the pie has been baked and cooled through a hole in the center of the pastry lid.

The pastry case

Sift all-purpose flour and salt into a deep bowl and make a well in the center. Bring the pure lard and water to a boil and when boiling, steadily tip into the bowl, mixing with the flour. As soon as the hot alabaster paste is cool enough to handle, work it vigorously until smooth – pummel, pound and knead. Leave in a warm place to rest for 15 minutes. Shape the dough into a lump, and hollow it out from the middle with a coaxing finger, keeping it thick and solid until there is enough space to set inside a suitable mold, such as a glass jar, to model round. Turn the mold upside down with the dough over the base, and work downwards. Or you can place the dough inside a hinged metal mold and begin working it up the sides gradually. Aim to keep the crust even throughout and no more than $\frac{1}{4}$ inch thick or the finished pastry will be stodgy. To loosen the case from the jar, lay it on its side and roll gently. Snip around the top of the case with scissors to neaten. Pack with the prepared meat filling, closely but not ramming it in or you will make bulges in the case. Roll a lid from the dough trimmings. Dampen the edges before laying the lid on top and pressing together firmly – use your thumb to make a piecrust edging. Now cut a neat hole in the middle of the lid and decorate with leaves, scrolls or acorns made from the leftover scraps of dough. Dampen these before placing on the lid. A tiny twist of paper set in the hole keeps it open while cooking. Brush over the outside of the pie with beaten egg for a golden finish. Bake at 325 degrees for 2 to $2\frac{1}{2}$ hours. If the top is browning too much, cover with a loose lid of foil. Leave the pie to cool for an hour, while the crust stiffens, before pouring in the stock. The stock should be warm, not hot. If in doubt about the strength of the side of the pastry case, a foil belt helps. Leave overnight to become cold before serving.

Galantines

A boned chicken, pork picnic shoulder, or breast of veal makes a neat pocket which you simply pack with the chosen ingredients, sew shut, then simmer, tied in a floured cloth. The meat envelope bastes the forcemeat as it cooks. Sliced when cold and pressed to reveal its variegated filling, the galantine is an altogether excellent choice for party food.

Cooking galantines

Boning a chicken is not as difficult as it sounds (full instructions on page 153). The forcemeat and other ingredients are packed into the boned bird or meat cut, and built up with an eye to the effect when cooked and sliced through. Stitch the bird or meat cut into shape, parcel into cheesecloth or sheeting and cook in stock. Cool, lightly press, cut off wrapping and stitching and glaze with the reduced stock.

Pâtés, terrines and potted meats

There are many classic recipes in the field to use as a yardstick for gauging relative proportions of lean meat to fat, salty to bland, seasoning to overall bulk, but try experimenting now with a splash of brandy, another time fresh herbs or greens.

Simple daily pâté
This pâté has the advantages of being cheap, tasty and endlessly variable: add a little spice, herbs or brandy.

½ lb bacon slices
1 lb pork, lamb or beef
1 lb fresh pork sides
1 small onion
2 cloves garlic
2 teaspoons juniper berries
1 egg
1 teaspoon salt
½ teaspoon pepper

Line an earthenware dish with strips of bacon – reserving some for the cover. Grind the liver and the pork sides, which you have trimmed of skin and bone, finely with the onion and the garlic. Roughly crush the berries and stir them in with the well beaten egg, salt and pepper. Turn the mixture into the dish, cover with the remaining bacon strips, then the lid and bake in a *bain marie* for about 1 hour, or until the meat shrinks away from the sides of the dish, at 325 degrees. Cool under a weight, and leave overnight.

Rabbit pâté
Rabbit meat, so often disappointing on its own (unless the rabbits are young, wild and herb scented), makes a light, pleasant pâté, eked out with veal and pork.

1 lb boneless rabbit meat
1 lb boneless veal
1 lb fresh pork sides
1 onion
3 cloves garlic
white wine or wine vinegar
1 tablespoon each chopped parsley and thyme
grated rind of 1 lemon
½ lb speck or hard fat back
a pinch of salt, pepper
1 tablespoon flour

Dice all the meats roughly (not the speck), removing gristle and membranes. Grind them together with the onion and the garlic. Meanwhile boil any bones and scraps with a little white wine or wine vinegar to make a stock. Mix the ground meats with the herbs, the grated lemon rind and the speck, cut into small cubes, and season with salt and pepper. Add ½ cup of the strained reduced stock, mixed with the flour. Pack into a dish, cover with foil and then the lid, place in a pan of water and bake at 325 degrees for 1½ to 2 hours. Press with weights overnight.

Game pâté
French cooking is especially rich in pâtés made with game, and these are an excellent way of stretching an old bird, and relieving its dryness. Use pheasant, partridge, or grouse.

1 game bird
½ lb boneless veal
1½ lb speck or hard fat back
3 eggs
⅔ cup brandy or whiskey
a handful of fresh parsley
1 tablespoon chopped fresh thyme
1 teaspoon each juniper berries and coriander seeds
salt, pepper
grated nutmeg

Bone the bird carefully, reserving the best pieces whole. Grind the scraps with the veal and just over 1 lb of the speck, reserving enough to line the dish. Beat the eggs with the brandy (or whiskey) and mix into the meat with the chopped herbs, crushed spices, salt, pepper and nutmeg. Leave in a cool place for a few hours for the flavors to mature. Then line a large terrine with strips of fat, and build up layers of alternate forcemeat and pieces of game, ending with forcemeat. Cover with more strips of fat, then foil, then a lid, place in a pan of water and bake at 325 degrees for 2½ hours. Cool under a light weight and eat the next day.

Veal and ham terrine with fresh herbs

The charm of this summery pâté is the contrast between pink meat and tender green herbs – use a large handful of mixed fresh herbs.

1 lb ham
1 lb fresh pork sides
1 lb boneless veal
3 cloves garlic
a handful fresh herbs finely chopped
a handful of fresh watercress or spinach
salt, pepper and grated nutmeg
½ cup brandy or whiskey
¼ lb bacon slices
1 egg

Finely dice the ham. Grind the pork and the veal together coarsely, or chop by hand. Crush the garlic, and add to the mixed meats along with the herbs, watercress or spinach, salt, pepper, nutmeg and brandy or whiskey. Leave for a few hours or overnight. Line a terrine with a lattice of bacon slices, cut in half. Stir the well beaten egg into the meat mixture and then pack it into the terrine. Cover with more bacon lattices, then the lid and bake at 325 degrees for 2 hours. Leave to cool unpressed. Serve with a potato salad.

Rillettes

One of a clutch of dishes which are not strictly pâtés or terrines but more in the nature of potted meats. This dish of fresh pork sides cooked long and slowly and lightly flavored is very good eaten with hot toast.

2 lb fresh pork sides
1 clove garlic
salt, pepper and grated nutmeg or mace
a sprig of fresh thyme or rosemary

Remove the skin and any bones from the meat, cut into small cubes and put them into a heavy cast iron pot with the other ingredients. Cook in the oven at the lowest setting or on top of the stove over a gentle heat, for at least 4 hours until all the fat is liquid and the meat is brown scraps. By then the pork bits should be just crisping and swimming in their own fat. Strain off the fat into a pan. Pound the meat in a pestle and mortar. Season well. Pack into small jars and when cold pour over a thick layer – ¾ inch – of its own fat. Cover with foil. Store in a cold dry place, the pantry rather than the refrigerator.

Confit d'oie (preserved goose)

Though not many readers will have a surplus goose problem, this recipe ought to be included in any book on preserving food. The same technique may be used with other meats – rabbits, large pieces of pork, sausages. The pieces of meat are cooked very slowly in lard or their own fat (in the case of a goose) until tender, then packed into a deep stoneware or glass jar with a wide mouth and covered with hot fat, which makes a perfect seal when cold and hard. Covered with foil, these will keep for months in a cold dry place. A bonus is that the fat itself will be deliciously flavored for frying potatoes, or cooking other meat. To retrieve the confit, heat the jar gently and scoop out what you need, making sure the rest stays covered with lard. Before you eat it you must heat the *confit* for 3 minutes at 158 degrees to ensure potential bacteria is killed off.

1 goose (10lb), cut into 6 pieces with all fat
* removed*
2 lb pure lard, enough to cover the goose pieces,
* together with the goose fat itself.*
To each pound of meat allow:
1 heaping tablespoon coarse salt
¼ teaspoon saltpeter
½ teaspoon dried thyme
1 crumbled bayleaf

Mix together the salt and other dry ingredients, rub into the pieces of goose and leave in a cool place, covered, for 24 hours. The next day, rinse the goose pieces free of salt and dry them. Then melt all the goose fat slowly in a heavy pan, add the pieces of meat, and enough pure lard to float the pieces. Cook very slowly for about 2½ hours, until a skewer stuck into the goose shows no juice bubbling out. Put a little fat into a large, cleaned and scalded canning jar, then pack in the drained pieces of meat, and cover with hot fat. Leave to cool, until the meat is imprisoned in cold fat, then top up generously with more of the fat. Press foil down onto the lard and store in a cool place.

Pies and galantines

Galantines and the raised pie pastry case both make edible sturdy containers for meat fillings. They seal in the meat juices while the dish cooks, as well as making it more substantial and attractive. Yield: 8–10 servings.

Melton Mowbray raised pork pie

The most celebrated British raised pork pie, firm, juicy and made rosy by the use of a little anchovy paste in the stock.

Stock or jelly

1 pair pig's feet, veal shank, pig's ears or tail, odd bones or trimmings of the meat
a bundle of herbs – sage, marjoram, parsley, bay leaf
1 onion stuck with 2 cloves
a bowlful of apple cores (optional but traditional, the seeds give a faint almond taste)
$\frac{1}{4}$ teaspoon anchovy paste
salt and pepper

Filling

$2\frac{3}{4}$ lb boneless pork picnic shoulder
$\frac{1}{4}$ lb ham or salt pork
1 teaspoon each of salt and ground white peppercorns
3 leaves of sage and a sprig of marjoram, chopped

Pastry crust

5 cups all-purpose flour
1 cup plus 2 tablespoons lard
1 cup water
$\frac{1}{2}$ teaspoon salt

Start by making the stock. Put all the ingredients except the anchovy paste and salt and pepper, into a large pan with cold water to cover. Bring to a boil, skim, then cover and simmer for 3 to 4 hours. Strain through a cloth into a clean pan and boil hard until reduced to about $2\frac{1}{2}$ cups. Season with the anchovy paste, pepper and salt if needed. When cold, skim off the fat.

To prepare the filling, trim the meat of gristle but leave on any firm white fat. Cut into neat small dice – about $\frac{3}{4}$ inch. Grind or finely chop the ham or salt pork. Mix with the pork dice, sprinkle over the salt, pepper and herbs. Leave overnight to mingle the flavors.

Next day make the raised crust (see page 149). Strengthen the pastry sides with a foil belt. Fill the pie shell with the meat mixture and bake for $2\frac{1}{2}$ hours at 325 degrees. Cover with foil for the first hour. When cooled, pour in the stock through the hole in the pastry case. Serve cold.

Galantine of pork, boned and stuffed

A coarser textured galantine than the next recipe, but full of flavor. A fresh pork picnic shoulder is a large, but not expensive, cut that makes a capacious cover for the stuffing.

1 fresh pork picnic shoulder, boned

Forcemeat stuffing

1 pork tongue (cooked)
1 lb fresh pork sides
1 lb boneless veal
2 cloves garlic
$\frac{1}{2}$ lb mushrooms
1 truffle (optional)
a bunch of parsley
salt, pepper, grated nutmeg and ground cinnamon

Stock

2 pig's feet
2 onions stuck with cloves
3 carrots
3 cloves garlic
$\frac{1}{2}$ bottle white wine
$1\frac{3}{4}$ pints water

Open out the pork, cut off any large chunks of meat which spoil its symmetry and grind these with the cooked tongue, pork sides and veal. (Or add the tongue separately, as a *salpicon*, diced with whole mushrooms and bits of truffle.) Add crushed garlic, slivers of mushroom and truffle, chopped parsley, spices and seasonings and leave while you make the stock. Boil in the stock ingredients in $1\frac{3}{4}$ pints of water until well cooked and tasty, then add the wine. Lay the pork flat, stuff with the forcemeat and tie with string. Then cover with a piece of linen or cheesecloth, tie and simmer for 4 to 5 hours, exceedingly gently. Leave to cool in the stock for a while, then remove, press and leave to cool. Use the jellied stock to glaze and decorate.

Note: It would be a pity not to use the truffle as the flavor is beautiful with pork, but for a cheaper alternative you might try adding peeled cooked chestnuts and pitted prunes (not too many) to the forcemeat, or some pitted black and green olives.

Chicken galantine

A resplendent dish for grand occasions. Use a fresh chicken or substitute a small turkey.

6–7 lb chicken, boned

Stock

2 pig's feet
bones for stock
1 onion stuck with 2 cloves
1 carrot
½ bottle dry white wine
a bouquet garni
1¾ pints water

Salpicon layer

½ cup pistachio nuts
¼ lb ham
a small can foie gras
1 chicken liver
¼ cup brandy, sherry or white wine

Forcemeat stuffing

2 lb lean boneless pork and 1 lb hard fat back
  or 1 lb lean boneless pork and 2 lb fresh pork sides
¼ lb bacon slices
a sprig each of thyme, marjoram and tarragon
salt, pepper, grated nutmeg and ground coriander
2 eggs

Put the chicken carcass, scraps and bones into a large pot with the other stock ingredients and simmer gently for 1 or 2 hours, covered. Strain and set aside.

Meanwhile make the *salpicon* layer. Blanch the pistachio nuts in boiling water and skin them. Cut the ham into strips. Cut the foie gras into cubes. Lightly fry the sliced chicken liver and put all these into a bowl with the brandy or wine, and leave to marinate.

To make the forcemeat, finely grind the lean and fat meats, without any skin and bones, together with the bacon. Add the chopped herbs, spices and seasonings, and mix in the beaten eggs.

Now lay the boned bird breast down, season lightly inside with salt and pepper, and pack it with a thick layer of forcemeat. Then add the *salpicon* in a thick layer from front to back. Finish with forcemeat, stitch as shown below and wrap in a piece of linen or cheesecloth. Put into the strained stock and gently simmer for 2 hours. Remove, press lightly between 2 boards to extract surplus liquid. Next day, remove wrapping and stitching and glaze with aspic. Decorate with bay leaves and truffles as shown on page 146 in the photograph.

To bone a chicken for a galantine, split the chicken with a sharp knife the entire length of the back. Loosen the carcass, being careful not to pierce the skin further. Gently detach the flesh from the bones. Leave the wing bones in, but prize the leg bone out of the socket with a knife. Lay the forcemeat on the boned bird, breast side down on the board, and sandwich with layers of *salpicon* for contrast. Wrap the skin back over the filling and stitch.

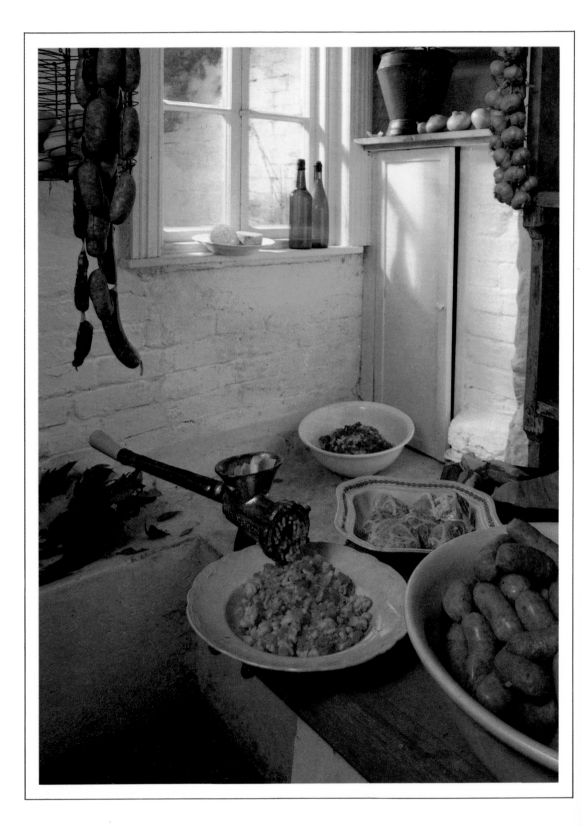

Sausages

'One gentle bite and it surrendered with an opulent pop
and a portion fell easily into the mouth.
It was a delicious mixture of tender meats
and mouth-melting fats concocted by an artist in gastronomy.'

101 Jubilee Road: A Book of London Yesterdays   Frederick Willis   1948

There is scarcely a country in the world which does not claim at least one distinctively national sausage, and some like France, Germany and Italy have developed sausage making into a highly specialized branch of charcuterie. Its popularity is hardly surprising when you consider that the sausage is probably as neat, handy and adaptable a food package as has ever been invented, and, if dried, keeps well too. In the days when every household was pressed for new ways of preserving food, dried sausages emerged as an excellent way of preserving meat, the gut casing allowing the natural moisture to dry out gradually while guarding the contents against dust, flies and bacteria. *Chorizo* made with wine, garlic and spices and dried in a warm airy place, keeps indefinitely and goes on getting more pungent and exciting all the time – one chunk of a well matured *chorizo* is enough to put new life into a bean casserole (and incidentally your kitchen, too).

Homemade sausages stuffed with pure meat, fresh herbs or spices and laced with wine, garlic or whatever else the cook may feel inspired to try, are superb food, and a revelation to anyone brought up on the degraded factory product with its permitted 'cereal' content, standardized seasoning and distinct twang of preservative.

A certain insouciance seems to go with sausage making. Knowing that nothing can go wrong should encourage you to experiment, and invent – there are scores of traditional recipes to browse through, of course, but do not be shy of altering or adapting to suit your needs, likes and budget. If you dote on garlic, for instance, use twice as much; if you are trying to economize use a cheaper, fattier cut of pork, beef or whatever (a good proportion of fat makes any sausage more succulent); if the recipe says marjoram when your garden is buried in basil, make the switch, with confidence. You can always fry up a morsel to taste how it is going.

One sausage-making suggestion – the time and trouble which goes into making your own sausages is likely to seem more justified when making something a bit different. That is not to say that pure pork sausages discreetly livened with nutmeg and herbs are not a joy to encounter, but you must expect the whole batch to disappear at a sitting, whereas the pungent *chorizo* imposes restraints and thus lasts for months.

Argentinian *chorizos* hang from the rafters, maturing; bowls of freshly ground sausage-meat contain a rosy Scandinavian game mix based on venison (center, back) and a pork sausage mix for the Pennsylvania Dutch sausages (right); and in the center are faggots, parceled in lacy caul.

Sausage making

Equipment

A butcher's sausage machine pumps filling into gut at the rate of a foot a second, and costs a vast amount. An obliging butcher will sometimes fill sausage casings with your own prepared stuffing, but you would need to think big – 20 pounds of meat, say – to make it worth his while. No domestic-sized machine can compete with these for speed and efficiency, as they have not got the push, but there are several modest models to choose from. Simplest, and cheapest, is an outsize syringe affair – the plunger forces meat out into gut threaded over the nozzle. Some brands of electric meat grinders come with a sausage funnel. Smaller versions of the butcher's machine can be found quite cheaply, if they are old models reconditioned.

To fill sausage by hand you need only a plastic funnel and long smooth wooden stick, or spoon handle, to push the meat through into the gut. An electric grinder or chopper, cuts down immensely on the time spent preparing the stuffing, but it can improve the texture of sausages to incorporate some coarser chopped meat, or fat cubes, and for this you need a very sharp knife. Large bowls are needed to take sausagemeat.

The most vital item, however, is of course the basic gut or casing, which comes in three sizes depending whether it belonged to a sheep (link size), pig (standard sausage size) or ox (hefty *mortadella* size). Pig casing is the easiest to buy – butchers who make their own sausages will usually sell you what you need. For sheep or ox gut you may have to contact butchers' suppliers – see your local yellow pages. If ox gut is unobtainable you can substitute stitched cheesecloth tubes, made by yourself. Casings come dried and salted, and need soaking before use.

Ingredients

Almost any meat, or combination of meats, can be used for sausages, but pork is the universal favorite because of its bland flavor, texture and succulence. It is a perfect background for special effects with spices and wine. A fresh pork picnic shoulder is a cheap cut, meaty and quite lean, or there is Boston shoulder, leaner still. Fresh pork sides, usually about half fat, half lean, is the most economical and tasty basic sausagemeat and should be added if you are making sausages from dry meat such as venison.

Cuts like beef shank, which generally need prolonged cooking to tenderize them, are fine ground for sausages as long as you carefully remove stringy tendons and membranes. Used with discretion, some cereal mixed in adds smoothness to a meat stuffing. Use homemade breadcrumbs (not from a package), oatmeal or barley, or mashed potato.

For a complete change from all-meat, try an all-cereal sausage such as the traditional English white pudding, well seasoned with herbs. It is pleasant sliced and fried with bacon. Blood sausages can be very good, but they are outside the scope of most people since the blood needs to be quite fresh and kept constantly stirred to prevent clotting. British faggots (or in France, *crépinettes*) are bundles of forcemeat wrapped in 'caul' – the pretty lacy fat lining the stomach, which bastes the meat as it cooks. Get caul fat from your butcher.

Herbs
Fresh or dried herbs can be used, remembering that fresh are much less pungent.
Thyme, savory, marjoram, sage and basil are all good, used singly or mixed.

Spices
Whole spices, freshly ground have most potency. Coriander, mace, nutmeg, cloves,
peppercorns and cinnamon are all used, in various combinations. Paprika has a
special use in sausage making – adding color as well as spiciness. If you want red or
rosy sausages, and do not like the idea of using saltpeter, be generous with paprika, or
its Spanish equivalent, pimenton. Use fresh onions and garlic, rather than onion or
garlic salt; however convenient they give that monosodium taste again.

Wine and spirits
A splash of wine adds excitement to any sausage mixture, and helps preserve it too;
use the cheapest, or homemade. Cooking sherry or port give alcoholic mellowness
much more cheaply than brandy.

Storing and drying
To make the breaks between sausages, just twist the casings. For long-term storage,
tie with thread as shown on next page. Sausages made from highly perishable meat,
such as brains or liver, or intended to be eaten fresh should be kept in the refrigerator
overnight for flavors to mature, then used as soon as possible. Since they do not
contain preservative, fresh pork sausages should be eaten sooner than the
commercial sort, and always stored in the refrigerator. Most sausages can be frozen
for up to a month or 6 weeks, but the flavor and texture may not be quite so good. To
dry sausages – these should be the spicy kind, preferably containing some beef which
dries fast, as well as pork, and wine too – simply hang them high up in a warm, dry
but drafty spot. The opposite end of the kitchen from your stove, range or boiler is as
good as any. After 3 or 4 days they will have darkened and shrunk noticeably, and
after 10 days they should be quite hard and dry, and may be moved to a cool, dry
place.

Another simple and attractive old method of storing sausages is to fry them first
and then cover with melted lard, in a stoneware or glass jar – as with *confit d'oie* (see
page 151). Make sure you cover them to a depth of 1 inch at the top. Seal with
aluminum foil. The charm of this method is that the lard will be flavored nicely (use
for frying) and the sausages tastier than if they were frozen. Before eating them, heat
the sausages at 158 degrees for 3 minutes in a skillet.

Smoking
This is a traditional way of flavoring and drying some sausages, much used in
Germany for their large *Würste*. A sausage for smoking should be dried slowly for a
few days in a warm dry place. Finally cool smoke for about 5 hours – when it has lost
about 25 per cent weight it should be done.

Making farmhouse sausages, preserved in lard

1. The ideal gut casing for the ordinary frying sausage comes from the pig. A comfortable length to work with is 2 yards, kept moist and pliable by soaking in a bowl of water. Pork meat is traditionally used for country sausages. Take either 4 lb of fresh pork sides, or for a leaner mixture, 3 lb of fresh pork sides and 1 lb of lean meat (shoulder for example), and grind.

2. $\frac{1}{2}$ lb speck, or pork fat back may be added to the meat, cut into manageable cubes. When you get to the stuffing stage, it gives you a more solid filling.

3. Spices and herbs add original flavor to sausages, and here the cook can take the initiative: the standard mixture of spices is nutmeg, cloves and cinnamon, pounded in a mortar and pestle with salt and black peppercorns. For herbs, one handful of parsley, finely chopped, is a staple, to be embellished with chopped thyme, marjoram, sage or basil. 8 cups fresh breadcrumbs may also be included to contribute a smoothness to the meat stuffing. Mix all these ingredients in a large bowl.

4. In the absence of sophisticated gadgetry to fill the casings, all you need is a simple funnel and a wooden spoon (it helps if the neck of the funnel and the handle of the spoon are roughly the same diameter). Thread the entire length of soaked gut on to the neck of the funnel to form a ruff, and knot the end of the length.

5. Fill the funnel with sausagemeat, and push into the casing, forcing the meat down with the handle of the spoon until a respectable sized sausage is formed (about 4 inches long).

6. To eliminate air bubbles and pack the meat firmly into the case, use your hands. As sausages swell while cooking under rather than over fill.

7. There are various ways of fastening sausages. The simplest is to twist the gut but this will not hold for smoking, or hanging sausages to dry. Using string, you can tie a knot at each intersection, or to give a professional finish, continue the string up the length of your whole run of sausages.

8. Your farmhouse sausages are now ready to be cooked and eaten, or they may be preserved after thorough cooking (frying is probably best).

9. Pour off the fat given off during cooking and fill a glass canning jar with the sausages. Pour melted lard (8 tablespoons will probably be enough) over the sausages. Allow the lard to set, imprisoning the sausages by 1 inch.

Note: Before eating, the sausages must be heated through thoroughly for 3 minutes at 158 degrees.

Sausages

The sausage is one of the most convenient forms of packaged food – a pleasure to make, delicious to eat in either its simplest form or with subtle variations and if properly dried and possibly smoked easy to keep.

Scandinavian game sausage

Venison is a good substitute for the traditional reindeer or elk. Not an everyday sausage but an exceptionally fine flavored one – marvelous barbecue food.

3 lb fresh pork sides
4 lb boneless venison
½ lb speck, or hard fat back
1 tablespoon coriander seeds
1 tablespoon allspice berries
1 teaspoon cloves
4 cloves garlic
4 tablespoons salt
2 tablespoons crushed black peppercorns
1¼ cups red wine or port
pig casings

Remove the rind and rib bones from the pork sides and put through your grinder with the game meat. Cut the speck into ¾ inch cubes by hand and mix into the ground meat. Pound all the spices and mix into the meat mixture with the crushed garlic, salt and pepper – use your hands to mix really thoroughly. Pour over the wine or port. Leave for a few hours, then stuff the casings, making short fat links. Leave in a cool place for 24 hours before eating, to allow the flavors to develop. Best cooked over charcoal.

Pennsylvania Dutch sausage

Strongly spiced pure pork sausage to eat fresh, freeze, smoke or store in lard.

4 lb fresh pork sides
2 lb boneless fresh pork, Boston or picnic shoulder
2 tablespoons cloves
3 tablespoons coriander seeds
1 teaspoon grated nutmeg
3 tablespoons salt
2 teaspoons pepper
large handful chopped fresh sage, or 6 tablespoons
  dry rubbed sage
pig casings

Cut the skin and rib bones from the pork sides. Roughly chop all the meat then grind medium fine. Pound all the spices to a powder, then add to the meat with salt, the pepper and finely chopped fresh or dried sage. Stuff the casings, making short fat links – about 4 inches. Hang in a cool place overnight to develop the flavor. Eat fresh or freeze. For smoking, leave the sausages to dry in a cool airy place for 2 to 3 days, then smoke at 70 degrees for 5 hours.

Schwäbischewurst

A fine textured, large sausage (use a cheesecloth bag if you cannot get ox casing), good fresh or smoked. Spice with caraway seeds for a distinctly European flavor. This sausage is good eaten fresh with dill pickles, or smoked.

2 lb boneless fresh pork Boston shoulder
1 lb speck or hard fat back
1 teaspoon sugar
2 tablespoons salt
½ tablespoon black pepper
3 cloves garlic
1 tablespoon caraway seeds
¼ cup white wine
ox casing

Roughly cut up the lean pork and speck, and put through your grinder once. Sprinkle over the sugar, salt and pepper, working in well with both hands, then grind twice more, until pasty and smooth. Crush the garlic and caraway seeds, and pound them with the wine to a mush. Work this well into the meat mixture. If you are using a blender give it another few seconds to blend. Stuff into soaked ox casings or two cheesecloth tubes about 1 foot long and 3 inches diameter, tying both ends. Lower the *Würste* into simmering water, increase the heat until boiling, then turn down and simmer gently for 45 minutes. Drain and serve hot (cut off the covers of course) or leave to cool, then smoke for 8 hours at 60 to 70 degrees.

Argentine chorizo

A first class sausage for drying, which concentrates the spicy, garlicky flavor. This is an old family recipe. Being Argentinian, it naturally includes beef which also helps the drying out process, as beef dries quicker than pork. Paprika gives the orangey-red color.

4 lb fresh pork sides
1¼ cups red wine
6 cloves garlic
½ nutmeg
1 teaspoon cloves
2 tablespoons paprika or pimento
1 tablespoon finely chopped fresh thyme or marjoram, or
* ½ tablespoon dried herbs*
3 tablespoons salt
½ tablespoon black peppercorns
2 lb beef shank or flank
pig casing

Remove the rind and bones from the pork sides and cut off the thick outer strip of fat. Dice the strip of fat. Bring the wine to a boil with the crushed garlic, pounded spices and herbs, add salt, peppercorns and paprika and leave to cool. Cut off as much gristle from the beef as possible, then roughly dice it with the lean pork sides and grind quite finely. Pick out any strings of membraneous fat which refuse to be ground up. Strain the wine marinade and pour on to the ground meat. Mix in the diced pork fat and leave overnight. Next day stuff into 6 inch links, twisting or tying off. Hang in a warm dry place for a week or two, until hard and knobbly, then transfer to a cool dry spot. As they dry harder, they will need longer cooking.

White pudding

Cooked and dried these oatmeal sausages keep for weeks. The best fat to use is 'flead' – a hard white fat surrounding the kidneys.

2 lb coarse oatmeal
2 onions
3 tablespoons chopped parsley
mint, thyme (for lamb) or sage, rosemary (for pork)
1 lb pork or lamb flead
salt and pepper
pig casing

Spread the oats out on a baking sheet and dry thoroughly in the oven at the lowest setting for 10 minutes. Very finely chop the onions, herbs and flead and add to the oats, with salt and pepper. Stuff the casings, leaving 1 inch space in each link for the oats to swell in cooking. Drop into boiling water and cook for 40 minutes, pricking here and there with a needle as they swell, to prevent bursting. Drain and hang up to dry.

Faggots

The answer for cooks who like sausage-meat but cannot get casings from their butcher.

A variety on the theme: sausage-meat parceled up in lacy caul fat instead of being stuffed into casings. The fat melts during cooking, and bastes the contents. Buy caul fat – usually frozen – from your butcher, and soak in salty water before use. ¼ lb wraps about 18 faggots.

1 lb fresh pork sides
1 lb pork liver
1 large or 2 small onions
1 clove garlic
lard or butter
1 tablespoon dried sage
½ teaspoon each grated nutmeg and ground cinnamon
salt
black pepper
2 eggs
2 cups fresh breadcrumbs
caul fat

Remove the skin and any rib bones from the pork sides and put through a coarse grinder with the liver, onion and garlic. Tip the mixture into a large skillet with a pat of lard or butter and fry over gentle heat for 20 minutes, stirring now and then. Remove from the heat, drain any liquid off and grind again, more finely. Add the herbs, spices and seasonings. Mix in the eggs, well beaten, then the breadcrumbs. Wrap egg-sized lumps of meat mixture in caul fat and arrange them in a greased shallow baking dish, touching each other. Add just enough water, stock or wine to cover the bottom of the dish. Bake at 375 degrees for 45 minutes, pouring off all the liquid after 30 minutes. Blot the fat with paper towels, return to the dish. Eat hot or cold. They look as good as they taste (see p. 154).

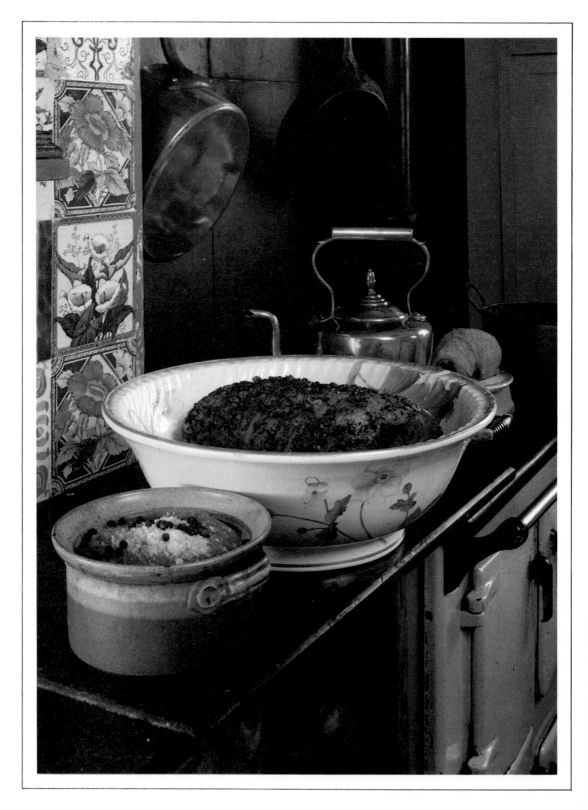

Dry Salted Meats

*'Then my grandmother decided how much salt should be rubbed into each piece
before it was pressed with heavy stones in a huge, open-mouthed earthen jar
and left for ten days or more. After ten days or so
my grandmother asked the servants to take the pork out and look at it.
If it was still as red, or redder than originally, it would be very good.'*

A Chinese Childhood   Chiang Yee   1940

There are two approaches to dry salting meat: one is mainly preservative, the other mainly for flavor. The preservative method, used in living memory to keep cut-up parts of the family pig over the winter, was simply to bury the cuts in a snow drift of salt. Stone troughs were specially scooped out for the purpose (stone is naturally cool). Treated like this the meat stayed good for several months. Of course, certain rules were followed in all this: pigs were slaughtered (often by a local butcher who did the rounds) after the cold weather set in, never in muggy or unsettled weather. The whole family helped prepare the meat for the salt trough, and the pieces went in as quickly as possible. The trough itself was naturally kept in a cool place. As preservatives went, this was quick, cheap and reliable, but of course it did little for the meat except make it saltier, needing to be soaked for days to make it eatable.

The flavoring method of dry salting is the one most likely to appeal today.

Briefly, what dry salting, or dry curing or dry spicing as it's called in some old recipes, involves is rubbing the fresh meat liberally and thoroughly with a mixture, usually of coarse salt (pickling salt must be used), sugar, spices and saltpeter (ascorbic acid if you prefer). It is then kept in a cool place, turned and rubbed daily with the mixture (a little more liquid each day, as the natural lymph drains out) for varying lengths of time, depending on the size and the degree of flavoring wanted. The point of *dry* salting like this, as compared with the wet pickle (sometimes called wet salting, to confuse everyone a bit more) is that it strikes into a large piece of meat more quickly, encouraging the lymph, or natural fluids, to drain rapidly. For this reason it was often done to hams for a day or two before they went into a slow pickle cure. So much fluid is released from a large ham that the pickle would have been much diluted otherwise, and this risked spoiling the meat. In this case, salt alone was used, and the salted ham pressed overnight under a weighted board.

Various meats dry salted and spiced for flavor: dry salted tongue in the foreground; topround of beef rubbed with spices and juniper berries, ready to be cooked in pastry (center); and, at the back a bath chap (miniature ham), cooked and rolled in golden breadcrumbs.

Dry salting and spicing

Unlike pickling, which is good for preserving several pieces of meat at a time and takes up space, dry salting is ideal for a single large roll of beef, or pork, or ham, and has the advantage that the meat can be kept in a bowl in the bottom of the refrigerator. Mix the specified ingredients in a large bowl, preferably a crock made of glass, china or glazed earthenware, and rub every get-at-able surface of your piece of meat vigorously for a minute or two. Rub the inside of birds, as well as the outside (you can always slip on rubber gloves). Push a good bit of your mixture down into any bone or socket cavities, as around a bone is where trouble starts, so butchers will tell you, especially with big hunks like a ham. Tongues are sometimes dry cured, but I would emphasize that they must be very fresh (from recently slaughtered beasts), be pricked all over with a sterile needle to help the cure penetrate, then rubbed very thoroughly, then stored in the refrigerator. As tongues are laden with bacteria, you need to work fast, and thoroughly; do not leave one in its plastic bag in a warm room overnight while you meditate what to do with it. Having finished the dry rub, cover the meat and leave in a cool place. Turn and rub it well daily, and if you are not storing it in the refrigerator but in a basement or pantry, *keep it covered*, with a proper old fashioned fly-cover of cheesecloth stretched over wire. Or put it in a deeper container than a bowl, and secure a clean cheesecloth over the top. Flies are not often mentioned in books on home preserving, but I cannot imagine why, since they are a persistent pest in certain seasons and it only takes one fly a minute or so alone with a piece of meat to produce a maggoty thing you will not wish to touch let alone eat. So – either take care, or keep your dry salting for cold weather, when the fly risk is over. Go on for as long as your recipe suggests; the time usually varies with the weight as well as nature of the meat being treated. As the days pass some liquid will collect in the bowl – this is to be expected. The amount varies with the animal, and the cut. Leave it, just spoon the whole lot over several times as if basting and rub a bit less. When the meat is done, brush off the spices, wipe over with paper and cook/smoke or put into pickle, as the recipe bids.

To cure a beef tongue, ensure first that it is very fresh, then sterilize a sharp skewer by dipping it in boiling water. Prick the tongue all over and put in a bowl. Sprinkle with pickling salt, scatter over a handful of juniper berries and leave overnight. Rinse off the salt and put the tongue in a cast iron kettle with a couple of onions (leave on their skins to color the dish), chopped parsnips, celery stalks and peppercorns. Cover with water and simmer all day long, then strain the liquid through cheesecloth. Skin and trim the tongue. Roll up and eat hot, served with a piquant mustard sauce or capers; or render down the stock by boiling it until it thickens, add 1 tablespoon of unflavored gelatin and pour into a mold around the cooled tongue.

Dry salted meats

Also called dry curing, or dry spicing, this method of preserving is really a protracted form of marinade. All sorts of meat can be treated like this, and the results range from the rich mellow flavor of spiced beef to the exquisite delicacy of Welsh salt duck.

Lamb ham

Smaller, cheaper and less unwieldly than a pork ham, a large leg of lamb was traditionally smoked to keep longer. I often omit the smoking, and simply simmer, press and eat the spiced lamb cold.

¾ cup pickling salt
⅔ cup dark brown sugar
2 teaspoons saltpeter
1 tablespoon each black peppercorns, coriander seed,
  allspice berries
1 large (5 to 6 lb) leg of lamb

Mix the salt, sugar and saltpeter with the crushed spices. Rub the leg thoroughly all over with this, pushing it in around the bone. Keep in a cool place for 10–14 days, rubbing daily with the spicy liquid which it yields, and turning it often.

Cook as for a ham, in a flavored stock (or water with vegetables, garlic and a little wine), simmering very gently for 3 to 4 hours, depending on the size. Leave to cool in the cooking liquid. Then remove, wrap tightly in a clean cloth, lay a board on top and weight overnight.

Spiced or dry-salted beef

10 lb beef rump, plate or brisket
⅔ cup brown sugar
½ teaspoon allspice berries
1 teaspoon grated nutmeg
2 teaspoons saltpeter
6 tablespoons pickling salt
1 tablespoon black peppercorns and juniper berries
8 cups flour
beef suet, drippings or butter

Rub the meat all over with the sugar to tenderize it, before the salt gets to work, put it in a bowl in a cool, clean place, covered, and leave for 2 days. Then crush the spices, saltpeter, salt, peppercorns and berries together and rub the meat all over with this. Repeat daily, keeping the meat

both cool and covered, for at least 10 days – this meat is better left longer than less time. To cook, wipe off the spices, then make a rough 'huff' paste with the flour and enough water to bind. Roll this out fairly thickly, lay the beef on top, then generously cover the meat with either grated beef suet, drippings or butter. Close the paste over it, dampen the edges and pinch shut. Bake in a roasting pan at 250 degrees for 1 hour per pound of beef. Leave to cool for 1–2 hours, then peel off the 'huff'. Wrap the meat in foil and leave under a weighted board overnight. Slice thinly.

Bath chaps

These miniature hams made from pig's cheek or jaw are cured along with the tongue. Ask your butcher to cut and bone the jaw.

1 boned jowl of pork and tongue
½ cup pickling salt
½ cup sugar
2 teaspoons saltpeter
2 teaspoons each coriander seeds, peppercorns and
  allspice berries
1 onion stuck with 2 cloves
1 leek
1 bouquet garni

The tongue should be skinned before curing. Trim off the root and gristle, prick with a sterile needle, then put into a bowl with the jowl. Mix together the dry ingredients, coarsely crushing the spices, and rub this well into the meat. Keep in a cool place covered and repeat daily for 1 week. At the end of this time roll up the chap with the tongue inside, tie with string to hold the shape, and cook like this – which is a fairly standard method for all salt meat: put in a large pan of cold water, bring to a boil slowly (to remove excess salt), throw the water away, and cover again with fresh cold water, adding the vegetables and herbs for flavoring. Bring to a boil slowly, then simmer gently for 4 hours. Cool under a weight, and roll in crumbs.

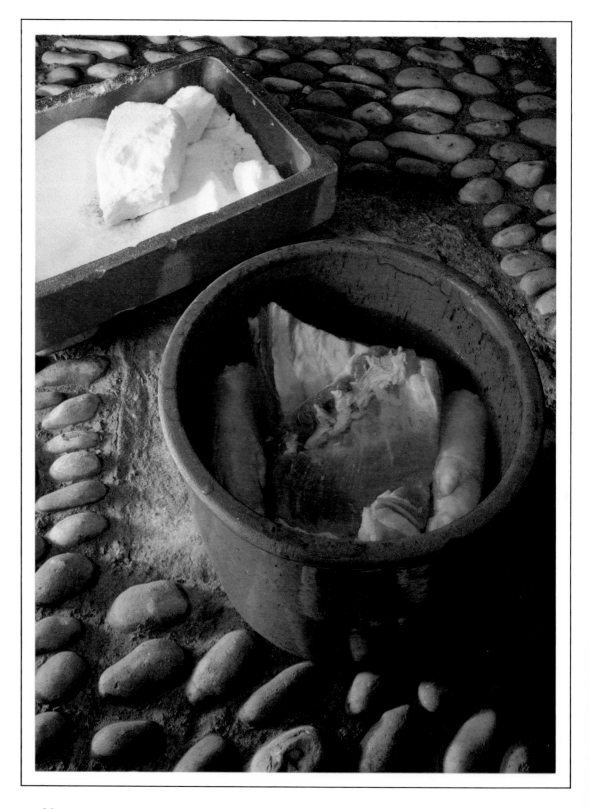

Brined & Pickled Meats

*'To have sweet and fine bacon
the fitches must not be sopping in brine
which gives it the sort of taste that barrel pork and sea junk have,
than which nothing is more villainous.'*

William Cobbett   1830

A brine or pickle tub, where cuts of meat submerged in strongly salted water can be stored for weeks, is a simple and effective old method of preservation that does not just keep meat from spoiling as a freezer would, but also adds to its flavor and makes it more tender. Some butchers keep a brine or pickle going in which tongues and cuts of pork and beef are left for several days to absorb piquant flavor and rosy color. Brining is such a straightforward business that it would be a pity if you did not try out the process for yourself. Assuming the salt strength is checked from time to time and elementary hygiene observed, meat left in brine pretty well looks after itself. Brine provides a two-way protection since salt checks the bacterial activity, while water excludes air and flies, which are the home preserver's most tireless saboteur. All of which readily explains why pickling has been popular since the Romans imported hams into Britain from Gaul.

Brine is a basic salt and water solution, while pickles (not to be confused with the vinegar solution for vegetables and fruit) are brine to which sugar or some other sweetener has been added. The reason for this is that salt and saltpeter (often used for the rosy color it gives meat) have a decidedly hardening effect on meat as time goes on and sugar, which softens meat as well as mellowing the overall flavor, is the ideal antidote. Adding sugar (or honey or molasses) was just the start of improvements on the basic brine formula. People were soon titivating it in other ways, adding herbs or spices, or strongly flavored berries that grow wild, like juniper. Alcohol, also a preservative, was bound to find its way into a meat pickle sooner or later; wine from the wine-growing districts, beer and stout in other parts. Spanish *jambon serrano* and hams from Modena in Italy both spend weeks in white wine pickle, while the famous Suffolk sweet cured hams in England were pickled for six weeks in stout or porter. A 'cure' in this context is the general term for whatever treatment meat (usually pork) undergoes in being turned into ham or bacon.

Pork curing in a pickling barrel: feet, ears, top of the head, ribs, all brine salted for immediate use in making head cheese. The all-purpose pickle permeates the pork with piquant flavor and tenderizes the meat before cooking it.

Curing

Pork has always been the favorite meat for pickle tubs partly because pigs were plentiful, being the easiest animal to raise on a smallholding, and partly because fatty pork is ideally suited to pickling, becoming more tender and delicate in texture. The fat soaks up the flavor – compare a slice of green (that is, cured and not smoked) bacon with a slice of fresh pork sides. You can leave a cut of pork overnight in pickle just to improve the flavor and texture before roasting. A longer stay in the pickle makes the flavor change more emphatic; a couple of weeks makes the joint taste more like a ham, best simmered then glazed in the oven with honey and mustard, or cider and brown sugar. Like ham, it is especially succulent eaten cold.

Any cuts of pork can be pickled with advantage but most effective are the less expensive parts – fresh pork sides, feet, pig's head (for brawn), jowl, even ears – because the fat and gelatinous meat is so much tastier after curing. Making bacon which tastes the way it did in the good old days is an enterprise which people buying half a carcass for the freezer might well consider. The pork for bacon must be hung for 5 days first otherwise the cure will not permeate. Then cure with the all-purpose pickle or the bacon pickle with white wine.

The benefits of a sweet pickle can also be extended usefully to other meats besides pork, especially when intended to be smoked later. Beef, game, poultry at the 'stewing' stage can all be softened and flavored by a short pickle cure. Tongues – lamb, pork, beef – are traditionally pickled for flavor and tenderness and should be really fresh and pricked all over with a sterilized needle (hold it over a flame) to help the pickle penetrate, then immersed without delay. The smaller the cut of meat the less time it will take for the pickle to take effect, so when planning the contents of a pickle or brine tub allow for this. Use up the smaller pieces first but give something as large as a pig's haunch a week. Really large hams are best dry salted first (page 170).

Equipment and ingredients
Traditionally, a brine tub or pickle barrel was used but today any large scrubbable container in plastic or china is suitable. A glazed stoneware crock is ideal. Sterilize everything before use by scalding with boiling water. You will need to keep the contents of the tub pressed down below the level of the pickle at all times. A wood or plastic lid weighted by a large stone is suitable. Scald these too.

The basic ingredients are water (preferably soft rain water) and salt (medium coarse pickling salt). White or brown sugar can be used.

Saltpeter
Saltpeter, usually sodium nitrate, occasionally potassium nitrate which makes the meat look more appetizing, rosy rather than brownish grey, can be bought from drug stores and small amounts used. There have been reservations about nitrates in food, the fear being that excessive amounts could be harmful. I continue using it because the amount called for in a pickle formula is insignificant and well within the safety factor. If you prefer, substitute ascorbic acid or vitamin C in crystal form. Buy from a drug store and use 1 g per every $4\frac{1}{2}$ lb meat instead of the saltpeter specified

Using brines and pickles

Ingredients for the pickle should be boiled up (many writers in old cook-books dispense with this stage but it seems to be a sensible insurance against possible mishaps where fresh meat is concerned), then left to become cold. Bacteria breeds in warmth. The cuts of meat should be packed in the bucket, or crock, and the pickle or brine mixture poured over. There should be enough to cover the meat by at least 1 inch. Then set your scalded board, or plastic lid, on top and a heavy stone or jar on top of that, so that the meat is well pressed down. The container should be kept in a cool place like a cellar or basement. Pickling, in any case, is best undertaken in cool weather. Small-scale pickling can stay in the refrigerator. After a few days check the tub and contents and give them a stir with a scalded wooden spoon. Saltier water tends to drop in level so this helps even out the treatment. The meat can now be left for as long as a couple of weeks, provided you keep the salt level up. Salt is really the most effective disinfectant.

Testing the salt levels

The chief risk with brining occurs when a piece is removed from the brine. The salinity level drops accordingly so while a pair of pig's feet is unlikely to make any difference, a haunch will have absorbed much of the salt. The drill for these occasions involves testing the salt by floating an egg on top before taking out the meat, then again afterwards. It should bob easily on the surface, not half drown. If it half sinks, the brine needs topping up. Make up a booster solution by boiling roughly one fifth the total of water with about three times as much salt per quart as in the original salt solution. Add a handful of spices too, and a tablespoon of sugar. Leave to become cold, then add to the brine. Repeat the egg test, which should now be favorable. The technique is shown overleaf.

Better safe than sorry applies particularly with a food like meat, not so much because anything horrid is likely to happen but because we are unfamiliar with handling meat, compared to our ancestors, and so much more likely to panic if there is even the slightest hint of trouble. Remember: provided the salt content is high, there is nothing to worry about.

If at any time during the cure you find the brine has soured, it is no great expense or labor to take out the meat, rinse it, clean the tub and make up a whole new pickle solution. Scald the barrel or crock again, chill it thoroughly and return the meat, covering it with the fresh, chilly solution.

Curing time

A minimum of 28 days is needed for a large shoulder or haunch. As a rough rule of thumb, allow $3\frac{1}{2}$ to 4 days for each 1 lb of meat.

For small pieces like the loin or bacon, allow 20 days for 10 lb slab of bacon but 25 days for a thicker piece, like the loin. The guideline here is 2 days per 1 lb. The pig's feet, ears, and top of the pig's head can be brine salted for immediate use in making brawns.

Curing a ham Italian style

Really large hams – about 12 lb are best dry-salted first, then given the slow pickle cure before smoking or drying. Dry salting encourages the lymph gland to release fluids – too much of that fluid in the sweet pickle later would dilute it and cause the meat to spoil. Smaller cuts, like those for bacon, can cure without this dry salting first.

1. Weigh the ham and record the weight. At the end of curing, the weight loss will tell you how long to continue smoking.

2. Scald a large crock, the wooden lid and the weight with boiling water.

3. Rub coarse pickling salt into the surface of the ham – $\frac{3}{4}$ cup salt to every 12 lb of ham. Push the salt down into any bone or socket cavities.

4. Place the ham in the scalded bowl, put the lid on and weight it for quick draining overnight.

5. Make up the Italian white wine pickle with: 2 quarts water, 3 cups pickling salt, 1 tablespoon baking soda and 2 tablespoons saltpeter (or 3 grams of Vitamin C, ascorbic acid) boiled together. Then add 2 quarts white wine, 1 tablespoon allspice and $\frac{1}{2}$ tablespoon peppercorns and leave to get quite cold: it is important that the ham, cold and compressed from the first salting, should go quickly into the pickle which should be just slightly warmer. If the pickle were colder than the ham, it would continue the extracting process, rather than the permeating one.

6. Drain the salt cure off the ham. Replace it in the bowl and pour over the pickle, straining it through cheesecloth.

7. Put on the lid, weight it down with a stone, and leave for 28 days.

8. To test the brine for saltiness, at the end of each week float a fresh egg on the solution. If the egg half sinks, the salt level needs topping up. Boost by boiling up roughly one-fifth the total of water with three times as much salt per quart as in the original formula. Leave to get cool before adding.

9. Every 4 or 5 days, remove the ham and stir the brine with a scalded wooden spoon as the salt needs a stir-up. Quickly scald the board, lid and weight and replace them.

10. Remove the ham from the cure after 28 days. Scrub off surface salt with a brush.

11. Hang in a cool airy place for about 1 week. Simmer for 2 hours in water, then for another hour with vegetables for flavor.

11

10

9

6

7/8

Brines and pickles

Soaking beef, pork or tongue in a brine (a basic salt and water solution) or a pickle (a brine to which a sweetener is added), gives the meat piquant flavor and rosy color. It is a way both of preserving and tenderizing cuts before cooking or smoking.

All-purpose pickle
This produces a mild, sweet cure suitable for bacon, (or any cut of pork) or for poultry.

1½ gallons water
2 lb (3 cups) pickling salt
4 cups sugar
2 tablespoons saltpeter
1 tablespoon juniper berries
½ nutmeg
1 teaspoon each cloves and black peppercorns
1 large sprig of fresh thyme, rosemary or marjoram
3 bay leaves

Bring the water, salt, sugar and saltpeter slowly to a boil, stirring occasionally. Add the other ingredients roughly crushed and tied up in cheesecloth. Boil for 3 minutes, then remove from the heat and cool. Discard the spice bag and pour the liquid over the meat in a crock or tub. Weight cover to keep meat submerged.
Note: For mildly salted small pieces, 3 days in this pickle will be enough. Slightly larger cuts – loin, bacon – can stay for a week, if you want a mild cure. Shoulder or leg will be mild cured after 10 days or so, but can of course be left much longer as long as you check on the salt level. They will get saltier, but slowly.

General brine
This is sweetened, but very slightly. Use it for beef, venison and poultry which is to be smoked. Leave meats in for 2 to 5 days depending on size, and dry overnight before smoking.

3 gallons water
3 lb (4½ cups) pickling salt
1 cup sugar
2 teaspoons saltpeter
1 tablespoon juniper berries.

Bring all the ingredients to a boil, the berries tied up in cheesecloth. Leave until quite cold before pouring over the meats.

Sweet beer pickle
This is a hearty, robust tasting cure for a small ham or jowl, or fresh pork sides to be smoked for bacon.

1 tablespoon allspice berries
1½ quarts strong beer
1½ quarts water
½ cup pickling salt
1 tablespoon saltpeter
¾ cup molasses

Tie the allspice, roughly crushed, in cheesecloth and boil with the remaining ingredients for 5 minutes. Skim if necessary, leave until cold, then pour over the meat. Small pieces will need 1 week or 10 days, larger ones can stay 3 weeks to a month for a good ham. Hams or bacon should be dried for 1–2 days after curing, and cool smoked for several days in a smoke house, or for several weeks in a chimney.

Italian white wine pickle
More delicate than the beer pickle, and unsweetened, this is ideal for a really special ham for Christmas or a boned, rolled shoulder or loin of pork. The meat will have a fine flavor, and need not be smoked. Cook as you would ham, but rather plainly – in a stock flavored with vegetables, but no fancy glazes which would obscure the steeped-in taste.

2 quarts water
2 tablespoons saltpeter
2 lb (3 cups) pickling salt
1 tablespoon baking soda
2 quarts white wine
1 tablespoon allspice berries
½ tablespoon peppercorns

Bring the water, salt, saltpeter and soda to a boil, remove from the heat, add the wine and spices and leave to become cold. Strain through cheesecloth into a crock or a bin, over the meat.

Leave a smaller cut – shoulder, loin – 2 weeks; a ham (leg), 4 weeks. Hang to dry in a cool airy place for about 1 week before cooking and eating. Italians store these hams – when unsmoked – by immersing them in olive oil; pure vegetable oil could substitute. Or smoke them. Full instructions for smoking hams are given on page 177.

Bacon

This is a basic dry salting recipe to which the white wine is added to pickle the pork for bacon. Eliza Acton, writing in the mid-19th century, makes enthusiastic claims for the addition of a bottle of good wine vinegar to the cure after 3 or 4 days and says it 'gives incomparable flavor'. A side of sweet cured bacon – smoked or green (unsmoked) which is milder in flavor – keeps for a long time in a warm, dry place.

For 12 lb meat allow :
1 lb (1½ cups) pickling salt
2⅔ cups brown sugar
2 tablespoons saltpeter
¼ cup peppercorns
1 quart wine vinegar
Mix up all the dry ingredients and halve.

After hanging the pork for 5 days after slaughtering, rub half the dry mixture into the meat and leave for 4 days, rubbing and turning daily. Then apply the rest of the dry ingredients mixed with the wine vinegar. Keep turning and rubbing daily until done. For green bacon brush off any spices and salt and keep in a dry place (hung from the ceiling) at room temperature.

Recipe using pickled pork:
Head cheese (*Fromage de tête*)
Though not an undertaking for the squeamish, a well made brawn is a dish with great style for a buffet supper or summer lunch party, especially when the pig's head is given 3 days in pickle first to heighten the flavor and some wine is used to flavor the jelly. It is a handsome dish – like pink marble set in clear jelly and quite absurdly cheap (pig's head is usually sold off at rock bottom prices for pet meat). In France, however, where sensibility never interferes with

good eating, *Fromage de tête* is a prized dish. This dish serves about 12 people.

1 pig's head
1 pair pig's feet
2 each of onions, carrots, leeks
a bouquet garni of thyme, parsley, bay leaf
1 teaspoon peppercorns
¼ cup wine vinegar
3 cloves garlic
1 quart white wine
lemon juice
a small pinch each of grated nutmeg and ground allspice
salt, pepper

Ask the butcher to prepare the head of brawn, leaving in the tongue – the brains can make a separate dish. Put the head and the feet in an all-purpose pickle for 2 to 3 days. Drain, then put in a pan, cover with cold water, bring to a boil and throw away the water – this removes any excess salt. Return to the pan, add the vegetables, chopped, herbs, peppercorns, vinegar and garlic. Add enough water to cover well, cover the pan and bring to a boil very slowly – the cool end of an old-fashioned range is ideal for cooking this type of dish. Simmer as slowly as possible, so the water hardly moves, for about 5 hours, or until the meat falls off the bones.

For the jelly you have to reduce 1½ quarts of stock and white wine by one third by boiling the water away. Drain off the liquid from the meat and measure 2½ cups into a clean pan, add the quart of wine and a squeeze of lemon and reduce by simmering until only 2½ cups are left. Season to taste with spices, salt and pepper. Meanwhile sort out chunks of meat from the cooked head. The tongue stays whole, but should be skinned and trimmed neatly. Cut the meat into neat pieces, discarding any gristle and bone. Add the meat to the reduced stock and wine mixture and simmer very gently for about 15 minutes to let it absorb the flavor, then cool.

When cool, but before it sets, prepare the final 'cheese' by ladling a thick layer of meat over the bottom of a dish. Set the tongue (whole or sliced, as you prefer) on top, cover with the remaining meat and then pour over the liquid. Turn out when set. In France this is covered with breadcrumbs, but I prefer to see the brawn in all its simplicity.

Smoked meat

Meat is smoked both for flavor and for preservation. As it dries out very slowly over a period of days or weeks, up the chimney or in the smokehouse, it takes on a distinctive tang and assimilates minute amounts of preservative chemicals, which also deter flies and other pests. The snag, however, at least where a large cut like a ham is concerned, is the time that the smoking takes – at the very least several days' continuous smoking, or several weeks of intermittent exposure.

If you live in an old house with one of those immense chimneys which used to take an open fire, range or bread oven and you burn wood over the winter months, your smoking problem is solved – simply hook up the ham securely to a beam, or string peg driven into the brickwork, at a point where it is as far away and high above the fire as it can be, but still in the path of the rising smoke. Distancing is necessary because if the ham itself is heated the fat will start to melt (dangerous flare-ups) and the lean to cook. This is of course how people have always smoked a ham or two without the trouble of keeping a smokehouse going, but it is necessary to keep an eye on even the simplest process. The wood burned needs to be of the right type, i.e. hardwood – oak, beech, elm, sycamore etc. Resinous woods spoil the taste of the meat. A fire does not need to be kept going *permanently*, but of course the smoking process takes longer when it is intermittent.

There are no hard and fast rules about how long to smoke meat in this more casual fashion. Much depends on how strongly flavored you want it to be, and how long you want it to keep. A fairly reliable guide is weight loss – a large cut like a ham should lose between one quarter and one third of its initial weight (before curing that is) by the time it is smoked through, so if you can, weigh the meat before and after curing and again after a week or two smoking.

Once your ham is smoked you can complete the good work of the 'cure' by stitching the ham into a stout cotton cover (they used to limewash these as extra protection) or other moisture-vapor-proof material before hanging it in a dry, airy place. If thoroughly smoked, ham should keep like this for months, even a year or more. Old timers will tell you that they remember eating hams which had hung a couple of years and they were 'sweet as a nut', and 'beautiful tender eating'.

If you do not have an appropriate chimney for smoking hams, there are still many sorts of meat which can be smoked successfully and deliciously using a homemade cool smoker (see illustration on page 134). A ham *can* be smoked in one of these, of course, but I think that it would be more trouble than it is worth keeping the smoker going for the necessary length of time. Opt instead for meat which can be smoked much more rapidly, either because it is smaller in volume (a side of bacon takes far less time than a ham), or less fleshy (poultry – ducks, geese and turkeys especially) or small and tender (beef or pork tenderloin).

Game is also a good candidate for the kiln, smoking being an interesting way of handling elderly game which respond particularly well to a few days in sweet pickle followed by smoking. Again, birds or small cuts take less time – a haunch of venison needs to be smoked for about a week. However, I should add that it is not vital to smoke meat continuously after it has begun drying off – an overnight break will not ruin the effect in the home smoker any more than in the chimney. But during the critical period before the preservative process has got a good hold, and the meat is dry to the touch and somewhat shrunken in weight, you do need to safeguard it against flies and other such pests and against sudden changes in temperature, like a sudden heatwave or spell of warm, damp weather. This means bringing the meat in at night and keeping it under cover meanwhile. One of those old style meat safes with flyscreen doors would be a very useful adjunct to a smoker, for storing meat and fish.

Equipment

Your homemade smoker operates in exactly the same way for meat as for fish (see page 124/5). Your hooks, however, will have to be strong enough to support greater weights. Use butchers' hooks, or bailing twine or strong stainless steel wire in several thicknesses; tie or double twist the ends to form a loop after running them through the meat. More sawdust will be needed, as most meat cuts take longer to smoke thoroughly. Hot smoking is more often used in finishing smoked meat than fish, and the design for your cool smoker should take into account the need to introduce a source of heat directly below the food being smoked. If this is altogether too much trouble it is quite in order to finish cool smoked meats in the ordinary domestic oven (at 325 degrees) after rubbing them over well with oil. For dry birds such as turkey, wrap foil around them too to prevent drying out.

Method

All meat, game and poultry to be smoked are first put into a brine or pickle solution (see page 172/3) or dry salted and spiced (see page 164), before being left to drain and dry for a while. Timing varies with the variety and cut of meat, as described overleaf. The meat is then ready to be hung appropriately in the cool smoker to smoke for as long as necessary to preserve it, or if you are only concerned with *taste* and the meat is to be eaten soon, to give a pleasant flavor. Incidentally, most smoked food develops *more* flavor if left a few hours before eating. Smoked meats are almost always cooked after cool smoking. This is especially true of pork, because of the risk of trichinosis where uncooked pork is concerned (the raw ham curers have their own way around these difficulties).

A string of sausages for smoking is first weighed, then dried slowly in a warm dry place for a few days. After this, the sausages are smoked for about 5 hours until they lose about 25 percent body weight.

Having tried smoking a variety of meats, my own feeling is that the fattiest meats are those which taste finest when smoked – succulent and with their own flavor enhanced rather than overpowered as can happen with delicately flavored chicken, for instance. Besides which, the curing/smoking process definitely plays down their inherent greasiness, improves their texture and makes them much more digestible. In this list I would include pork, goose, duck, old fat pheasants and other elderly game birds. Some of the larger game animals, too, would come under this heading – moose, elk, reindeer, wild boar.

Game animals

Venison and wild boar should be hung for a week or so before beginning the pre-smoking cure, but they should not be allowed to get 'high' at all. The haunch is the best cut to smoke with all these animals, but a well fleshed shoulder or saddle is another possibility. For the richest flavor, put the cuts in a sweet pickle for a week, turning them often. Then rinse, and leave to dry in a cool airy place for a day or two. Smoke for at least a week in a cool smoker (longer in short bursts), or until the surface is blackened. Rub drier meats with oil and finish in a low oven, or step up the temperature in the cool smoker to around 225 degrees and hot smoke for about 3 hours.

Game birds

Full instructions and artwork showing the preparation of game birds are given on p. 145. Hang game birds for 2 or 3 days only – they should never be smoked 'high'. Small, young birds need only 1 to 2 hours in brine (make up a simple mixture of salt and water with only a little sugar added, as the usual sweet pickle spices would overpower the flavor) before cool smoking. Old dry birds go into a pickle pricked all over first. Small birds like quail need about 12 hours' cool smoking, larger ones like pheasant or elderly grouse need about 3 days. If dry looking, the birds can be brushed over with vegetable oil several times before and during smoking. Hot smoke for 1 to 2 hours to finish, or transfer to a domestic oven and cook in foil at a low setting for 30 minutes to 3 hours, depending on the size.

Poultry

Ducks and geese smoke excellently, their meat never drying out. Some care needs to be taken with both birds however, to see that they are not over smoked because this turns the fat rancid and inedible. Ducks should be pricked all over before being left in brine or a plainish pickle for 3 hours. Hang them to dry for a day and then cool smoke at between 75 to 80 degrees for 36 hours exactly. Finish in the oven at 325 degrees.

Smoked breast of goose is a Christmas feast dish in Germany, sliced thinly and eaten with rye bread and a scrape of clarified goose fat. Goose breast, divided into fillets, is rubbed with salt and a pinch of saltpeter, and left covered in a cool place for 5 days, the rubbing process continued often. Then it is dried for half a day and finally cool smoked until it looks and feels quite dry, which takes about 12 hours of continuous smoking, after which time it will look brown and slightly translucent, resembling ptarmigan.

Smoked turkey is an ideal bird for a party, as all the meat is tasty, and there is no danger of having smoky leftovers going moldy in the refrigerator – incidentally, the carcass, bones and leftovers of all smoked birds make the most excellent stock for soup, cooked just as you would usual leftovers. Turkey for smoking can be elderly hen birds, cheaper than young roasters. Prick the flesh with a fork, steep in brine for 4 hours, string up by the wings and drain for a day, then cook smoke for up to a week. Finish in the oven, as described above.

Beef and pork tenderloin

Beef should be pricked and brined for about 2 hours, then tied up with a string noose and dried overnight. Weigh, if possible, before smoking and cool smoke at 80 degrees or less for around 5 days, or until blackened, and about 25 per cent less heavy. Pork tenderloin is delicious given 12 hours in sweet pickle, dried all day, then lightly cool smoked for up to 68 hours before baking, wrapped in puff pastry, or brioche dough.

Corned beef

Tougher, fattier cuts of beef such as brisket, rump and plate are all suitable for curing and smoking by this old fashioned method – the results are infinitely superior to the ubiquitous canned article. The beef should be kept in a spiced sweet pickle (molasses can be used instead of brown sugar) for 10 days, weighted down. Turn occasionally. Hang up to drain and dry for a day or two. Cool smoke for a week or until dark, dry and about 25 percent lighter than at first. Cook as you please.

Bacon

Mild cured bacon (see the cure on page 173) should be cool smoked at just below 60 to 70 degrees for 24 hours, for a mild smoke flavor, or up to a week for a strong one.

Rabbit

These are plentiful in most country places, but can be a bit tasteless. Curing and smoking changes all that. The rabbit should have been dead 3 days, hung in a cold place, or kept in the refrigerator. After skinning (it will have been cleaned as soon as shot), soak in salt water for a couple of hours to remove blood, then put into a brine or pickle for 5 hours. Cool smoke without drying, for a day. Finish by roasting in foil.

Smoking a ham

Casually, hung above the fire in a chimney a ham smokes well, but a large one needs smoking for so long in a home smoker that it is more trouble than it is worth. Smoking is ideal if you have one of those immense chimneys which used to take an open fire, bread oven or range. Simply hook up the ham to a beam or peg in the brickwork, far away and high above the fire, but still in the path of the rising smoke. Weight loss is the guide to how long the ham needs to be smoked. Large cuts like a ham should lose between a quarter and a third of their initial weight. Once smoked, stitch the ham into a stout cotton cover (these were traditionally lime-washed for extra protection) and hang in a dry airy place for months. The cover helps keep the moisture in the ham and protects it.

Fruit & Vegetables

Harvesting the crop

Few sights do more to restore a cook's equanimity, and induce self-complacency than a cupboard ranged with jars and bottles, polished and labelled, in which the scents and flavors, colors and textures of summer kitchen garden, fall orchard and hedgerow are distilled, imprisoned and perfected. No treasure hoard was ever come by so innocently, assembled so lovingly, or dismantled so enjoyably. Biting into a fat red strawberry, or a crisp young cucumber is a delight, but to meet them again in mid-winter, bobbing in a sugary syrup, or piquant with herbs and vinegar, is luxury. My grandmother used to can fruit as a matter of course, hoards of great rose-flushed plums ending up in row upon row of dignified jars on the pantry shelves, the fruit bronze like goldfish within their transparent bellies. The sumptuous flavor of those canned plums haunted me for years, and it was not until fate arranged the coincidence of a bumper harvest and the discovery of a crate of dusty canning jars in a local junk store, that I discovered what my granny always knew – that certain fruit of luscious texture are more delicious preserved in a light syrup even than when eaten straight from the tree.

Nowadays, we can afford to think of preserves as luxuries, delicious non-essentials all the nicer – and of course cheaper – for being homemade. But it is only a hundred years or so since a well stocked cupboard was a bastion, the housewife's arsenal, and the surest proof of her skill. Winter must have fallen upon the land like a seizure, in grim contrast to the ease and plenty of summer and fall. It was a time when hens went off lay, cows gave little or no milk (if they were not slaughtered for meat) and fresh food was limited to such hardy vegetables as could stand up to severe frosts. Shops were few and far between, their stock restricted in any case largely to dry goods. In most households, especially in remote country areas, work began early in summer, salting down butter and making cheeses, waxing or pickling eggs, making soft fruit into preserves, with sugar, honey or spiced vinegar, pickling vegetables or turning them into powerfully seasoned sauces, ketchups and chutneys. As the months passed there would be barley and malt to brew for beer and ale, wheat to be milled and stored in mouseproof bins – rats, mice, weevils, cockroaches and similar voracious pests were a perennial headache – fish and meat to be salted, dried, cured or smoked, orchard fruit to be dried or canned (in simple corked jars, cooked in the oven) beans and cabbages to be salted, root vegetables to be stored in 'clamps', herbs hung in bunches from the roof beams, walnuts husked and buried in wet salt. To think that they also found time to gather wild flowers and fruit for country wines and liqueurs, to grow, gather and distill herbs for – often effective – remedies or 'simples', not to mention making all their own soap, candles, household linen and clothes! Small wonder that 'strong and strapping' was high praise where a marriageable wench was concerned, and that the untimely death of one of those powerful women plunged her family and household into chaos and confusion from which the looked-for escape was for the widower to find a successor as soon as custom allowed. 'Huswifery' in those times was, indisputably, a highly and variously skilled occupation.

All the same, I cannot help feeling relieved that we can take life more easily today, thanks to modern conveniences. To preserve or not to preserve is a proposition one can toy with, safe from the rather alarming consequences that might well have followed on neglect or incompetence in these matters once upon a time – scurvy, for instance, due to lack of the vitamins which even preserved foods supply quite generously; rickets, from calcium deficiency (cheese is a pre-eminent source of calcium), and other deficiency diseases from which to-day most of us are comfortably insulated.

Whatever the motivation might be – economy, nostalgia, revolt against overpriced, tasteless commercial products – there is sure evidence that the old fashioned methods of preserving food, and especially fruit and vegetables, are enjoying a considerable revival. The disappearance of distilled vinegar and preserving equipment generally from shop shelves in the late summer is exasperating proof. This is not to say that everyone has suddenly fallen in love with the idea of homemade jams, jellies and pickles but that more and more people are making their own hedge against inflation by growing as many fruit and vegetables as their gardens can sustain. What this leads to, as every gardener knows, is over-production, green beans, zucchini and tomatoes fruiting in the extravagant way they do, not to mention the gooseberry bushes sagging with fruit, the strawberry beds running amok and all the other agreeable problems gardens give rise to. Much of this surplus can go straight into the freezer of course, and simple, safe and effective a method it is too. But not very interesting or imaginative, dare I say, compared with the rich variety of treatments, each contributing distinctive texture, flavoring and character, perfected by our ancestors. Besides, even freezers get overcrowded, and some fresh produce – zucchini, tomatoes, orchard fruit – just does not stand up to freezing well. There is a place in any kitchen for canned fruit, homemade jams and jellies, pickles and chutney, unusual delicacies like damson cheese and apple butter, the surprising pungency of dried mushrooms or morello cherries, the epicureanism of whole fruit conserves in brandy flavored syrups, or the lively individuality of fruit vinegars, marmalades, homemade mustard, spiced crab apples, elderflower wine, sloe gin and raspberry cordial.

The dearth in our eating today is not one of variety and quantity – a short stroll around any supermarket shows a greater range of foodstuffs than many of our ancestors encountered in a lifetime. But that there is a sameness, a processed 'tastiness' about it all, nobody could deny. The real value of homemade foods and preserves, as with all things made by people rather than machines, is that they redress the balance in favor of *non*-conformity, the things taste of themselves, the ground they grew in, the air they breathed, the way you cooked them, a whole host of variables which make the opening of each new jar, or pot, something of an event. Late ripening blackberries picked along the seashore taste quite different, when made into jelly, from fat squashy berries culled from sheltered bushes inland. It is small surprises like these which make the hours of picking, the tedious coring, peeling or otherwise preparing, seem like nothing in retrospect. The rewards are so real that a passing enthusiasm can easily grow into a lifelong hobby.

Food from the wild

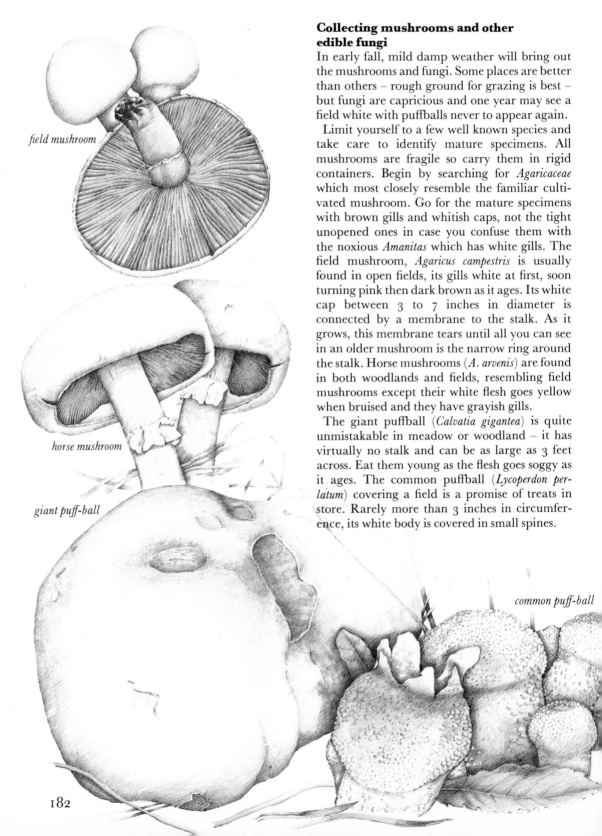

field mushroom

horse mushroom

giant puff-ball

common puff-ball

Collecting mushrooms and other edible fungi

In early fall, mild damp weather will bring out the mushrooms and fungi. Some places are better than others – rough ground for grazing is best – but fungi are capricious and one year may see a field white with puffballs never to appear again.

Limit yourself to a few well known species and take care to identify mature specimens. All mushrooms are fragile so carry them in rigid containers. Begin by searching for *Agaricaceae* which most closely resemble the familiar cultivated mushroom. Go for the mature specimens with brown gills and whitish caps, not the tight unopened ones in case you confuse them with the noxious *Amanitas* which has white gills. The field mushroom, *Agaricus campestris* is usually found in open fields, its gills white at first, soon turning pink then dark brown as it ages. Its white cap between 3 to 7 inches in diameter is connected by a membrane to the stalk. As it grows, this membrane tears until all you can see in an older mushroom is the narrow ring around the stalk. Horse mushrooms (*A. arvensis*) are found in both woodlands and fields, resembling field mushrooms except their white flesh goes yellow when bruised and they have grayish gills.

The giant puffball (*Calvatia gigantea*) is quite unmistakable in meadow or woodland – it has virtually no stalk and can be as large as 3 feet across. Eat them young as the flesh goes soggy as it ages. The common puffball (*Lycoperdon perlatum*) covering a field is a promise of treats in store. Rarely more than 3 inches in circumference, its white body is covered in small spines.

Blewits often appear in late fall, later than other fungi. *Lepista saeva* is mushroom shaped, has a beige cap 2 to 6 inches in diameter, white to grayish pink gills and a violet tinge to the stout and ringless stalk. It is found in fields. Wood blewits (*Lepista nuda*) are an astonishing purplish bruised color when young, though cap and gills often turn beige as the fungus ages. Another woodland species chanterelle (*Cantharellus cibarius*) has a tawny yellow body and funnel shaped caps, 1 to 4 inches in diameter which make these blewits unmistakable.

Coniferous woods in summer and fall can yield a delicacy: cep or *Boletus edulis*, with dark brown, moisty, shiny cap 2 to 8 inches in diameter and spongy mass of tubes beneath. White at first, these turn green/yellow later. All members of the *Boletus* family are identified by these vertical tubes resembling foam beneath the caps. Beware of the *Boletus satanas* – identifiable by its red stalk and tubes – as it is poisonous when eaten raw.

Parasol mushrooms (*Lepiota procera*) are well worth looking out for. They occur in clearings, or the fringes of woods. The caps are veiled when young but later can open out to as much as 10 inches across in an umbrella shape, and the long, striped stalk has a loose double ring. The cap is covered in large dark scales, the gills are white and detached from the stem and the spores are colorless. The shaggy parasol (*Lepiota rhacodes*) has a less scaly cap than the other, the stipe or stalk is smooth and if its surface is scratched, particularly near the base, it soon turns yellow, then reddish. Both fungi are strongly flavored and delicious.

chanterelle

cep

blewit

parasol mushroom

carrageen

nettle tip

laver

knotted wrack

dandelion

furze

primrose

hawthorn

silver birch leaves
and catkins

may

elder

Spring

Birch sap rises just before spring's official start, and this is the time to tap trees carefully for an exhilarating wine. Early spring is a sucession of wild flowers, all yellow, and excellent for wine: primroses, furze, dandelions. Do not pick more than a bucket of primroses, and only then if you happen on a mass at once. Brave furze thorns for the coconut-smelling flowers which make a delicate golden wine of great distinction. Dandelion petals make a fine wine.

Edible seaweeds like laver (*Porphyta umbilicalis*), carrageen or sea moss (*Chondrus crispus*), and knotted wrack (*Aescophyllum nodosum*) are all commonly found in temperate waters in the late spring. Laver fronds are purplish, thin and irregularly shaped. Washed and boiled until it looks like dark-brown spinach purée, this sea-weed can be cooked in butter and rolled in oats for breakfast biscuits. Carrageen or 'sea moss' which is purple-brown, more clump than moss, and knotted wrack with its branching fronds are both traditionally used to set jellies and blanc-manges. Rock samphire (*Chrithmum maritimum*), a handsome pale-green clump of fleshy forked leaves with yellow flower cushions, clings to cliff sides, has a fiery-acid taste and can be boiled with spice and vinegar for pickles.

Inland, meanwhile, pick a bucket or two of may blossoms for wine, filmy young beech leaves for *noyau* and hawthorn buds for an equally potent liqueur. Wild greens are sprouting in profusion; pick nettle tips, in gloves, to make a sharp, tonic broth with sorrel, spinach and cream. Put a flowerpot over a convenient dandelion to blanch young leaves for a salad. Allow yourself a few wild violets, to crystallize.

Summer

Early to mid-summer is elderblossom time. A mere quart of the creamy talcum scented blossom makes 1 gallon of elderflower wine, most fragrant and brilliant of country wines. A few heads will give you elderflower champagne which is frothy, quick and fun. A few more dipped with gooseberries and strawberries make beautiful muscat flavored jam. Or, simplest of all, dip the heads.in batter for a flower fritter, scented and charming. Lime blossom may be dried to make a sedative and refreshing tisane.

Wild horseradish, a tallish plant with a white spire of flowers and big crinkled dock-like leaves, grows in sunny sheltered waste land. The root – dig down and cut a length off – is pungent enough to make several jars of sauce. Or grate a mound and eat fresh with or without cream to eat with beef. Search along stream beds in shady places for wild garlic, or ramsons, a starry white flower with green blade leaves. The smell is unmistakable. It can be used just like the cultivated sort but more freely, leaves, stems and all chopped into salads or soft cheeses.

Mid-summer is the time to search for wild soft berries: raspberries and strawberries, tiny, sweet and beautiful with curd cream. Look for them in light woodland, grassy heath and in sunny sheltered corners. The raspberry can be distinguished from red blackberries by its smooth stems. Wild strawberries creep down low in grass and bracken so need to be hunted for. Just a few of either will transform a dessert or a jam. On high ground, hunt for the thinly scattered blueberries (known as huckleberries when darker blue or nearly black). They are marvelously juicy and good in tarts or with cream.

horseradish

blueberry

wild strawberry

sweet violet

ramsons (wild garlic)

sloe

crabapple

elderberry

haw

truffle

hazel

Fall

Gardeners are almost too busy to chase up all the wild fruits on offer in the pauses between preserving all the cultivated ones, like apples and pears. Elderberries and blackberries ripen about the same time: elderberries are ready to pick for wine, syrup or sauce when the flat heads of juicy berries hang down like tassels. Wild blackberries are everywhere. The first of the season are best for eating raw, the mid-season fruits make nice tarts, jams and wine and the late autumn ones can be sieved with apple for blackberry jelly. Coastal blackberries ripen later but have a keener flavor. In the fields, blackberries on the sheltered side may be twice as big as those on the other, so look around. Do not forget the bright haws, fruit of the hawthorn. Although too dry to use for anything but jelly or wine, they have a smoky strange flavor which grows on you. The same applies to rowan berries, fruit of the mountain ash, which are ripe around this time of year though they may take longer in cold climates. The green berries of the cranberry plant ripen in late fall, ready for making into the much loved cranberry sauce to serve with the Thanksgiving turkey. Hickory nuts, cobnuts and walnuts must be picked early in fall if they are to be pickled green for a delectable relish.

Winter

Mild damp weather can raise a flush of fungi in fields and woods, so take a plastic bag in your pocket when you go for a walk. After a downpour the odd truffle may sometimes – rarely – be discerned just surfacing through leafmold at the foot of beech trees. Truffles are hunted and found by trained dogs and greedy pigs all over Europe. Black and white truffles are roughly spherical, mostly about the size of a ping pong ball, with warty and crinkled skin. They usually grow some inches below ground, but heavy rain can uncover them.

After the frosts is the best time to pick rosehips for wine, syrups and jellies as they are more tender and have a better flavor. This also applies to sloes for making into the crimson sloe gin. Sloes cling to the branches but you cannot mistake their misty blue among the pale green leaves in early winter.

A few nuts such as hazel or cobnuts may have escaped the squirrels while the bigger nuts from the hickory are improved after being left out for a winter, ready for an early spring pickling. While in the colder climates winter offers little in the way of edible food to be picked out of doors, it is a good time of the year for putting away the fruits of sunnier climes.

rowan

blackberry

rose hip

walnut

...et chestnut

Salted vegetables

Salting is a cheap and effective way of preserving some vegetables which do not stand up to drying very well – green beans and cabbage in particular. It is an ideal method for those who do not have, or want, deep freezes.

Salting beans

Preserving raw green beans in salt is uncomplicated – the beans are merely buried in lots of salt. Also useful is the fact that more beans can be added as the season progresses. They keep well like this for 6 months. Rinse well in cold running water before use, though, and do not salt the cooking water.

You will need an earthenware crock, or glass jars, and pickling salt; table salt is not suitable. Allow 1 lb (1½ cups) of salt to 3 lb beans. Alternate layers of salt and layers of beans in the jar or crock, beginning and ending with salt. Press the beans down well, and cover with wax paper or plastic wrap.

Salting cabbage

Sauerkraut – German for pickled cabbage – is a deservedly popular traditional method of preserving cabbage by fermenting it in salt, a process which not only keeps molds and bacteria at bay but turns the shredded cabbage into a piquant vegetable delicacy. Use it as a winter salad, or serve it in the plain, hearty style of Alsace, where a mound of sauerkraut appears with steaming boiled potatoes and carrots, a selection of smoked sausages and lots of spicy mustard.

Equipment

To make a bulk amount of sauerkraut, you need a large crock or glass jars, a wooden board to fit down inside the container like a lid, a large smooth, scalded stone, and a very sharp knife to shred the cabbage finely. The shredding attachment to your food processor will perform this task admirably. Also, you need a generous supply of hard white cabbages (no others will do) and pickling salt. Iodized salt is unsuitable. Several large sheets of clean white cloth or cheesecloth are needed, too.

If in doubt as to how many cabbages your crock will hold, start small – 15 to 20 pounds – and add more later.

Heat processing: the boiling water bath method

Sauerkraut will keep for up to 2 to 3 months so long as you make sure the cabbage is covered with brine, and the cheesecloth cover is scaled and washed regularly. But to keep longer, it must be heat processed. Pack the sauerkraut into large, sterilized canning jars, filling to within 2 inches of the rim. Stand the jars (with loosely fitted lids) on a rack or layer of cloth in a large deep kettle or pan up to their shoulders in cold water. Bring the water gently to a boil. Remove from the heat. Wipe around the jar rims and top up with a little extra boiling brine, leaving ½ inch of headroom. Adjust the lids and follow the boiling water bath method (see Canned Fruit, page 200), allowing 15 minutes for pint jars and 20 minutes for quarts. Remove from the kettle and complete the seals if necessary.

Sauerkraut making

1. Peel coarse outer leaves and shred the cabbage very finely.

2. Measure it as you shred, and pack down into a large crock or earthenware jar (at least 12 inches in diameter at the mouth) 12 cups (2 lb) at a time, mixing in $2\frac{1}{2}$ tablespoons of pickling salt to each layer. A little crushed cumin or caraway seed can be added for flavor. Layer until 3 inches from the top. By this time the cabbage should have yielded a fair bit of juice. Press down until the juice easily covers the cabbage.

Cover the crock with several layers of scalded cheesecloth. Then choose a scalded wooden board which can fit down inside the container. Weight it down with a smooth, scalded stone so that the air is excluded. Keep the crock in a warm place (70 degrees) to encourage the fermentation evidenced by busy bubbling beneath a skin. After a few days, even the lid should be submerged. Keep the kraut at this temperature for 2 to 3 weeks, regularly washing and scalding the cloth and board and skimming off the skin. When the bubbles stop, transfer the crock to a cool place (38 degrees). It will keep for 2 or 3 months.

3. To preserve sauerkraut for longer, or store it at temperatures higher than 38 degrees, pack it down tightly into large, sterilized canning jars and process in a boiling water bath as described opposite and on page 200.

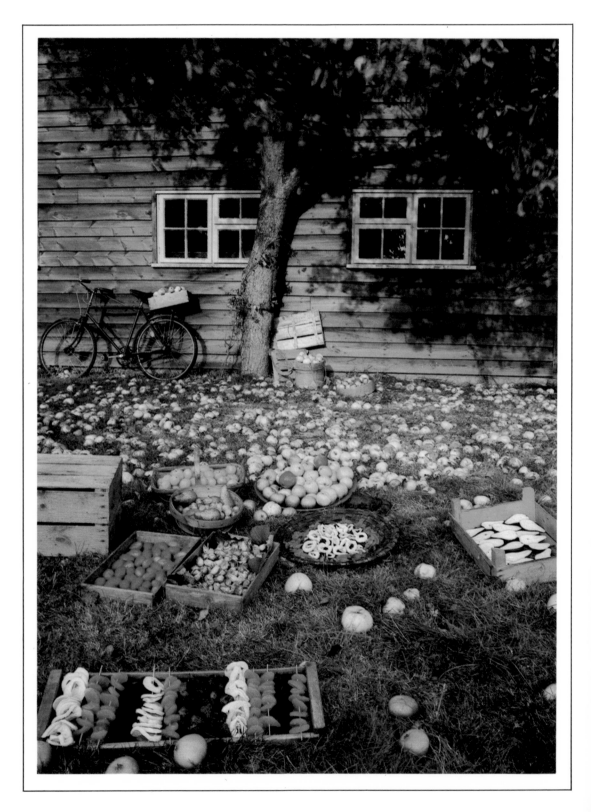

Dried Fruit

*'Of the two downstairs rooms, one was used as a kind of kitchen storeroom,
with pots and pans and a big red crockery water vessel at one end,
and potatoes in sacks and peas and beans spread out to dry at the other.
The apple crop was stored on racks suspended beneath the ceiling,
and bunches of herbs dangled below.'*

Lark Rise to Candleford   Flora Thompson   1945

Preserving fruit by drying is the oldest, easiest and most natural way of all. It is also the most satisfactory for long-term storage as the various molds, yeasts and bacteria which spoil fruit need moisture to thrive and multiply. By drying out whatever natural moisture is in the fruit, the action of the bacteria is stopped.

The easy, cheap way to dry fruit is in the sun's heat but it needs to be a hot sun burning out of a cloudless sky for the process to continue unchecked. Sun drying, as well as costing nothing and being highly convenient, produces fruit with the truest flavor: sun-dried apricots from Kashmir are the best in the world.

So much for drying under optimum conditions. People living in more variable climates can still dry fruit successfully by making the best use of such natural sunshine and wind as comes their way, together with a judicious back-up from artificial sources of heat. Festoons of apple rings slowly turning leathery in the heat of the old kitchen stove used to be a common feature of country kitchens; in sunnier climates there would be trays of plums and cherries.

In the case of foods that dry particularly well, this is a straightforward and satisfactory way of taking care of a sudden glut, or of dealing with food left over from canning or pickling. The enormous advantage of dried food is that it takes up so little room – a hoard of fresh plums will fit into a glass jar when dried into prunes and several jars will last the winter through. Containers for drying fruit must, however, be airtight, since anything dried is likely to absorb whatever moisture is floating about in the air. Apple rings over a kitchen range in constant use are one thing, apple rings in a damp kitchen full of steam quite another.

In theory anything may be dried. In practice, I think the field can be limited to perhaps half a dozen different sorts of fruit. The ones I have chosen are the ones I think most people would find most useful, and which stand up to drying best.

Late summer sunshine steadily warms and dries prepared fruits: plump apricots; windfall apples, peeled, cored and skewered; and pears, halved and brushed with ascorbic acid to prevent discoloration. The plums and nuts have been harvested for indoor drying.

Fruit drying

Equipment

For drying in the sun, some kind of large, light tray to spread out the produce is needed. The air must be able to circulate freely, so light, rigid wooden frames covered with wire, gauze or cheesecloth stapled on for strength are a handy solution. Make them so they can be stacked on top of each other indoors, allowing air to circulate, above an artificial heat source: convector heater, hot plate, radiator. If you are drying fruit out of doors, provide some sort of protection against flies too – cheesecloth thrown over the top of the trays. Bring it all indoors if it rains. Another expedient, useful where the weather is variable, is to set the food out under glass, which concentrates the sun's heat – use a glazed cold frame, or the shelves of a greenhouse.

For indoor drying, equipment can range from your own stove, turned to a low setting, to expensive, but convenient, electrically powered drying cabinets with thermometers, fans to circulate air and slatted shelves. In my experience an ordinary domestic oven will dry average amounts of food quite satisfactorily and inexpensively. Depending on the size of the fruit, it can be dried on the usual oven grids, with a piece of cheesecloth laid over the trays, or in baking pans, or in specially made stacking trays designed to fit the oven.

Not vital to success, but handy, is a thermometer for checking oven temperature or heat over the drying trays.

Some fruits tend to darken or discolor as they dry – it is arguable whether this affects the flavor but, in some people's view, it makes them unattractive. There are various ways of checking this. The simplest is a salt water dip (2 tablespoons of salt per gallon of water), which is suitable for apples. Or you can use ascorbic acid, available in crystal form. Added to water at the rate of 1 teaspoon per $2\frac{1}{2}$ cups and sprinkled over the prepared fruit (apricots, peaches, pears, apples) it helps preserve their natural color without altering the flavor.

Peaches and nectarines

Peel, halve and pit the peaches and nectarines. Sprinkle with ascorbic acid to prevent darkening. Lay on trays, hollow side uppermost (sugary juice collects here at first), and dry at a very mild heat (125 to 150 degrees). Lower the heat towards the end to prevent them scorching. After about 15 hours the fruit will be dry but pliable and leathery.

Apricots

Slit the top carefully, remove the pit but do not peel. Sprinkle with ascorbic acid to prevent discoloration then dry, as for peaches, except they need less time and less heat.

Grapes

Dry these in bunches, after picking off any bad ones. Dip them in boiling water to speed things up. A mild heat as for peaches, then dry out for 8 hours.

Drying fruit

First clean, wash and trim the fruit, cutting into manageable slices or pieces unless really small. To dry the fruit out entirely you need a steady source of heat – the sun is best, but sadly usually unreliable – plus a slight draft if possible. Fruit can be dried in short bursts, as it contains enough acid and sugar to inhibit molds. When the fruit has dried, leave it at room temperature overnight to 'condition', and then store.

1. Apples. Use ripe apples, eaters or cookers. Peel, core and slice into $\frac{1}{4}$ inch rings, dropping them into lightly salted water (2 tablespoons per 1 gallon to prevent browning. Shake off the water, and thread on sticks or spread on trays. The sticks can then be propped up above the stove, or supported on trays in the oven. The oven heat should be no more than 140 degrees. If heat is continuous, the rings take 4–6 hours to dry; if intermittent, 2 to 3 days. They are ready when their texture is like a chamois.

2. Pears. Pears should be peeled, quartered and cored, sprinkled with ascorbic acid to prevent darkening, and spread on stacking trays covered with cheesecloth. Dry as for apples, never allowing the temperature to exceed 150 degrees.

3. Plums. If small, dry whole, first scalding with boiling water to split the skins. Large plums can be halved and pitted. Proceed as for pears.

4. Cherries. Sour or Morello cherries dry best, with the most flavor. Leave the stalks on, do not pit, and spread on trays and dry at 130 degrees for 6 hours.

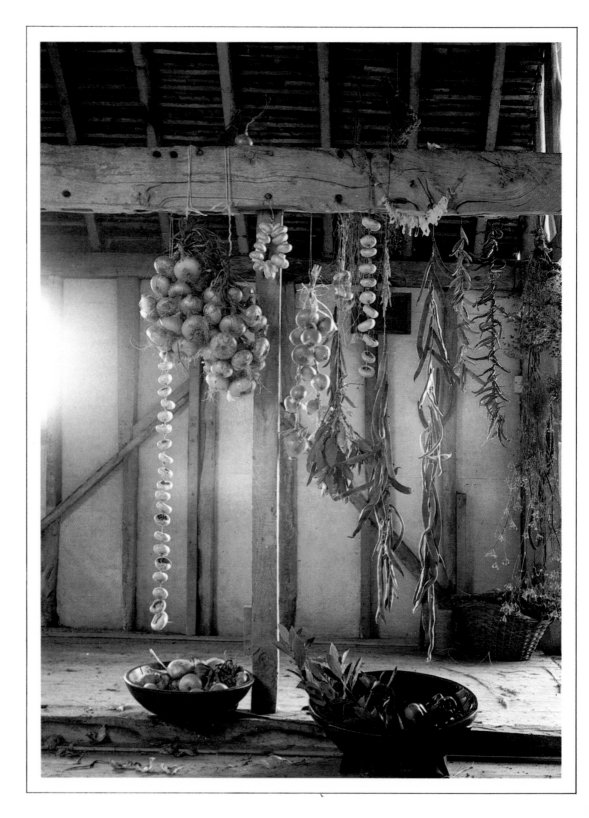

Dried Vegetables

'Other jams, jellies and pickles already stood on the pantry shelves.
Big yellow vegetable marrows dangled from hooks and bunches
of drying thyme and sage. The faggot pile was being replenished
and the lamp was lighted after tea.'

Lark Rise to Candleford   Flora Thompson   1945

Vegetables are a little trickier to dry than fruit, as they contain less acid and almost no natural sugar. If the drying process is interrupted, or does not get going properly, they can go moldy before they dry. I find that onions, peppers and mushrooms are the best vegetables – legumes excepted – to dry, and seem to avoid this problem.

Cut vegetables smaller than fruits when preparing them for drying as more water will be lost and the process takes longer. When they are quite dried, leave the vegetables at room temperature overnight to 'condition', and then store in airtight containers, in a cool, dark place. Obviously some things dry faster than others, and the type of heat makes a difference too, so it is impossible to give precise times. Keep an eye on your vegetables to begin with, looking over your handiwork every hour or so, and change the trays round to encourage everything to dry evenly.

Nearly all garden herbs, except parsley and chives, can be dried successfully. The best time to pick herbs for drying is early in the summer, just before they flower. They should be cut in the morning on a fine day. Small leaved herbs – thyme, savory, marjoram – need only to be tied loosely in bundles and hung up to dry in a warm place, preferably wrapped in a loose cheesecloth cover to keep off the dust. Bunches of herbs can be hung outdoors in the half shade during the warmest part of the day for several days. Large leaved herbs like sage, may be dipped in boiling water for 1 minute, then removed, the water shaken off, and dried in a cool oven until brittle. Basil can be dried as for thyme – it tastes different dry, but is still good for cooking. If you are drying for seeds – fennel, dill, coriander – cut the stems with the seed heads as soon as they are ripe. Dry the whole stalk then thresh them out over a sheet of clean paper. Dry the seeds for a further 2 hours in the sun or in a warm, dry place.

Run a roller over dried herbs to crush them, pick out stalks and store in dark glass jars or cans, away from the light. Keep different herbs separate or their flavors will blend, with disappointing results.

A warm, dry barn for drying the fall crop of vegetables and herbs: onions knotted in bunches, garlanded in rings from the rafters; threaded mushrooms to flavor winter soups; lima beans left to dry in their pods; bunches of herbs; and sweet peppers ready to be sliced for drying.

Vegetable drying

Garlic
Dry, string and store homegrown garlic bulbs exactly as for onions. Because of their natural oil, garlic bulbs keep perfectly in a dry place for months.

Tomatoes
This is a Tunisian method of preserving ripe tomatoes in the form of a salty paste. Cut the tomatoes in half, scoop out the seeds and remove the skins. Mix three handfuls of salt with the thick, red juice, turn into a jellybag and leave to drip all night over a bowl. Next day, scrape off the red paste, mix with one handful of salt, spread on flat earthenware dishes or plates (do not use metal plates) and leave in the sun or in a cool oven to evaporate the remaining moisture. It should not be allowed to dry hard, but remain pasty and soft. Cool. Spoon into jars, cover with $\frac{1}{2}$ inch of oil, cover and store. Add no salt when cooking with this paste.

Peppers
Buy peppers at their cheapest in summer, and dry them to use throughout the year. Home-grown peppers also dry well and retain their flavor better than commercially dried peppers. Prepare the peppers – red and green – by slicing across into rings, removing the stalk, seeds and partitions. Best to spread on trays and dry in the oven – they take approximately 3 hours in the oven. They are ready when brittle. Condition, pack and store.

Edible fungi
The right weather conditions raise wild fungi like dragon seed – too much at once. Drying is the best way to preserve wild mushrooms and other edible fungi and their flavor is concentrated enough for one of two dried specimens to flavor a whole stew. To dry, simply rub any dirt off the stalks, discarding really tough ones, spread out on trays and dry slowly, at not more than 120 degrees, in the sun or an oven until dry and leathery. Or thread them on strings without stalks and suspend them over the range, or in another warm, dry place.
Note: if the oven is too warm, or the mushrooms exceptionally juicy, you may find precious juice oozing out of them, so it is a good idea to put a pan beneath to catch it. Boiled up with nutmeg, mace, cayenne and a spoonful of brandy, and sterilized in boiling water for 15 minutes, this makes superb ketchup. You *must* process mushroom ketchup as it grows mold very quickly otherwise.

Legumes
All the legume family (chick peas, soybeans, lentils, peas and navy beans) are dried in much the same way. Leave them on the plant to dry naturally as long as possible, then take the pods indoors or into a greenhouse to dry for another few days. Finally, shell them, spread them out on trays and allow them to dry completely hard in the sun or an oven. It takes many plants to get much to show for your work. Mature beans and peas dry easily out of doors.

Drying onions

Onions can be dried either whole and strung up in skeins, or peeled and sliced. The bulbs themselves will keep for months in a dry place, as will the slices in an airtight container.

1. For the first method, spread out the onion bulbs (still on their stems) on raised wire mesh to allow the air to circulate and leave them to dry for several days out of doors in the sun. Cover them if it rains. They are ready when their skins are bronzed and papery and the stalks have shrivelled.

2. To string onions, take a length of stout string or twine and tie it to form a loop. Hang the loop over a hook at a convenient height for working.

Knot the first few onions as shown in the illustration. Continue until the string has been used up. Alternatively push the onions into old stockings to store them. Hang the bunches in a warm dry place. Dryness is the vital factor; they will sprout in a damp spot.

3. Only sound onions are suitable for stringing up whole, since those with soft patches will rot. Any that are bruised or damaged can be dried in peeled slices of $\frac{1}{2}$ inch thickness. Spread them on trays covered with cheesecloth and dry for 3 hours in an oven, or 8 hours in the sun. They are ready when brittle.

Leave them overnight at room temperature to 'condition', then store them in plastic bags. Use as a convenience food in stews and soups; they are marvelously tasty fried for a second or two.

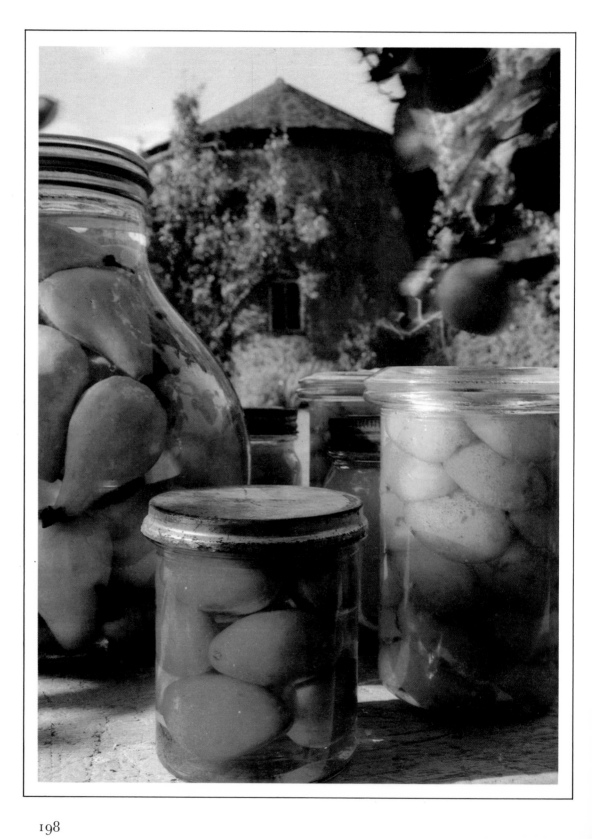

Canned Fruit

"'It's very strong" said Miss Pole as she put down her empty glass.
"I do believe there's spirit in it."
"Only a drop, just necessary to make it keep" said Miss Barker.
"You know we put brandy paper over preserves to make them keep.
I often feel tipsy myself from eating damson tart."'

Cranford   Mrs Gaskell   1851–3

With the advent of tin canning, then in latter years, freezing, the thrifty practice of packing away ripe orchard fruit in jars for winter use seems to have fallen from favor. This is a pity, I think, because the fruit that cans well tastes fresher and truer to itself preserved that way than any other. Fruit of luscious texture are even more delicious preserved in a light syrup than when eaten straight from the tree. I would put peaches, apricots, nectarines, pears and cherries in this class, and in other climates I imagine mangoes, guavas and litchi nuts would respond well too. It is a waste of time canning soft fruit such as gooseberries, strawberries and raspberries because they emerge tough, or flimsy, and seem to be all seed. Blackberries, sieved to a purée and canned with puréed apple, are an honorable exception. Canned apple purée is a good standby, and useful and pleasant to have on hand for turning into charlottes, betties and pies at a moment's notice. Rhubarb, too, cans excellently due to its high acid content.

It is the natural acid in fruit which makes it so perfect for canning. *Clostridium botulinum*, the bogey of home canning, cannot survive in acid conditions though it can survive heat processing and airless vacuum seals. Vegetables, due to their low acid content, are risky subjects for home canning except where vinegar, lemon juice or some other acid is supplied, as in pickling. Properly canned fruit will keep safely for a long time, but it should be heat processed to destroy the enzymes and micro-organisms which could spoil the flavor and the fruit.

This is not difficult to do, but it is one of those kitchen activities which needs full concentration, proper equipment, careful preparation and a conscientious eye on the clock. Do not try to weave it in with the usual day's routine, but set aside a whole morning or afternoon for the job, at least for the first few times. You will find full instructions overleaf.

Rosy damsons and golden plums float within the transparent canning jars; large pears soak up clear sugary syrup, more delicious even than when eaten straight from the tree; and apple purée has been bottled with cinnamon and lemon peel as a useful standby for pies and charlottes.

Fruit canning

Equipment

The *sine qua non* of canning is proper jars, made of glass strong enough to withstand high temperatures, large enough to contain a reasonable quantity of fruit (enough to fill a pie pan, say), and supplied with suitable lids for creating a vacuum seal. Purpose made canning jars fulfill these requirements and will last for years if you look after them, but they are expensive initially, and the metal lids need replacing every time they are used. Old-style mason jars and bailed jars are no longer being manufactured, but there are lots of them around. If you buy some secondhand, be sure that rubber rings are still being manufactured to fit their lids.

Other equipment you should have includes a deep round pan of heavy enameled ware or stainless steel with a cover and a rack, or a steam pressure canner, and a jar-lifter. Finally, you need a wooden board to stand the hot jars on – and a clock.

Making syrup

Make the syrup with water and ordinary granulated sugar, adding a little honey to canned pears, if you feel like it. Do not make the syrup too strong because the fruit will crowd at the top of the jar if you do. As an average guide use 1 cup sugar to 1 pint of water. Dissolve the sugar in the water by stirring over a low heat before bringing it to a boil, then simmer for a couple of minutes. It should be added, boiling, to the jars. Add a little spice – cinnamon, lemon rind – to the syrup.

Preparing and packing the fruit

Fruit should be cleaned and trimmed of brown or squashy bits. They can be canned whole or peeled, cored and quartered – cut-up fruit packs down tighter. Pears and apples should be kept in a large bowl of slightly salted water with a squeeze of lemon juice until you are ready to pack them down, to stop them browning. Fill jars, leaving headroom to allow for expansion, or bubbling up during processing.

Heat processing: the boiling water bath method

To process foods safely, the water must be kept at a full rolling boil and must cover the tops of the jars of food being processed by at least 1 to 2 inches. So choose a deep kettle or pan that is $4\frac{1}{2}$ to 5 inches deeper than your jars. A kettle will come with a wire rack, otherwise use a round cake-cooling rack to stand the jars on. Follow the method given opposite for canning peaches. Pack the food to be canned in sterilized containers, leaving headroom as specified. If using jars with the modern 'dome', 'snap' or 'self-sealing' 2-piece screwband metal closures, give a $\frac{1}{4}$ inch counter-turn to the lid to allow the jar to vent during processing. Jars containing hot food may be put directly into boiling water; those containing raw food should be placed in cooler water to prevent breakage. When the processing time is up, remove the jars immediately with a jar-lifter. Complete the seals if necessary and leave to cool on a rack, wooden board or pile of newspapers for 12 hours, then test the seals (see page 229). To use a pressure canner for a boiling water bath, follow the manufacturer's instructions.

Canning peaches: the boiling-water bath process

1. Make a syrup from 1 quart of water and 2 cups of sugar.

2. Clean and trim the peaches, which can be canned whole or peeled, halved and pitted. If you cut up the fruit it will pack down tighter.

3. Pack the fruit into sterilized jars, leaving $\frac{1}{2}$ inch of headroom. Pour in the boiling syrup, again leaving $\frac{1}{2}$ inch headroom. Give the jars a quick shake to release any trapped air, wipe clean the sealing edges and cover.

4. Put the rack in the kettle, half fill the kettle with water and put it on the stove (the water can be heated while packing the jars). Lower the jars into the kettle, placing them about 1 inch apart and away from the sides. Pour enough hot water around the jars to bring the water level up to 1 to 2 inches above the tops of the jars and bring to a full rolling boil. Start timing now, allowing 25 minutes for pint jars and 30 minutes for quarts (do *not* include the minutes taken to bring the water to boiling). Remove the jars from the pan immediately after processing and complete the seals if necessary. Leave to cool, then seal.

Preserves

'And the Quangle Wangle said
To himself on the crumpetty tree
"Jam and jelly and bread
are the best of foods for me"'

The Quangle Wangle   Edward Lear   1846

If preserves did not exist it would be a priority matter to invent them because they provide the simplest, longest lasting method of preserving a quantity of fruit in a small compass. This was discovered way back in medieval times – indeed Chaucer was present at the coronation banquet for Henry IV, at which comfits of candied quince, among other dainties, regaled the company.

In those times fruit seems usually to have been made into fruit cheeses – sliced rather than spread – instead of jams and jellies, because this method, being so highly concentrated, makes the most of whatever natural sugar may be in the fruit itself (a fact New England farmers' wives thriftily turned to account a few centuries later) and thus requires less extra sweetening in the way of sugar or honey.

It was not until the West Indian sugarcane plantations were in full swing that sugar became cheap and commonplace enough to be used extravagantly. Sugar was a luxury until then, sold in apothecary shops by the ounce and the poor had to satisfy their craving for sweetness with honey and dried fruit.

Homemade preserves today, however luxurious they may be, are not necessarily expensive. Hedgerow jams, jellies, butters and cheeses can be made from all the wild fruits and berries – blackberries, blueberries, cloudberries, hips and haws, elderberries – which are there for the picking, on country expeditions, weekend walks and if you look carefully, in many of the less formal parks. Preserves like these have a fresh, innocent wild savor all their own and are one of the nearest things I know to a free treat. Fruit farms where you pick your own raspberries, strawberries and other soft fruit are well worth a visit as the prices are rock bottom, but I suggest that you ring up first to check that they still have what you want, as soft fruit seasons are short.

I have been using the word 'preserve' very loosely to cover the whole range of jams and their more refined, more clearly defined compatriots such as jellies, butters and cheeses. However, I should add that a 'preserve' is in fact a distinctive type of jam. If this sounds confusing, I had better quickly say that cooks are not linguistic philosophers and pass on to some of the basic definitions.

Damson fruit cheese, foreground left, and sweet black butter, right, made from any surplus soft fruits in summer. Then, at the back, crabapple jellies with the fruits suspended in amber jelly, lemon curd, beside rowan and redcurrant jellies, and two jars of purpled damson jam.

Preserving

Jams: whole fruit or fruit pulp boiled with sugar until such time as the acid and pectin in the fruit combine with the thickening sugar syrup to make the mixture set.

Preserves: in its specific, rather than generic, meaning this refers to a rather stately sort of jam, intended for 'best' rather than everyday eating, to which nuts, candied peel, dried fruit, lemon or orange slices, ginger or alcohol are added.

Conserves: whole fruit preserved in a fair amount of syrup or a light jelly to be eaten with a spoon together with fresh curd cream at the end of a good meal. This is a peculiarly French type of preserve and the word descends, I would guess, from the French 'compote de fruits en conserve'.

Jellies: essentially the same as jam, except that the cooked fruit pulp is strained in a bag, and the strained juice alone boiled up with sugar until it reaches setting point. A good way of getting rid of seeds, pits and extracting the flavor of certain dry berries like hips, haws and rowanberries and certain juicy ones like cranberries or elderberries though it has a lower yield per pound of fruit than jam.

Fruit cheeses and butters: descendants of the medieval sweetmeats, the fruit pulp cooked slowly with sugar until stiff, solid and almost dry. Fruit butters are cooked for a shorter time until thick but not stiff, and are used for spreads whereas fruit cheeses are eaten in small slices.

Marmalades: normally a preserve made with citrus fruit, in which the cut rind is embedded in a jelly flavored with the juice. It is the ideal breakfast time preserve as the astringent flavor helps to unclog a drowsy palate.

Equipment

The single most important piece of equipment is a suitable kettle for cooking preserves. It needs to be large ($1\frac{1}{2}$ to 2 gallon capacity), shallow but wide to help evaporation and solid to distribute heat and guard against sticking and burning. This may seem very large but the golden rule in jam making is never to have the kettle more than half full. Boiling sugar splutters, foams and boils up with alarming suddenness. A good quality, stainless steel, enameled or aluminum preserving kettle, with a thick bottom, is not cheap but it is a well designed piece of equipment which lasts. A kettle of 2 quart capacity is useful for small quantities of jelly.

Also vital are a deep kettle for heat processing jam, canning jars in prime condition (jelly jars or other strong glass jars can be used for jelly), a jelly thermometer, household scales for weighing fruit pulp for jam and a long handled wooden spoon for stirring (most jams should be stirred in the last few minutes to prevent scorching). Other items which will be needed are a strainer or sieve, a ladle, a plastic funnel, a jar-lifter and a jug for transferring the cooked jam into pots. A commercial or homemade jellybag is the neatest way of straining fruit pulp for jellies. More advanced jam makers will probably want to try the pectin test, to work out the setting capacity of a particular batch of fruit, and for this a little rubbing alcohol will be needed.

Fruit cheeses should be pressed into oiled pottery dishes or molds so they can be turned out easily. For the everyday type of jam. I find the standard 1 pint canning jar is the best size. For the special herb scented or wild berry jellies to eat with game and meat, very small glass jars are best, as they provide just enough for one meal.

To keep well, all preserves should be given an airtight seal. Jelly in jelly jars needs $\frac{1}{2}$ inch of headroom before the sterilized caps and screwbands are put on; leave $\frac{1}{8}$ inch of headroom if you are sealing with paraffin wax. Leave $\frac{1}{2}$ inch of headroom for jams in hot sterilized canning jars. Check the seals before storing. The jar itself can be covered with pretty paper doilies, or smart rounds of check gingham. Polish the jars and, label them neatly with the name of the jam and the date.

Making preserves

Some methodology is helpful. Let us deal first with the pectin and acid question: pectin is a gummy substance naturally found in fruit, in some fruit more than others. Ditto for acid. Acid helps leach out the pectin during cooking. The pectin then combines with the sugar to produce a good jell or set, so it follows that fruit high in both is good for jam.

Tart cooking apples, blackcurrants, redcurrants, damsons, plums, gooseberries, crabapples, cranberries, loganberries and quinces are all high in pectin and acid. All these jell, or jam, effortlessly.

Fresh apricots, loganberries, raspberries, greengages and early blackberries have a medium pectin/acid content.

Strawberries, rhubarb, late blackberries, pears, cherries and pumpkin have a low pectin/acid content.

Slightly underripe fruit is at its peak for pectin/acid and this is the best to use. Testing fruit for pectin is simple and can be useful in deciding how much sugar to use. A simple rule of thumb is that high pectin sets more sugar equals more jam. However, a more accurate version with measures is:

High pectin fruits – $2\frac{1}{2}$–3 cups sugar to 1 lb fruit
Medium pectin fruits – 2 cups sugar to 1 lb fruit
Low pectin fruits – $1\frac{1}{2}$ cups sugar to 1 lb fruit.

To test for pectin, take one teaspoon of juices from the pre-cooked fruit (before adding the sugar) and put it into a small glass jar with 1 tablespoon rubbing alcohol. Shake. If one jelly blob forms, the fruit is rich in pectin, if two or three smaller ones, it is moderately well off, if small beads, or none at all, it is so low that you must mix it with a high pectin fruit, or commercial pectin. A lack of acid is easily made up by a squeeze of lemon juice, lemon slices or a little citric acid. Commercial pectin can be added to any jam of doubtful setting properties.

Medium to low pectin fruit, as the following recipes will show, generally uses a greater weight of fruit than sugar.

Making everyday strawberry jam

1. Take 4 lb of ripe but sound fruit, pick over for stalks and leaves and remove the hulls.

2. Strawberries should not be washed, but should be wiped instead with a clean cloth.

3. Put the prepared fruit into a preserving kettle with the squeezed juice of 4 lemons. Strawberries are low in pectin/acid, and the sharp juice helps the jam to set. Simmer over a low heat until the strawberries are quite soft and mushy – about 30 minutes. Warm the sugar before adding it to the fruit. Draw the kettle off the heat for a minute, add $3\frac{1}{2}$ lb (7 cups) warmed sugar to the fruit, stir vigorously to dissolve, turn up the heat, return the kettle and bring quickly back to a boil. This jam takes approximately 15 minutes to set.

4. A jam-making thermometer is not essential but helps to give you an instant progress report. Before plunging it into boiling jam, it should always be warmed in a jug of hot water. The red line will shoot up to within a couple of degrees of 'setting point', 221 degrees, the last degree always taking the longest to reach. When the jam is nearly done, unclip the thermometer, and take the reading from the centre of the pan.

5. Alternatively if you do not have a jam thermometer, do the saucer test. Drop a tiny bit of boiling jam on to a clean saucer, blow to cool, push with your fingertip, and if it crinkles because a skin has formed on top, the jam is done.

6. When the jam is judged ready, remove the kettle from the heat. The jars, clean and sterilized, should be standing by on a tray or large wooden chopping board, which helps stop the jars cracking. Leave the jam to cool for 5 minutes and then ladle into a jug and either funnel or pour into the jars to within $\frac{1}{2}$ inch (for jam in canning jars or jam to be sealed with paraffin) or $\frac{1}{8}$ inch (for modern jelly jars) of the rim. Wipe off drips with a hot damp cloth.

7. A disk of waxed paper can be placed on the jam surface to seal.

8. Alternatively, cover with $\frac{1}{8}$ inch layer of hot paraffin wax and allow to cool and set.

9. Place a plastic lid or metal cap on each jar. Jams should be heat processed for 10 minutes in a boiling water bath (see page 200).

Note: in Britain jams are commonly covered with plastic wrap. This is not a recommended covering in America and is obviously unsuitable for processing in a boiling water bath.

Jams

Homemade jam has never really lost ground to the commercial product. A good jam appeals to the artist in every cook; fine color and brilliance count for almost as much as good flavor.

Damson jam

Damsons are a natural jam fruit, and make a jam of episcopal purple, firm texture and intense plummy flavor – splendid with buttered toast and biscuits. The pits are one of the small inconveniences you have to put up with to enjoy the rest – do not attempt to pit the raw fruit, just skim off as many pits as you can as they rise while cooking.

5 lb damsons
1 quart water
6 lb (12 cups) sugar

Put the damsons in a large bowl and cover with cold water to float off stalks and leaves. Pick off any remaining stalks. Put into a preserving kettle with the water and simmer until quite soft. Add the warmed sugar, bring to a boil and boil hard until the jam sets, skimming off any pits as they rise, with a slotted spoon. Ladle into jars, cover and process. This will make about 10 lb of jam.
Note: a refinement is to crack some of the damson pits and add the kernels for a hint of bitter almonds.

Rose petal jam

This jam is a fitting end for any richly scented roses (preferably red). Spread out the petals on newspaper and dry them in a cool place. You need the same weight of petals as sugar, not less than $\frac{1}{2}$ lb to justify the trouble involved. An old fashioned, sweet, fragrant jam to grace a poet's tea.

$\frac{1}{2}$ lb rose petals
1 cup sugar
$\frac{2}{3}$ cup rosewater (available from drugstores)
1 tablespoon orangeflower water

Put the dried petals into a large bowl and pour a kettleful of boiling water on them. After 1 minute, drain off the water, shake the petals and leave them to dry.

Make a syrup from the sugar and the rosewater. Use just enough rosewater to dissolve the sugar. When the sugar is completely dissolved, stir in the rose petals and the orangeflower water and boil until the jam has reached setting point. Leave to cool for a few minutes, then ladle into jars, cover and process.

Strawberry jam

Unlike the everyday strawberry jam, this uses commercial pectin, the best choice if strawberries are scarce and expensive and you do not want to risk a flop. It looks handsome too because the fruit remains whole.

4 lb strawberries
6 lb (12 cups) sugar
1 small bottle of commercial liquid pectin

Put the fruit in the kettle and bring slowly to a boil. Add the warmed sugar, stir well but gently until the sugar is dissolved, then boil for 6 minutes. Add the pectin, bring again to a full rolling boil and boil for 1 minute, stirring constantly. Skim. Leave for 5 minutes. Ladle into jars, cover and process. This will make about 10 lb of jam.

Raspberry jam

Seeds or no, this is one of the most perfect jams, as fragrant as it is richly flavored and royally crimson.

4 lb raspberries
4 lb (8 cups) sugar

Put the berries and sugar into a heatproof bowl in a 350 degree oven for 10 to 15 minutes. Then turn them into the preserving kettle, bring to a boil and cook stirring slowly, for 3 to 5 minutes or until it reaches setting point. Ladle into jars, cover and process. This will make approximately 6 lb of jam.

Dumpsideary jam

A traditional English country jam, made with mixed orchard fruit. The Irish version, 'Mixty Maxty', omits the spices.

2 lb tart cooking apples
2 lb pears
2 lb plums
2½ cups water
sugar (2 cups to every 1 lb of fruit pulp)
2 lemons
6 cloves
1 small stick cinnamon

Quarter the apples, slicing off the core and any brown parts. Do not peel. Chop the pears somewhat smaller, also removing soft or brown parts. Put them all, with the whole plums, into a large pan, with the measured water and cook gently and slowly until the flesh is all soft. Pour into a strainer or sieve, and rub through into a preserving kettle. Keep some of the plum pits, cracking them with a hammer to extract the kernels. Weigh the pulp and warm the sugar. Add grated lemon rind and squeezed juice to the fruit. Tie the bruised spices in a cheesecloth bag and add. Stir in the warmed sugar and put the kettle over a moderate heat, stirring until the sugar dissolves, then boil rapidly, stirring often, until the jam reaches setting point. Stir in the plum kernels, ladle into jars, cover and process.

Blackcurrant jam

A classic and unfailingly successful jam. One of the most economical too, as the yield in jam is two and a half times the weight in fruit.

4 lb blackcurrants
2 quarts water
6 lb (12 cups) sugar

Pick over the fruit, removing stalks and leaves. Rinse under cold running water, then turn into a pan with the water and simmer gently until the skins are soft, stirring now and then. This may take 45 minutes. Add the warmed sugar and boil rapidly until it sets. Ladle into jars, cover and process.
Note: unripen green grapes can be used instead, but with an equal weight of sugar and fruit.

Gooseberry and elderflower jam

Elderflower heads dipped into cooking gooseberries confer an elusive, elegant muscatel grape flavor. If you cannot manage the elderflowers try a sprig of rosemary, a few blackcurrant leaves or a teaspoon of crushed coriander seed, all aromatic in their different ways. Unadorned, gooseberries still make one of the best jams, of keen flavor, tawny port color and good set.

Note the large proportion of sugar to fruit. Gooseberries are high in acid and pectin so perfect for jam.

4 lb gooseberries
6 lb (12 cups) sugar
5 heads of elderflower

Top and tail the berries, then put them with enough water to cover in a preserving kettle and cook gently for 20 to 40 minutes, until the skins are quite tender. Add the warmed sugar, and elderflower heads, rosemary, blackcurrant leaves or coriander tied in a small piece of cheesecloth. Stir to dissolve the sugar, bring to a boil, then boil hard until the jam sets. Remove the cheesecloth bag, ladle into jars, cover and process. This will make approximately 10 lb of jam.

Dried apricot jam

The best all-the-year-round jam as dried apricots have no season, and they make a rich strongly flavored preserve. The grapefruit supplies acid – 2 lemons can be substituted to help the set.

1 lb (2 cups) dried apricots
3 pints boiling water
2 lb (4 cups) sugar
1 large grapefruit or 2 lemons

Wash the fruit, put them in a large bowl and pour over the boiling water. Leave for 1 to 3 days, until swollen and soft. Pour into a kettle and simmer until tender. Add the sugar and squeezed grapefruit juice, bring to a boil and boil until it sets. Ladle into jars, cover and process. This will make approximately 3 lb of jam.
Note: a few shredded almonds are often added with the sugar.

Rhubarb, squash and ginger jam

Squash makes a dull jam on its own, even with the help of ginger. The addition of rhubarb enlivens the flavor considerably.

3 lb hard, yellow summer squash
3 lb rhubarb
6 lb (12 cups) sugar
¾ cup chopped preserved ginger
3 lemons

Skin the squash, remove seeds if necessary and cut it into small cubes. Cut the rhubarb into short segments, and layer the squash and rhubarb in a large bowl, with layers of sugar between. Leave overnight to draw out the juices. Pour it all into the preserving kettle, and add the chopped ginger, the squeezed lemon juice and the rind tied up in cheesecloth. Bring to a boil rapidly and boil for about 30 minutes, or until the jam reaches setting point. Remove the cheesecloth bag. Ladle into jars, cover and process. This makes about 5 lb of jam.

Hedgerow jam

This is the attractive, omnibus name for jam made from a mixture of wild fruits, the sort you might bring back from a casual country stroll in the fall. Sloes, blueberries and elderberries can be cooked up together to make a wine-dark jam of intense, wild fruit flavor. Strengthen this if you like with a handful of hips and haws, but then the jam must be sieved, because rose hip seeds are like infinitesimal burrs. In any case sieving is advisable, to get rid of the sloe pits and blackberry seeds. You can add a few tart apples, or wild crabapples.

4 lb wild fruit of your choice
sugar (2 cups to every 1 lb of fruit pulp)

Remove the stalks and dry leaves, and chop apples into quarters. Put all the fruit into a kettle with enough water barely to cover and gently simmer until soft – 30 minutes. Put through a sieve. Weigh the pulp, and return to the kettle with 2 cups sugar to every pound of pulp. Stir to dissolve the sugar, bring to a boil and boil hard until the jam reaches setting point. Ladle into jars, cover and process.

Blackberry and apple jam

Blackberry seeds add nothing to a jam (and are torture to denture wearers) so I usually sieve this classic mixture, to make a smooth pulp halfway to a jelly. The proportions of apple to blackberry can be varied depending on your haul – more blackberry than apple gives stronger flavor and needs more sugar to compensate for the lack of pectin in the berries. Include some red (unripe) berries to sharpen the flavor.

4 lb blackberries
2 lb apples
1¼ cups water
sugar (2 cups to every 1 lb of fruit pulp)

Pick over the berries, removing the leaves and stalks. Cut unpeeled apples into quarters, removing any brown parts. Combine the fruit in a pan with the measured water, and simmer very gently until the fruit is soft and the apple peel floats loose. Pour into a strainer or sieve, and rub through into a preserving kettle. Weigh the pulp, and add 2 cups of sugar to each pound. Stir to dissolve. Bring to a boil rapidly and boil hard until it sets. Ladle into jars, cover and process.

Lemon curd

Not really a jam, as much as a lemony custard, but too good and useful to leave out. It makes a delicious pie filling. Children love it on anything in the roll or bread line.

6 tablespoons unsalted butter
1½ cups sugar
2 large lemons
3 eggs

Make the curd in the top of a double boiler. Melt the butter with the sugar and add the lemon juice and grated rind of both lemons. Stir over simmering water until the sugar has dissolved, then add the eggs (lightly beaten) and stir constantly until the curd is thick. Ladle into jars, cover and process.
Note: lemon curd does not keep as long as jams and jellies and should really be eaten within 3 to 4 months. This will make approximately 1¼ lb of curd.

Conserves

Conserves and preserves are elegant jams with sophisticated additions like ginger, nuts, brandy or rum, or exquisite refinements like seeding each gooseberry. The method and equipment are the same as for jams and jellies.

Currant conserve Bar-le-Duc

The gourmet version is made from currants as big as cherries (from specially pruned bushes) seeded with a goose quill. More realistically, we can substitute a medley of red and white currants and leave the seeds in – but take care not to squash or mash the fruit.

2 lb red and white currants
2 lb (4 cups) sugar

Pick over the fruit, removing the stalks and leaves. Do not squash. Put them into a kettle and heat very gradually until the fruit is soft, shaking the kettle instead of stirring. Now sprinkle on the warmed sugar little by little so one batch dissolves before adding the next. Shake the kettle to prevent sticking. Bring just to boiling point, no more, then ladle immediately into jars. Cover and process. This will make approximately 3 lb of conserve.

Raisiné

A Burgundian preserve, and very choice.

4 lb ripe juicy grapes
2 lb dessert pears
3 lb (6 cups) sugar

Put the grapes into a pan and simmer very slowly until the juices flow, mashing from time to time. When soft, pour into a strainer or sieve and press the juice out into a bowl. Meanwhile peel, quarter, core and thinly slice the pears and poach them for 3 or 4 minutes in just enough simmering water to cover. Drain when just tender. Weigh the grape juice and allow 2 cups of sugar to every 2 lb of juice. Put the juice and the sugar into a preserving kettle, bring to a boil and simmer until reduced by about one third. Add the drained pear slices and continue simmering, stirring constantly, until the mixture is thick. Ladle into jars, cover and process. This will make approximately 5 lb of raisiné.

Plum, orange and walnut preserve

An elegant preserve, bobbing with plums and nuts, to be kept for special occasions.

2 oranges
3 lb plums
2 lb (4 cups) sugar
1 cup blanched, skinned and chopped walnuts

Wash the unpeeled oranges, and mince them finely, saving the juice. Pit the plums and tie the pits in a cheesecloth bag. Put the plums, the minced oranges, the juice and the sugar into a kettle and heat slowly to boiling point, stirring once or twice to make sure the sugar dissolves. Simmer over a gentle heat for 1 hour, or until the fruit and peel are soft. Add the walnuts and simmer for another 30 to 40 minutes. Ladle into jars, cover and process. This will make approximately 3 lb of preserve.

Apples in wine and brandy

If you can substitute some quinces – three or four – for apples, the flavor will be sumptuous. This is the quintessence of a conserve.

6 lemons
2½ cups white wine
4 lb (8 cups) sugar
4 lb apples
2 tablespoons brandy

Finely peel the lemons and marinate the rind in the wine plus an equal quantity of boiling water, for 30 minutes. Put this mixture plus the lemon juice and sugar into a kettle and boil hard for about 8 minutes, until slightly syrupy. Strain the syrup and return to the kettle. Drop in the peeled, cored and thinly sliced apples and simmer for 40 minutes or until the apples are tender and the syrup thick. Add the brandy, then ladle into jars, cover and process. Eat this with cream. It will make approximately 6 lb of conserve.

Jelly making

Jellies are the most pleasing and insouciant of all preserves to make. The fruit needs little or no preparation, the basic formula is easy to keep in your head, and they always seem to turn out right, setting well and keeping perfectly. They are *beautiful* to look at, as vividly translucent as stained glass: amber, rose gold, cornelian, ruby, purple. Wild fruits and berries, or the often disregarded fruit of decorative garden shrubs and trees – japonica, berberis, crabapple – make some of the best jellies, with a distinctive and appealing sharpness and intensity of flavor, and a subtle variation in color which gives the cook an almost painterly satisfaction to contemplate. Jelly making *feels* casual, no need to pick until your arms ache because a few handfuls of fruit or berries, eked out perhaps with some windfall apples, will make many tiny jars of jelly to eat with meat or game, or stuff into crêpes, or spread on toasted English muffins for tea.

Ingredients

Once you have mastered the absurdly simple basic procedure, you can make jelly from most things, starting with the free, wild offerings of woods, fields and hedgerows – blackberries, sloes, elderberries, rowan berries, hips and haws, blueberries, cranberries – and moving on to the domesticated flavors of your own garden – green grapes, unripe figs and guavas, currants white, black and red. Fruit sweet enough to enjoy without sugar makes insipid jelly, thus crabapples are better than apples, redcurrants than raspberries, damsons than plums. Sugar is added to strained juice either measure for measure or (marginally sweeter) at the rate of 2 cups sugar to $2\frac{1}{2}$ cups juice. Both jell equally well, and are blessedly simple to remember. Seal with lids or hot melted paraffin.

Method

Jelly making can be informal, or full dress, depending on your mood and the rarity of the ingredient. For an everyday sort of jelly, do not bother with strigging (taking off stalks), or lengthy straining through a jellybag – simmer the fruit as it comes then pour it into a strainer or sieve, and press the last drop through with a wooden spoon. Do not rub – that is going too far. For immaculate jelly turn to the jellybag, bought, homemade or improvised with a clean cotton square tied securely by all four corners to the four legs of an upended stool or chair so the juice drips into the pan beneath. The bag, or square, should first be scalded by pouring over boiling water. Wring out, then use – the dampness helps the juice pass through. Jars should be wide mouthed (the traditional jelly jar looks most elegant), not too big, and warmed before filling. Have them standing by – some jellies jell in a wink. Should the reverse occur – which it rarely does – simply tip it all back into the pan and boil for a few minutes longer.

To test when your jelly is ready to set, take the temperature of the boiling brew from the center of the pan with a jam thermometer, when the reading reaches 221 degrees you are there. Alternatively try the saucer test. Spoon a few drops on to a saucer, and if they wrinkle when pushed with a finger, the jelly is done. Ladle into jars and cover.

Making basic apple jelly with herbs

1. Take a mixed bag of apples – cookers, eaters, crabapples, windfalls – for the best flavored jelly. Quarter 4 lb of fruit, removing any bruised, discolored or brown parts, and chop roughly (no need to peel and core). Place in a preserving kettle with a handful of fresh herbs tied in a bunch, either mint or tarragon, or a large sprig of rosemary or thyme. Pour over enough water barely to cover, and simmer slowly until the fruit is soft.

2. Remove the herbs and strain the remaining fruit and juice into a bowl through a scalded sieve or jellybag.

3. The amount of sugar to be added is determined by the quantity of the juice. The proportions are either 2 cups sugar to 2 cups (1 pint) juice, or for a slightly sweeter jelly, add 2 cups sugar to each $2\frac{1}{2}$ cups (1 pint) of juice. Return the extracted juice and sugar to the preserving kettle and bring to a boil, stirring with a wooden spoon to dissolve the sugar.

4. Have warmed jelly glasses or jars ready to be filled (small jars are best, as one can be finished at one meal), standing on a baking sheet. Fill the jelly glasses with a jug and cover with the jelly glass lids, or melted hot paraffin. Cover the tops with plastic wrap, or attractive gingham squares secured with rubber bands, if you like. Serve rosemary and thyme jellies with pork or beef, mint with lamb, and tarragon jelly with roast chicken or chops.

Jellies

The fruit for jelly – unlike jam – is cooked until very soft then strained through a jellybag, or cheesecloth. The juice is then measured and cooked with the required amount of sugar as stated in the recipes.

Crabapple jelly

Cornelian colored, sharp and delicious. If you ask around you may find a neighbor who has a crabapple tree, with fruit to spare, as they crop prolifically.

4 lb crab apples
1 quart water
sugar

Wash and quarter the apples without peeling or coring. Put into a kettle with the water and cook gently until quite soft, which takes 1 hour or so. Check to see that the water does not boil away. Strain the apples, either through a jellybag or strainer or sieve – the jellybag method takes several hours, or overnight. Measure the juice and return to the kettle. Add 2 cups of sugar to every pint of juice, bring to a boil and boil briskly for about 10 minutes, or until it reaches setting point. Ladle into jars and cover.

Lemon and honey jelly

An excellent and unusual jelly, with a sweet flavor as refreshing to the palate as a fine marmalade. It is delicious on hot toast, or with biscuits, or as a filling in a layer cake. It needs commercial pectin to assist setting. Or you could substitute your own apple jelly base.

¾ cup lemon juice
1 tablespoon grated lemon rind
1 lb (1⅓ cups) honey
½ bottle (3 oz) commercial liquid pectin

Strain the lemon juice to remove any pulp. Stir the juice with the grated lemon rind and honey in a kettle over a moderate heat until fluid and well mixed, then bring to a boil. When bubbling hard, add the commercial pectin and boil for 1 minute, stirring constantly. Remove from the heat and stir for 3 minutes longer, then pour into clean, hot jelly glasses and cover. Makes about 2 pints jelly, or 4 glasses.

Rowan jelly

Rowans are the brave scarlet berries of the mountain ash, so decorative it is a surprise to find they are edible. As the berries are dryish, it is best to add apples for bulk. Rowan jelly has an interesting smoky flavor, and is traditionally served with venison in Scotland.

6 lb rowan berries
3 lb sharp apples
sugar

Pull the stalks off the berries. Put the berries with the quartered apples (do not peel or core these) in a kettle, add enough water just to cover and simmer gently until quite soft – about 1 hour. Tip into a scalded jellybag, and leave to drip overnight. Measure the juice and add 2 cups of sugar to each 2½ cups of juice. Put them both in the kettle, stir to dissolve the sugar, bring to a boil and boil hard until it reaches setting point – this jelly does not set hard so use the drop on a saucer test alongside the thermometer reading, to doublecheck. Ladle into jars and cover.

Cranberry jelly

Cranberries have always been a traditional accompaniment to the Thanksgiving turkey, and they make an agreeably tart jelly. Adding apples will help the set.

3 lb cooking apples
2 lb cranberries
sugar

Put the roughly chopped apples (do not peel or core) and the cranberries into a kettle with enough water just to cover them. Simmer until soft. Pour into a jellybag and leave to drip through overnight. Measure the juice, and return to the kettle with 2 cups of sugar to every 2½ cups of liquid. Bring to a boil and boil hard until setting point is reached. Ladle into jars and cover.

Hips and haws jelly

A handsome red jelly of strange, striking flavor: a little smoky, astringent and reminiscent of fall hedgerows after rain. Use the berries in equal proportions.

1 lb hips and haws
sugar
juice of 1 lemon

Rinse the berries under running cold water and remove bits of stalk and leaves. Put into a kettle with water just to cover. Simmer until soft and strain through a jellybag overnight. Weigh the juice and return to the kettle with 2 cups sugar to each pound, plus the juice of the squeezed lemon. Stir, bring to a boil, and boil to setting point. Ladle into jars and cover.

Blackberry jelly

This tastes of the fall to me, of damp earth, mist and woodsmoke. Add some red, unripe berries to help the set.

4 lb blackberries
1 pint water
sugar
2 lemons

Put the blackberries with the water in a kettle and simmer for 30 minutes, or until quite soft. Pour into a strainer or sieve and press to extract all the juice. Measure the juice, and add 2 cups of sugar to each $2\frac{1}{2}$ cups of juice. Put the juice, the sugar and the squeezed lemon juice into the kettle, bring to a boil and boil until it will set. Ladle into jars and cover.
Note: if the blackberries are late ones, add a few hard cooking apples to help the jelly set firm.

Redcurrant jelly

A rich, red, finely flavored accompaniment to venison, roast lamb and saddle of hare. This is the most extravagant way of making it, as it uses no water, but the gain in flavor makes it worthwhile.

6 lb redcurrants
sugar

Put the fruit into the kettle and heat slowly, squashing with a wooden spoon to help the juice flow. Continue simmering and squashing for about 45 minutes, until the fruit is quite pulped. Turn into a jellybag and leave to drip for several hours. Measure the extract and return to the preserving kettle. To every pint add 2 cups of warmed sugar, stir to dissolve, then bring back to a boil and boil hard for 5 minutes. Have warmed jars standing by, because this jelly sets almost at once. Ladle immediately into jars and cover.

Guava jelly

Reputed to be the most distinguished jelly of all for serving with cold meat, this fruit has large seeds so it takes a long time to drip through the cheesecloth.

4 lb green guavas
sugar

Wash the fruit, remove the stems and slice thinly. Place them in a kettle with enough water just to cover, and simmer until quite soft. Leave overnight in a jellybag to drip through. Measure the juice and return to the kettle with 2 cups of sugar to each pint of juice. Bring to a boil, and boil hard until the mixture sets. Ladle into jars and cover. This will make about 5 lb of jelly.

Japonica jelly

Many people do not realize that the small apple-like fruit of the japonica can be used to make an attractive, tawny jelly.

2 lb japonica fruit
1 lemon
sugar

Wash the japonica apples, remove stalks and cut into quarters. Finely peel the yellow lemon rind. Put the rind and the apples into a kettle, add enough water just to cover the fruit and simmer until soft. Strain the pulp – using a jellybag, strainer or sieve – then measure the juice. Use 2 cups of sugar to every pint of juice. Put the juice, the sugar and the lemon juice into the kettle and bring to a boil. Boil fast for about 6 minutes, or until it will set. Ladle into jars and cover.

Fruit butters and cheeses

Fruit cheeses and butters are simple, sugared fruit purées or jams with all the moisture cooked out of them. The cheeses, which use more sugar, are cooked until stiff enough to hold the impression of a spoon, and set firm when cooled. Butters are cooked until they can 'hold a trail' and although thick, soft and dryish they spread easily.

Traditionally in England, fruit cheeses appeared at Christmas, flanking the Stilton and crusted port. On one side the damson cheese, wickedly black, glossy and unadorned (though people tipped a little port over their slice sometimes), on the other, the russet quince or apple cheese, bristling with slivered almonds and flounced with whipped cream. Such aristocratic preserves were never *spread*, but cut into small fingers or cubes to nibble at along with the nuts, the ripe Stilton and the port or Madeira. Fruit butters, as the name suggests, are more utilitarian, designed to be spread on toast or muffins or used to fill tarts and crêpes.

Cheeses and butters must be cooked slowly otherwise they have a tendency to burn. Given a really good quality thick bottomed pan, you can produce a successful cheese or butter provided you simmer the sieved fruit long and slowly until almost dry *before* adding the sugar, as fruit alone is less likely to burn, and stir constantly *after* adding the sugar, as this helps drive out the remaining moisture rapidly, as well as preventing the mixture sticking to the pan. Asbestos mats would be useful under the pan to diffuse the heat.

Cooking either of these delicacies is a process not to be hurried, and one which needs watching over, but the results are distinguished and delicious.

Finishing, covering and storing cheeses and butters

Do *not* store fruit cheese in a canning jar, or you will lose the pleasure of turning it out onto a plate. Any fairly small, shallow container will do, such as a little pie pan or casserole, cereal bowls and even old teacups. Wash the container well, dry and rub over with a little almond oil or glycerine to prevent the cheese sticking. Fill with cheese and press wax paper cut to fit down onto the hot cheese, waxed side down. The wax melts on contact with the hot preserve to make an airtight seal. To make certain, you can invert the container to force out air. Then cover the pot or jelly jar with ordinary plastic wrap, and tie down with string. Store in a cool dry place. Keep for 3 months before eating, as the flavor improves with keeping. Fruit butter does not keep as well as cheese, as it contains less sugar and more moisture, so start eating it fairly promptly. It can be stored in ordinary canning jars, as it is soft enough to spoon out easily. Cover with wax paper to seal, then with plastic wrap tied down with string as for fruit cheeses.

Melted paraffin, poured over while the preserve is very hot, makes the most perfect airtight seal, but has the disadvantage that you cannot see how the preserve looks until you break the seal.

For one reason or another – curiosity, pleasure in the quaint names, a feeling for tradition – every imaginative cook I know is intrigued by any mention of fruit cheese and butter.

Comfits and sweetmeats, or what we now think of as fruit cheeses and butters, seem to have been the earliest sort of jam. Dating from medieval times, they enjoyed success in the Royal courts and in the countrywoman's kitchen.

Apple butter

This recipe converts a pile of windfalls into an excellent, russet colored, rich tasting spread, which is popular with children. The yield is less than with jams, but being more condensed a little goes a lot further. Cider is not essential, but improves the taste. Use crabapples instead of some of the apples if you can to produce a stronger flavor.

4 lb apples
2¼ cups hard cider
5 cloves
1 inch cinnamon stick
sugar
1 lemon

Quarter the apples, remove the stalks and any brown parts but do not peel or core. Put them into a kettle, pour over the cider, then enough water just to cover, add spices and simmer until the apples are soft and mushy. Sieve and weigh the pulp. Return to the kettle and continue simmering until thick and dryish before adding the warmed sugar – 1½ cups of sugar to each pound of pulp. Remove from the heat while stirring in the sugar. When the sugar has dissolved, add the squeezed lemon juice and grated rind, return to the heat and cook slowly, stirring all the time, until drawing a spoon across the surface leaves a trail. Spoon into wide mouthed jars. Press down wax paper or plastic wrap onto the butter surface, and reverse onto plates to force out air. When cool, cover with plastic wrap, tie down and store.

Sweet black butter

Make this from any surplus soft fruits in season – strawberries, redcurrants, raspberries, gooseberries, black currants – mixed together in varying proportions. For 'blackness', the blackcurrants should predominate slightly. This is rich and sticky. As the fruit is so sweet, this recipe uses less sugar.

2 lb mixed soft fruit
2 cups sugar

Put the soft fruit into a pan, without water, and heat gently until the juices flow, mashing now and then with a wooden spoon. Simmer until soft, sieve and return with the sugar to the pan. Cook, stirring, until the butter is thick enough to leave a trail. Pot as usual.

Damson cheese

4 lb damsons
1¼ cups water
sugar

Rinse the damsons under cold running water. Put them in the kettle with the water and simmer gently until quite soft, mashing occasionally. Sieve. Weigh the pulp, and measure out 1½ cups of sugar to every pound of pulp. Return the pulp to the kettle (do not put the sugar in yet) and cook very gently until thick, with no visible liquid. Pour in the warmed sugar, stirring hard to dissolve it, then turn up the heat just a little and go on cooking and stirring until pressing the spoon down on top of the mixture leaves a mark. This gives a cheese firm enough to turn out of a mold and slice. For a very firm, almost candied consistency, go on cooking until a spoon drawn across the kettle parts the mixture and the bottom shows. Turn into oiled molds and seal.

Cranberry cheese

2 lb cranberries
1 quart water
2 lb (4 cups) sugar

Pick over the cranberries, rinse them under running water then simmer them in the water until quite soft. Cook as for damson cheese, but stop short at the spoon stage. Pot and seal.

Marmalade making

For an explanation of why Scotland's renowned orange preserve should have borrowed a foreign name for a completely different fruit, we must visit the town of Dundee in the last years of the 19th century where a certain John Keiller, grocer, was wondering whether he had not acted a bit rashly in buying up a shipload of Seville oranges very cheaply. Fortunately, it occurred to his wife that by cooking them according to her mother's recipe for quince 'marmalet' (from the Portuguese 'marmelo' or quince), the best part of the cargo might be preserved. She experimented. The results were so gratifying that news of Mrs Keiller's orange preserve or marmalet soon spread. Thus the Keillers made their name and fortune, Seville oranges found their noblest use and marmalade became permanently associated with Scotland and citrus fruit – an unlikely partnership on the face of it.

Marmalade is a jam or preserve made from citrus fruit: lime, lemon, grapefruit, sweet and Seville oranges. In the traditional marmalade no particle of the fruit is wasted – the juice flavors the syrup or jelly, pith and seeds contribute pectin and their own bitter tang, while the rind, sliced thick or fine according to taste, lends the preserve its distinctive taste, texture and appearance.

Equipment
The equipment is the same as for jam, except that a really sharp knife is essential for slicing the rind, and an efficient vegetable peeler saves time in thinly paring off the outer rind. Some electric mixers or processors have a slicing and shredding attachment which can be used for this most arduous part of the process, but they do not make such a neat job of it as a sharp knife and a pair of hands. A very large bowl is needed for soaking the rind. A pressure cooker cuts down the time spent on preliminary softening of the rind from hours to minutes. Be sure to provide yourself with plenty of clean, hot canning jars and lids. Quantities of marmalade can result from what looks like a handful of fruit.

Method
The first step in marmalade making is to scrub the fruit well, to remove dirt and fungicides. Use a small stiff brush and plain warm water. There are various ways of preparing the fruit. Sometimes the fruit is simmered whole, before slicing; sometimes the outer rind is pared off finely and cooked separately before being added to the fruit; and sometimes the fruit is cut in half and squeezed, then the rind sliced, and the whole lot cooked together. The reasons for this have to do with varying traditions, cooks' caprices, and the coarseness and pithiness of the orange skins. Marmalade making is basically no more complicated than jam making, except that as the rind is so very thick and hard it needs long preliminary softening (by soaking overnight, long cooking, or a short spell in a pressure cooker) before the sugar is added. As with jam the golden rule is slow gentle cooking *before*, fast boiling *after*, adding sugar.

Marmalades, like jams, should be given a 10 minute process in a boiling-water bath as insurance against spoilage (see page 200). Leave $\frac{1}{2}$ inch headroom when filling jars.

Making pressure-cooked marmalade

1. Take 2 lb Seville oranges and 1 lemon and scrub the skins with a soft brush in water to remove any dirt and fungicides. Pare off the rind thinly with a sharp knife and slice into thin strips.

2. Peel off the pith and put by.

3. Place all the fruit on a large plate and cut up roughly, trying to keep all the juice and saving the seeds. Fill a small cheesecloth bag with the seeds and the pith, and tie up securely. The chopped fruit, juice, sliced rind, seeds and pith are now ready to be cooked under pressure. Bring to 10 lb pressure and cook for 10 minutes, after which time the hard rind should be soft enough to crush in your fingers – if not, cook a little longer as once rind meets sugar no further softening takes place.

4. Leave to cool at room temperature and remove the cheesecloth bag. (Use the pressure cooker if more convenient for the next stage of cooking, but *leave the lid off*.) Add 4 lb (8 cups) sugar and 1 quart of water and heat, stirring to dissolve the sugar. Bring the marmalade to a boil and boil fast until it reaches setting point.

5. Remove the kettle from the heat and let the marmalade stand for 15 minutes to thicken slightly. Stir to distribute the rind, and pour into warmed jars, cover and process.

Marmalades

Homemade marmalade is cheaper and better than any other. Now, with the aid of modern gadgets such as pressure cookers and shredding machines, the complete process has become uncomplicated and pleasurable.

Seville marmalade

This is the whole fruit method – easiest to grasp and the least tiring to prepare, as the cooked rind is soft.

2 lb Seville oranges
2 quarts water
juice of 1 large lemon
4 lb (8 cups) sugar

Wash the oranges, put them into a kettle with the water and simmer for about 2 hours, until the rind can be easily pierced with a fork. Take the oranges out, and when they are cool enough to handle cut them up into thick or fine shreds as you prefer, reserving all the seeds. Put the fruit aside in a preserving kettle. Tie the seeds in a cheesecloth bag, return this to the cooking liquid in the kettle, add the lemon juice and boil for 5 minutes. Strain the liquid, add it to the sliced fruit and boil until the contents are reduced one third – draw a line on the outside of the kettle to guide you – and the temperature reaches 221 degrees. Add the sugar, stir to dissolve, then bring to a boil and boil fast until setting point is reached. Ladle into jars, cover and process.

Lime marmalade

Made with fresh limes, this is a special and delicious marmalade. It is a particularly good recipe for the tropics.

12 limes
1½ quarts water
3 lb (6 cups) sugar

Peel the fruit, halve and squeeze out the juice. Slice the rind thinly. Chop the fruit pulp and tie in a cheesecloth bag with the seeds. Put the cheesecloth bag, rind, juice and water into a kettle and simmer for 1 hour. Remove the cheesecloth bag, squeezing hard. Stir in the sugar, bring to a boil and boil hard for 10 minutes. Ladle into jars, cover and process.

Superior Scotch marmalade

Here is a thoroughly old-fashioned recipe, slow and painstaking in the making – in marked contrast to the corner-cutting recipe on page 219 – but giving a preserve of outstanding flavor.

4 lb Seville oranges
5 lb (10 cups) sugar
3 lemons

Wash the oranges, halve and squeeze out the juice into a bowl, reserving the seeds. Scrape off any pulp clinging to the skins, and add this to the juice. Boil the skins in water to cover. After 30 minutes, change the water – this makes the preserve less bitter – and boil again in water to cover until the skins are tender enough to pierce with a matchstick. When quite cool, scrape any white thready bits off the skins and slice the skins thinly. Put the juice, pulp, sliced rind and cheesecloth bag with the seeds into a kettle. Heat slowly, adding warmed sugar after a few minutes. Stir to dissolve the sugar and bring to a boil. After it has boiled for 10 minutes add the squeezed, strained juice and finely grated rind of the lemons. Boil for a further 20 minutes or until the marmalade has reached setting point. This can be judged either with a jam thermometer (the setting point is 221 degrees) or by doing the saucer test. Cool for 15 minutes, then ladle into jars, cover and process. Yield about 10 jars.

Grapefruit and lemon marmalade

Sharp but refreshing.

3 grapefruit
4 lemons
2 quarts water
3 lb (6 cups) sugar

The method is precisely as for the three fruit marmalade. For a gingery snap, add about 1 cup of finely chopped crystallized ginger just after adding the sugar.

Grinder marmalade

The most objectionable part of marmalade making for most people is cutting up the rind. Mincing it (using either the old-fashioned hand one, or an electric grinder) saves time and an aching wrist though the resulting marmalade will not be crystal clear.

8 Seville oranges
2 lemons
1 gallon water
6 lb (12 cups) sugar

Wash and halve the fruit, then squeeze the juice into a large bowl. Collect the seeds and tie in a cheesecloth bag. Mince all the rinds, collecting up any juice, and add to the bowl with the water. Leave to soak overnight. Next day put the mixture into a kettle with the bag of seeds and gently simmer for about 2 hours or until the rind is quite soft and the liquid well reduced. Remove the seeds, add the warmed sugar, stir to dissolve the sugar, then bring to a boil fast and cook for about 25 minutes or until setting point is reached. Cool for 10 minutes, then ladle into jars, cover and process. Yield 10 jars.

Tangerine and lemon marmalade

A clean, sharp marmalade, less bitter than Seville, and with the pleasant sweet scent of tangerines.

2 lb tangerines
3 lemons
2 quarts water
3 lb (6 cups) sugar

Peel both fruit, removing white pith and strings. Slice the rind thinly and put it into a cheesecloth bag. Chop all the fruit roughly, put it into a kettle with the water and cheesecloth bags and simmer gently for 45 minutes. Remove the rind and reserve it and continue cooking for a further hour. Tip the cooked fruit pulp into a jellybag and leave to drip overnight. Next day put the strained juice and warmed sugar into the kettle and bring to a boil, stirring to dissolve the sugar. Empty the cheesecloth bag and add the reserved rind. Boil fast to setting point. Leave to cool for 15 minutes. Ladle into jars, cover and process.

Three fruit marmalade

The best all-year-round mixture.

2 grapefruit
2 sweet oranges
4 lemons
3 quarts water
6 lb (12 cups) sugar

Peel all the fruit quite finely, then cut them in half and extract the seeds. Put these, with the thick pith from the grapefruit and the oranges (if there is any) into a cheesecloth bag. Chop the fruit roughly on a plate. Cut all the rind finely into shreds. Put everything into a preserving kettle with the water and simmer for $1\frac{1}{2}$ hours, or until soft – you should be able to crush the rind in your fingers. Remove the cheesecloth bag, squeezing out any liquid. Stir in the sugar, bring to a boil, and boil fast until setting point is reached. Ladle into jars, cover and process.
Note : Vary this recipe by including a spoonful of coriander seeds in the cheesecloth bag.

Pineapple and lime marmalade

Here's a true exotic for warm climates, or as a special treat elsewhere.

1 large pineapple, ripe but sound
4 lb (8 cups) sugar
4 limes or lemons
2½ pints water

Peel and thinly slice the pineapple. Cut out the core and reserve. Chop the flesh into small pieces. Put in a bowl with half the sugar sprinkled over and leave overnight to extract the juice. Wash the limes or lemons, then slice them thinly, putting the seeds with the bits of pineapple core into a piece of cheesecloth. Put the lime, or lemon, slices and water into a kettle, with the cheesecloth bag, and simmer until the rind is soft. Squeeze the seed bag and remove, add the pineapple and the remaining sugar, stir over a low heat until the sugar is dissolved, then boil fast until setting point is reached. Skim, ladle into jars, cover and process. Yield about 6 jars.
Note : If you use the pressure cooker method for any marmalade, cook the fruit in quarters and when softened, slice them up in an egg slicer.

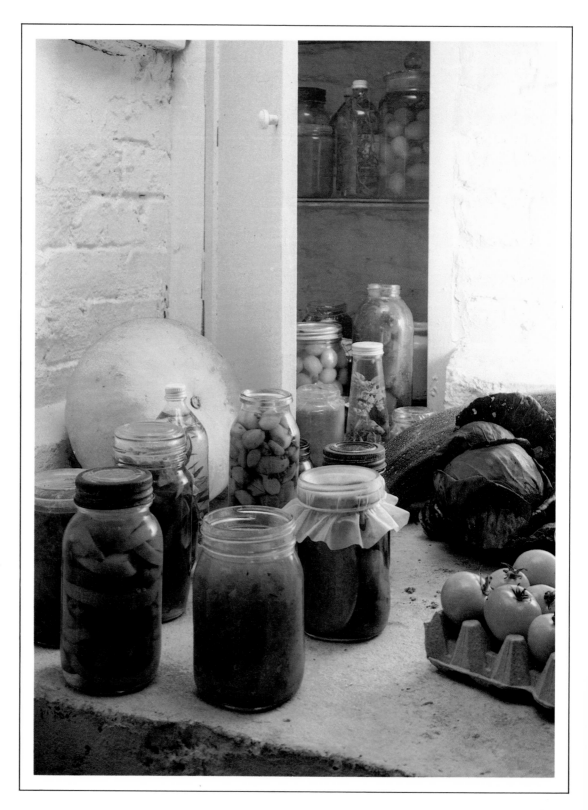

Pickles
& Chutneys

'I chose my wife as she did her wedding gown,
not for a fine glossy surface, but such qualities as would wear well.
She could read any English book without much spelling:
but for pickling, preserving and cookery, none could excel her.'

The Vicar of Wakefield   Oliver Goldsmith   1858

The first thing to be said about pickles and chutneys is that they are both endearingly *easy* to make. Jam making, even for the experienced, has its tensions and pitfalls, but making chutneys and pickles is a relaxing and rewarding business, nicely attuned to the mellow, winding-down atmosphere of the fall. The methods are simple, the materials are (or should be) cheap, and the results reliably excellent. A shelf packed with interesting, varied, homemade 'condiments' is immensely useful. It is remarkable what spiced pickled peaches will do for canned ham, and the difference a seasoned chutney (all chutneys improve with age) makes to sausages and meat balls, not to mention the cheering effect a plate of crisp pickles has on cheese and bread.

Pickles and chutneys both make use of vinegar and spices to flavor and preserve. But the pickle is international in character, with an honored place in the cooking of almost every country, whereas all chutneys are descended from a purely national invention, the Indian *chatni*. This is a spiced relish served alongside the bland *dal* or lentil dishes. Indians like their *chatni* both cooked and uncooked, and usually serve a bowl of each. For storage, however, the cooked chutney, a medley of ingredients simmered until reduced to a sort of savory jam, is more suitable.

One of the great delights of chutneys and pickles is their good tempered adaptability. Quantities are not really critical in chutney making, so there is no need to abandon the idea because you have not quite as much sugar as the recipe asks for, or only sugar of a different color. One dried fruit does as well as another and an extra handful will make up for any missing sugar. Equally with spices; it will not ruin a chutney to use, say, cloves and cinnamon instead of coriander seeds, or ground mustard instead of mustard seed, or preserved ginger instead of fresh. It will just be a slightly different – maybe better – chutney. Use the recipes as a guide to relative proportions and quantities of ingredients, by all means, but do not feel that you are imprisoned by them.

Foreground, left, sweet pepper pickle beside a jar of tomato chutney and, center, dill pickle sealed with oilskin. Jars of pickled onions cluster beside bottles of clear vinegar flavored with herb cuttings of tarragon and marjoram and a small jar of amber spiced pickled fruit.

Making pickles and chutneys

Equipment

The important point to be noted here is that chutneys and pickles contain a fair amount of vinegar and vinegar contains acetic acid which instantly attacks metals such as brass, copper and iron, and produces a taste as bitter as wormwood. It will also corrode any metal it is in contact with in time. So use aluminum or unchipped enamel pans for cooking chutneys and for boiling spiced vinegar for pickles. Use a nylon or hair strainer or sieve rather than a wire one for straining. Glass containers are safest for anything containing vinegar, and regular glass canning jars should be used. The cover must be airtight because vinegar evaporates in time and this shrinks and dries out your precious chutney and pickles. Those attractive glass jars with spring clip lids are unsuitable as they are not strong enough to withstand heat processing, also corrosion from the wire spring would discolor the pickles most unpleasantly. Heat processing for 10 minutes (for pint jars) in a boiling water bath (see page 200) is necessary to ensure sterilization and a good seal.

Other standard items of equipment which may be needed are a large bowl, household scales, ladle, sharp knife and chopping board. Some chutney recipes call for ingredients to be minced, or finely chopped – obviously a food grinder, operated by hand or electricity, will save time and effort here.

Pickle ingredients

The choice internationally is wide. But probably the most appealing pickles to Western palates are either crisp, onions, shallots, red cabbage, small pickling cucumbers, or sweet, beets, plums, peaches. Pickled walnuts are excellent if you can get hold of green walnuts, but other green nuts – hazel, cob, filbert – can be used instead. Some celebrated pickles – the Italian Mostarda di Cremona, Piccalilli – use a mixture of fruits or vegetables, highly seasoned. Sweet peppers, turnips and garlic can all be pickled and are both good and unusual. Ingredients for pickles should be as fresh and crisp as possible, and firm and sound.

Chutney ingredients

Chutneys are even more obliging than pickles in respect of ingredients as these need not be perfect, super fresh, or intrinisically tasty. Those huge overgrown zucchini, squash and pumpkins which are a problem to keep up with at the height of the growing season, make excellent chutney, with a luscious texture. Windfall apples, rhubarb past its prime and green tomatoes are obvious candidates too. Green gooseberries, under-ripe plums, green mangoes, hard peaches and apricots are all excellent if you have enough to spare. Use good white distilled vinegar for everyday chutney, a finer grade (wine or cider) for more delicate fruit chutneys. White or brown sugar are equally suitable, brown gives a deeper color and slight caramel taste. More important to a good chutney is to use whole, that is unground, spices, bought fresh for each pickling season. The difference in pungency between these and the relatively costly powdered spices put up commercially in pretty little jars is quite astonishing.

Making pickles and chutneys

Pickles, broadly speaking, are edibles of one sort or another stored in a liquid which preserves and flavors: vinegar, brine, oil. They preserve by excluding air and by destroying bacteria. Sugar is another preservative and, when added to pickling vinegar, acts as a further safeguard besides greatly improving the flavor.

There are various ways of pickling fruit and vegetables. The simplest, and one of the most popular methods, is to pack the jars with selected fruit or vegetables, and pour over enough spiced, sweetened vinegar to cover them. For crisp, sharp pickles – onions, cabbage, cucumbers – the vinegar may be poured over cold, for others which need softening, it is poured over boiling hot. In some cases this is repeated a few times over a period of days, draining off the vinegar, re-boiling and pouring over again. This both softens the pickle, and concentrates all the flavors. Alternatively, the pickle ingredient itself may be simmered until tender in water before going into the vinegar. This is essential with whole baby beets, for instance, some other vegetables, and with hard fruit like crabapples.

Chutney-making is simpler still: usually all the ingredients are very gently simmered together in a pan for several hours. The brew is stirred occasionally – *more* often when the chutney begins to thicken – and then it is ladled into jars when thick like jam.

Brining or salting before pickling

Salt has a way of drawing out moisture which is why sliced eggplants are salted as a matter of course before cooking. Salting vegetables before pickling them has the same effect, drawing out the moisture which would otherwise dilute the pickle and lessen its preservative properties. The salt can be applied straight on top of the vegetables – dry salting – or the vegetables can be steeped in a saline solution – wet salting. In dry salting the cleaned, peeled or otherwise prepared vegetables are packed in layers in a large bowl with salt sprinkled in between – approximately 3 tablespoons of salt to each pound of vegetables. The vegetables are then covered and left for between 12 to 24 hours as a rule. Now noticeably softer and slightly shrunken, the vegetables are rinsed under running water and dried before pickling. For wet salting, mix up a saline solution, using $\frac{3}{4}$ cup of salt to 2 quarts of water – you will need about $2\frac{1}{2}$ cups of salt solution to each pound of vegetables. Immerse the prepared vegetables, cover them with a weighted plate and leave for the stated time. Some traditional recipes from Central Europe and the Middle East leave the ingredients in brine long enough to allow natural fermentation to start, which not only drives out unwanted bacteria but creates a distinct, pleasant change in taste and texture of the vegetables concerned, making them mellow and rich.

It is important to keep the vegetables completely immersed throughout this lengthy brining, and to check now and then to make sure the solution has not been diluted too much by the moisture extracted from the vegetables. Before going into pickle, wet salted vegetables should also be well rinsed and dried.

Note: use pickling, dairy or kosher salt without additives; do not use table salt.

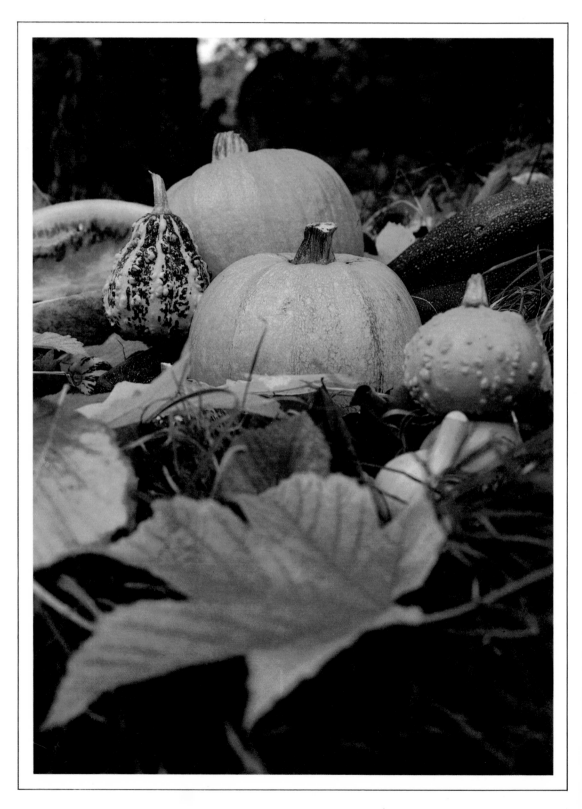

Vinegar

White distilled vinegar, of 4 to 6 percent acidity, is the cheapest available, and is fine for the more robust type of pickle such as eggs, onions, beets and cabbage, especially if you add enough sugar to soften the flavor. Keep the more expensive vinegars – cider and wine vinegar – for fancier efforts, where you are aiming for a subtler sweet-sour flavor, pickled fruits, for instance. Vinegar is usually spiced as well as sweetened, to add interest to pickles. Pickling spices are sold ready mixed, but it is usually cheaper and more interesting to mix up your own. For a change use just one spice instead of a mixture – coriander has a pungent, orangey taste which is delicious with cabbage; cloves and peppercorns are excellent with onions, a few cardamom pods complement pickled peaches. If you are planning to pickle on a lavish scale, save time by making up 1 gallon of spiced vinegar and leaving the spices to infuse for several weeks before use. A good basic spice mixture for 1 gallon of vinegar would be: $\frac{1}{4}$ cup each of allspice, cloves, black peppercorns, coriander, mustard seed and fresh ginger root or ground ginger, 3 dried chili peppers, 6 to 10 cloves garlic, 1 cup sugar. To maximize the flavor, bruise the spices lightly (tie them up in a cloth and hit them with a rolling pin), bring to boiling point in vinegar, then cool and store until needed. For people who only want to make a few jars at a time, it is more fun to mix up different spices to suit each batch of pickles, cooking them with the vinegar as above. You can leave them in or take them out before pickling, depending on how aromatic you want the pickle to finish up. I leave them in myself, but some people prefer their pickles free from seeds, pods or grains. The same applies to garlic cloves, ginger and chili peppers, all of which contribute a distinctive note to a harmonious pickle.

Warning note

The American FDA (Food and Drug Administration) has recommended that all pickles be heat processed in a boiling water bath (see Canned Fruit, page 200) before storage, to triple check against spoilage, infection or botulism. After processing check the seal carefully. On modern mason jars, the metal lids of the 2-piece screwband closure will have snapped down, pulled in by the vacuum that indicates a good seal. Press any lid that is not concave: if it springs back the seal has gone. Bailed jars and old-style masons should be tilted so the food pressed against the closure: bubbles appearing at the lids indicate a bad seal. Remove the screwband or release the bail from any jars you have doubts about and lift the jar by its sealed-on lid. The seals should remain intact.

If within 24 hours after processing you find the seals to be imperfect, boil up the pickles again and re-pack in sterilized canning jars and process again in a boiling water bath.

Melon, squashes, zucchini and pumpkin ripe for pickling and chutney making. Golden pumpkins and green squashes are simmered slowly with spices into a rich, mild chutney; huge rosy watermelon yields pithy rind for a spicy pickle.

Pickling onions

Delicious with bread and cheese, this pickle can be made with either small pearl onions or shallots. This method of draining off the brine and pouring it on again both softens the pickle and concentrates all the flavor.

1. Make a brine solution of 1 lb (1½ cups) pickling salt added to 1 gallon water in a plastic bucket. Half the solution will be used immediately and half kept until later. This saline solution draws out the moisture from the onions which would otherwise dilute the pickle and lessen its preservative qualities. Put 4 lb unpeeled pearl onions – or shallots which connoisseurs prefer – in another plastic bucket and cover with half the brine solution. Leave overnight.

2. Next day, pour off the first brine solution.

3. Peel the onions.

4. Put them back in the bucket with the second half of the brine. Test to see if it is sufficiently salty by floating a fresh egg on top – if it floats, the solution is salty enough. If it sinks or half bobs, top up with more salt. Weight the onions down with a plate and heavy can, or jar, so that they are completely covered by the salt solution. Leave for 2 to 3 days.

5. The onions are ready after 2 to 3 days to go into a solution of prepared cold vinegar. Take the onions from the brine, drain in a colander and rinse well – if you don't they will taste of not much besides salt. Leave to dry on towels.

6. Meanwhile make up the vinegar solution. To get the most flavor first bruise your pickling spices – 1 tablespoon cloves, 1 tablespoon white peppercorns, 2 dried red chili peppers – by tying them in a cloth and bashing them with a rolling pin. Then put them in an aluminum saucepan with $\frac{1}{2}$ cup sugar and 2 quarts vinegar and bring to the boil.

7. Pack the onions into pint glass canning jars and pour over the hot vinegar making sure the vinegar covers the onions and leaving $\frac{1}{2}$ inch of headroom. I leave the spices in to make the pickle more aromatic. Some people prefer their pickles free from seeds and pods in which case strain the solution first through a nylon sieve before adding to the pickle jars.

8. Put the lids on and adjust. Then process in a boiling water bath for 10 minutes (see page 200), the water at full boil covering the jars by 2 inches. Complete the seals if necessary and leave to cool. Check the seals carefully before storing; if they are imperfect either store the jars in the refrigerator for immediate use or boil the contents and re-process in sterilized jars.

Note: in Britain it is acceptable to seal jars of pickle and chutney with waxed paper and cotton dipped in melted paraffin wax. This is not recommended in America and will not survive a boiling water bath.

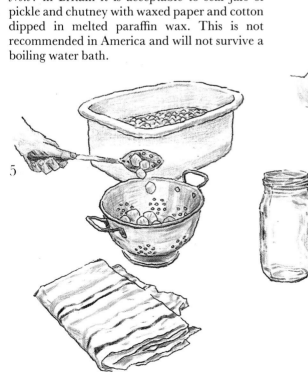

Pickles

There is room in any well stocked kitchen cupboard for a variety of pickles and I have added some Middle Eastern as well as traditional recipes. They are not difficult to make. Present them with quiet triumph to complement a plate of cold meat.

Sweet pepper pickle
Pickle a medley of red, yellow and green peppers when they are cheap to cheer you later in mid winter. This is a Turkish recipe, good with kabobs, hors d'oeuvre, and pilaffs.

6 red peppers
6 green peppers
6 yellow peppers
salt
sugar
sherry
white vinegar

Slice the peppers across and remove cores, seeds and white pith. Pack them into jars, and cover with a hot spiced vinegar made by stirring 1 teaspoon of salt, 4 teaspoons of sugar and $\frac{1}{2}$ cup of sherry into every $2\frac{1}{2}$ cups of vinegar. Cover and process.

Spiced pickled fruit
This is a sweet-sour pickle, delicious eaten with game, cold ham and pâtés. The syrup makes a good sauce for steamed puddings. Use brown sugar for peaches, white for pears or plums.

4 lb small ripe peaches, or small hard pears or
  small under-ripe plums
1 tablespoon each : allspice, cloves, cinnamon (powder
  or stick) and coriander seeds
2½ cups white vinegar
4 cups sugar

To prepare the fruit, wash and wipe but leave them whole, only cutting off any soft or brown parts. Tie the spices in cheesecloth, crush them slightly and boil with the vinegar and the sugar, stirring to dissolve the sugar. Add the fruit and simmer very gently until tender. Lift out with a slotted spoon and pack into warmed jars. Boil the vinegar hard for a few minutes to reduce it to a syrupy consistency, then pour it over the fruit. Cover at once and process.

Spiced crabapples
Too often these most decorative fruit are left to drop and rot. Cooked, they have a delicate tartness and superb color. Use them to stuff roast goose or duck, or eat with meat or game.

4 lb crabapples
water
lemon rind
sugar
white wine vinegar or distilled white vinegar
coriander seeds, cinnamon, peppercorns

Remove the stalks and any blemishes, wash the apples and put them into enough boiling water just to cover. Add strips of lemon rind. Simmer until just tender. Strain off the cooking water, and to each $2\frac{1}{2}$ cups add 2 cups of sugar, $\frac{2}{3}$ cup of vinegar and 1 teaspoon mixed spices, either ground or tied into cheesecloth whole. Boil this mixture, stirring well to dissolve the sugar, then add the crabapples and simmer uncovered over a gentle heat until the syrup is much reduced and the crabapples almost transparent. This will take about 40 minutes. Ladle into warmed jars, cover with syrup and process.
Note : Medieval recipes invariably added a little pepper to spiced mixtures like these.

Pickled grapes
The small, seedless variety of grapes are good for this pickle. Serve with smoked fish.

1¼ cups white vinegar
2½ cups water
1 cup sugar
1 teaspoon mixed cloves, cinnamon and allspice
2 lb grapes

Boil the vinegar, water and sugar with the spices and leave to cool. Wash the grapes, picking out any blemished ones, and dry them before packing into jars. Pour the hot spiced vinegar over them, cover and process.

Dill pickle

Ideally you should use tiny cucumbers 4 to 5 inches specially grown for pickling, but ordinary cucumbers cut into sticks can be substituted, though they will not be as crisp.

brine solution
4 lb small pickling cucumbers
6 cloves garlic
several sprays of fresh dill
1 teaspoon each allspice, cloves, cinnamon and caraway seeds
½ cup sugar
1 to 1½ quarts distilled white vinegar

Make up 1 gallon of brine (see previous page). Wash the cucumbers carefully, remove any flowers, pack them into the brine and leave, covered and weighted down, for 3 days. Remove, drain and pack into jars, with the garlic cloves and dill distributed among them. Boil the spices (tied in a cloth bag) and the sugar with the vinegar, stirring to dissolve the sugar. Pour the boiling spiced vinegar over the cucumbers. Cover tightly and leave in a warm place for 24 hours. Drain off the vinegar, boil it up again and pour over the cucumbers once more. Cover and leave in a warm place for another 24 hours. Repeat this again if necessary until the cucumbers are a fine green color. Top up with fresh hot vinegar, cover and process.

Pickled eggs

An excellent snack with winter salads and cold meats.

12 eggs
1 quart vinegar
6 cloves garlic
1 tablespoon white peppercorns
1 tablespoon allspice berries
small piece fresh ginger root (optional)

Cook the eggs in simmering water for 10 minutes, then leave to cool in cold water. Peel. Simmer the vinegar with all the other ingredients for 10 minutes. Pack the eggs into canning jars and pour over the hot vinegar which may be either strained or used complete with spices. Cover and process. They can be eaten after 1 month.

Pickled walnuts

Pickled walnuts are the most elegant accompaniment to a really good cheese. Wear fine rubber gloves to handle the walnuts – the stain is near indelible. Green cob nuts or hazel nuts may be pickled too.

4 lb green walnuts (or cob or hazel nuts)
pickling salt
spiced vinegar as for pickled eggs

Leave the walnuts in enough brine (see previous page) to cover them. Keep them submerged for 5 days, then drain and cover with fresh brine for another week. Drain and spread out on trays in the sun, turning occasionally until they are quite black and dry – about 1 day. Pack into jars and cover with hot spiced vinegar poured over hot. Cover and process. Eat after 1 month.

Pickled watermelon rind

This classic American pickle uses the part of the melon which is normally thrown away, the white strip between flesh and skin.

8 cups cubed watermelon rind (see below)
6 tablespoons pickling salt
1 teaspoon powdered alum
1 quart water
1 cinnamon stick
10 cloves
2 cups sugar
1 quart white or wine vinegar

To make the cubes, pare off the green outer skin (the red inside has all been eaten of course) and cut the white, hard flesh into ½ inch cubes. Put them all into a large bowl. Mix the salt, alum and cold water together, pour over the rind and add enough additional cold water to cover. Put a weighted plate on top and leave overnight. Drain, rinse under running water and shake off as much moisture as possible. Put the spices and half the sugar into the vinegar and simmer for 10 minutes. Add the watermelon cubes, bring to simmering point, remove from the heat and cool. Add the rest of the sugar, bring to simmering point again and cook gently until the cubes are transparent, stirring occasionally. Ladle into hot jars, cover and process.

Chutneys

Uncooked chutneys must be eaten within a month, but the cooked chutney, a medley of ingredients simmered until reduced to a sort of savory jam, is an ideal case for preserving, and actually improves on keeping.

Pumpkin or zucchini chutney

One of the best homemade chutney recipes, rich but mild, this will cope admirably with a glut of vegetables.

5 lb pumpkin or zucchini
2 lb fresh or canned tomatoes
1 lb onions
6 to 8 cloves garlic
3 lb (8 cups) light brown sugar
1 cup seedless white raisins
¼ cup salt
1 tablespoon each: peppercorns, allspice, ground ginger
 (or 1 piece crushed fresh ginger root)
2½ pints vinegar

Peel the pumpkin, but leave the skin on the zucchini. Slice thickly, remove the cottony centers and the seeds and cut lengthwise into strips 1 inch square and ½ inch thick (if the fruit is too thick it can refuse to soften in cooking). Roughly chop the tomatoes, if fresh. Slice the onions and chop the garlic. Put all the ingredients into a kettle and, bring slowly to a boil, stirring to dissolve the sugar. Cook slowly but steadily for 1 to 2 hours, until the mixture is tender (but not disintegrated) and thick, but not too dry. Ladle into jars, cover and process.

Apple chutney

A mild, fresh tasting chutney which improves with keeping. Children like it. I use windfalls and do not bother peeling them.

4 lb tart green apples
2 lb onions
2 tablespoons yellow mustard seed
1 tablespoon ground ginger or 1 piece of fresh ginger root
1½ cups seedless white raisins
3 cups brown sugar
6 red chili peppers or 1 teaspoon cayenne pepper
1 quart malt vinegar
1 tablespoon salt

Quarter the apples, core and chop roughly. Chop the onions. Heat the mustard seed lightly in a heavy kettle then grind to a powder in a mortar. Chop the ginger finely if using fresh root. Put all the ingredients into a large kettle and cook for several hours very gently until pulpy and brown. Ladle into jars, cover and process.
Note: Old recipes give an uncooked – or largely uncooked – variation on this chutney under the title of Bengal chutney. Usually all the ingredients are put through a food grinder, stirred up with vinegar, spices and sugar, then canned.

Tamatarr (tomato) chutney

A hot, spicy chutney which makes use of both green and red tomatoes.

2 lb each red and green tomatoes
1 lb onions
1 whole head of garlic
2 teaspoons fenugreek
3 tablespoons coriander
1 teaspoon each grated nutmeg, cardamom pods, chopped fresh basil
2 quarts vinegar
1 lb (3 cups) raisins
3 cups brown sugar
1 cup capers
1 tablespoon cayenne pepper
¼ cup salt

Chop the tomatoes roughly. Chop the onions and garlic. Roast the fenugreek and the coriander for a few minutes in the oven, then grind finely. Take the seeds from the cardamom pods. Cook the tomatoes in half the vinegar over a low heat until reduced to a thick mush – make sure it does not burn. Cook the raisins, the chopped onion, the garlic, sugar, spices, herbs, capers, cayenne pepper and salt in the rest of the vinegar until the onion is tender and the consistency reduced. Add the tomato mush, stir to mix and simmer for 10 minutes. Ladle into jars, cover and process. Store for 6 months.

Ketchups

The best way of dealing with a glut of ripe tomatoes or field mushrooms is to simmer them down into highly flavored sauces and catsups. These are a safe and easy way of preserving surplus vegetables and take up very little space.

Tomato ketchup

A hotter, spicier chutney which makes use of both green and red tomatoes. It should be kept for 6 months to allow flavors to mingle.

12 lb ripe outdoor tomatoes
2 cups sugar
2½ cups white vinegar
1 tablespoon salt
1 teaspoon each ground ginger, cloves, nutmeg, paprika and cayenne

Cut the tomatoes into quarters and either cook gently on the top of the stove, or bake at a low heat in the oven until soft enough to sieve. You should not need to add water if the tomatoes are juicy enough. Sieve the tomatoes. Then simmer the pulp in a large pan with all the remaining ingredients until thickened – it will thicken more when cool. Pour at once into canning jars, cover and process for 30 minutes.

Pontack sauce

This is a proper, pungent old fashioned 'store sauce'. Traditionally it was kept for 7 years to allow the true bouquet to mature.

2½ cups ripe elderberries
1 pint vinegar
1 tablespoon black peppercorns
¼ tablespoon allspice
1 teaspoon cloves
½ teaspoon grated nutmeg or mace
1 teaspoon salt
8 shallots

Put the berries into an earthenware jar or pot, cover with the vinegar and set in a warm oven for 2 hours to extract all the juice. Strain into a kettle, add the spices, seasonings and shallots and simmer for 30 minutes. Strain, return to the kettle and simmer for 5 minutes. Pour into hot jars, cover and process for 10 minutes. Leave for 2 months to mature.

Mushroom ketchup

Wild mushrooms make the best ketchup of all – a few drops in soups, sauces and gravy make an astonishing difference. Use sound mushrooms only – a good sized bucket or basket at least.

Weigh the mushrooms, then break them up and layer them in a crock with 1 tablespoon of pickling salt to every pound. Leave them to sweat out their juices for 2 or 3 days, pressing now and then. Then put the jar in a cool oven (at the lowest setting) for 3 hours to extract the last drops. Pour them into a nylon strainer or sieve over a bowl and squeeze as much juice from the mushrooms as possible. To every 1 quart of mushroom liquor allow:

1 teaspoon allspice
¼ teaspoon grated nutmeg
3 chopped garlic cloves
1 red chili pepper
¼ teaspoon ground ginger
1¼ cups red wine (homemade elderberry)

Put the spices and the garlic into cheesecloth, then add them to a kettle with the mushroom liquor and the wine. Simmer slowly for 2 or 3 hours until thickened. Turn into jars, cover and process for 20 minutes.

Mustard

Those fashionable old style mustards are simple to make at home. Wine vinegar simmered with the dregs from a wine bottle until slightly reduced makes a good base. The method is simple. Use a mixture of yellow and black mustard seed in a ratio of two yellow to one black. Pound or blend about half the mixture to a powder, more if you do not like the mixture too grainy. Stir the whole seed into the powdered seed, then add a pinch of sugar and blend in the reduced liquid. Using vinegar flavored with herbs or spices will vary the flavor, as will adding a little minced garlic, powdered turmeric and coriander, or peppercorns.

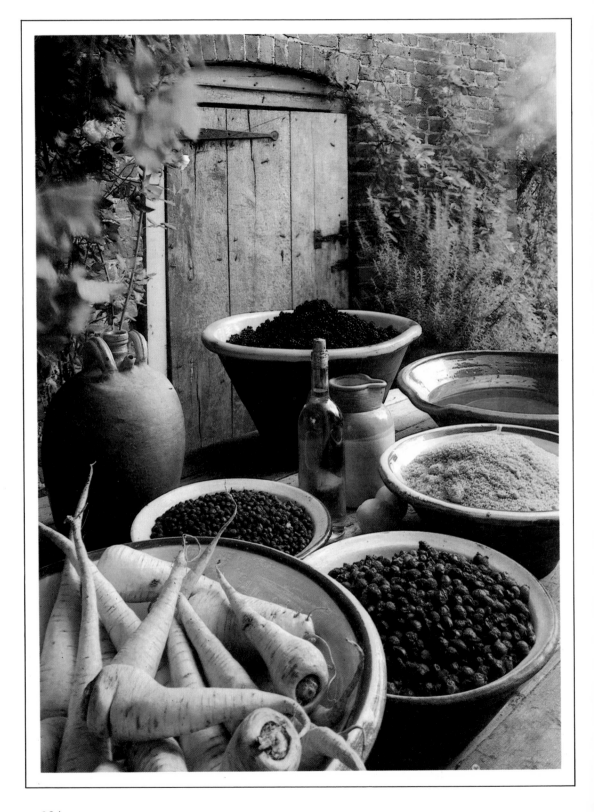

Wines

'"I want you to hev a look at my wine, gel; I ain't sure about it.'
Prissy went to the old man's house and her verdict was instantaneous:
'You want to take that there mould off the top right quick, you dew!
Thet will spoil it. Thet at the bottom's all right ..."'

Ask the Fellows who Cut the Hay   George Ewart Evans   1956

Home wine making has become one of the most popular hobbies, supported by a flourishing small industry turning out recipe books, magazines, and equipment ranging from the simplest cork to the most stream-lined insulated heater to keep the fermenting bucket at the ideal temperature. This popularity has brought about a timely reappraisal of amateur wine making methods; one result is the proliferation of grape concentrates, which are about the closest you can get to an instant wine mix. The traditional, country wine recipes based on the local fruits and flowers which were a frugal peasant's first choice, have been revised to produce wines quite unlike the syrupy, medicinal or brackish tasting concoctions which gave home-made wines a bad name and prevented them being taken seriously. Modern recipes aim for wines on the dryish side, nicely rounded and characterful without being heavy, in short, a pleasant drink to accompany a good meal. Next time you are offered a glass of parsley, mulberry or elderflower wine, just try it. It could surprise you. The fact is, a properly made country wine based on fruit, flowers or vegetables is a drink of much fresher flavor and charm than the acrid, chemical tasting grape products which wine merchants offer in the lower price range. An exquisite elderflower wine is an interesting drink, and a simple blackberry wine, light, dry and red, answers as well to what you expect of an agreeable table wine as anything you could find.

Country wines do not taste, in a crude or literal sense, of what goes into them. Pea pods make a light, fresh Rhine-style wine. Flower wines are fragrant, naturally, and a glass of one of these fine delicate scented wines on a hot summer evening is something to remember. The problem with all homemade wines is keeping them long enough to experience all the improvements which maturity confers in the way of smoothness, balance and subtlety.

I have deliberately emphasized the often impressive quality of homemade wines because I think the people who make them are apt to be too modest but, of course, the clinching fact in their favor, and the one which sets most people making their own, is their astonishing cheapness. Using the thriftiest means – wild or homegrown fruit say – one bottle of attractive wine costs little more than a pint of milk.

Bowls of fruit and vegetables ready for fermenting with yeast, water and sugar: parsnips for one of the best and strongest white wines, elderberries for a medium sweet red wine that improves with maturity and freshly picked blackberries for a light, fruity, dryish red wine.

Wine making

Equipment
For 1 gallon of wine, you need only buy a length of plastic tubing for siphoning purposes, as you will almost certainly have a plastic bucket, and several large empty bottles in the house, and these will serve, well cleaned and sterilized, to ferment the wine in and store it later.

If you want to make wine seriously, buy the largest size fermentation buckets and several 1 gallon glass jars. It is very little extra trouble to make larger amounts of wine, the fermentation usually goes better in bulk, and at the end of it you have enough wine to put by, and forget about for 6 months or a year. Two $5\frac{1}{2}$ gallon bins – white plastic, purpose made, with snap on lids – plus 10 jars is enough to make two batches of flower wines in spring, which will be ready to bottle by the time the next bout of wine making begins in the fall, with blackberries, elderberries, apples. Bottles are no problem: collect empties, wash and sterilize them and store in dust proof boxes until needed. Wine must be protected during its stay in the gallon jars, from outside air and possible bacterial infection, but it must not be sealed off, or the carbon dioxide given off during fermentation cannot escape. The cheap solution is to fasten a plastic garbage bag over the neck of the jar securing it with rubber bands to make a sort of balloon. Or buy proper fermentation locks; plastic ones with integral stoppers are handiest of all. Also needed is a length of plastic tubing for siphoning and racking, a large plastic sieve for straining, a long handled wooden spoon for stirring, a long handled bottle brush to clean the jars thoroughly and a gadget for driving in corks if you don't use screw caps. This equipment should be scalded or sterilized regularly and used only for wine. A hydrometer, which ascertains whether the wine has fermented out, is also useful though not essential.

Additives
Some chemicals are needed; potassium metabisulphite is essential, for sterilizing the equipment, adding to the wine itself at various stages to protect against infection, or wild yeast ferments, and to stabilize and clear it. Most winemakers buy potassium metabisulphite in crystal form, which is cheaper, or you can buy it in the form of Campden tablets. For sterilizing purposes, dissolve it in water – 2 oz of crystals or 2 tablets per gallon of water. Other chemical aids which are cheap and efficient are acid blend or ascorbic acid, sold in powder form, to use instead of the more expensive lemons, and pectinase, or pectic enzyme, which is used in some methods to prevent haze or clouding, caused by minute protein particles. All these can be bought from a wine supply store.

Definition
Wine is a fermented, flavored liquid. During fermentation the yeast converts the sugar present into alcohol. To produce a drink which tastes nice as well as alcoholic, most country wines need supplementing in one direction or another – only wine grapes are naturally endowed with the right proportions of acid, tannin and sugar. Thus to some fruit or flower wines you add acid (ascorbic or lemon juice), to others

tannin (cold tea or grape tannin, which is available from wine supply stores) and to others extra 'body' in the shape of dried fruit. Some flower wines need all three. By setting up a ferment in this way almost anything can be turned into wine. But some work better than others, and it is these reliable 'classics' I shall include in the recipe section.

Yeast

In the old days people spread brewer's or baker's yeast on a slice of toast and floated this on their open cask of 'must' – must, before we go any further, is the stuff in your fermentation bucket before siphoning off, embryo wine. The old way, for once, was quite wrong. Neither of these yeasts is powerful enough to produce the alcohol content wine needs, they muddy the wine flavor, and the remaining unfermented sugar makes the wine sickly sweet. Fermenting without a lid, too, was an open-house to bugs, molds, wild yeasts and sour flavors. Today we use proper wine yeasts, a spin-off from the wine trade. You can choose between dry yeast, which is cheaper, and liquid yeast in a wider variety of strains: chablis, pinot noir, etc. Wine yeast is more temperamental than beer yeast, and should be 'started' in the favorable microclimate of a bottle of boiled water before being added to the must (see overleaf). This helps to start the fermentation. Buy ready-made yeast starter kits, or make your own.

A day before preparing the must, make up the starter. Half fill a clean bottle with tepid boiled water, add a tiny pinch of acid blend or citric acid, sugar and yeast nutrient, then the yeast, and shake well. Plug the top with absorbent cotton, set in a warm place and after 24 hours the fermentation should have begun. Look for tiny clusters of bubbles on top and a cloudiness in the water.

Sugar

This is the essential partner to yeast. Use plain white granulated sugar, bought in bulk if possible for cheapness. Yeast can convert roughly 4 cups of sugar per 1 gallon of liquid into alcohol. For a dry wine add just this amount for a sweeter wine, add rather more. For a 1 gallon batch of wine, add all the sugar at once; for larger amounts it is best added by stages, so as not to overload the yeast.

What can go wrong

It is rare for wines to go wrong if you take reasonable care. The worst that can befall is for a wine to be invaded by the vinegar fly, which turns it all to vinegar and this is rare. Sour flavors – funny tastes – can happen, usually as a result of leaving the ingredients hanging about too long, or not being generous enough with the potassium metabisulphite. Sour flavors cannot be hidden, though I would leave any wine for several months to make sure it *is* a funny taste, and not just an awkward stage of development. If the ferments sticks, which means that the yeast gives up before the sugar is fermented out, leaving a flat, sweet mixture, correct it by putting the bucket in a warmer spot or stirring hard to aerate the must, or adding a little yeast nutrient and acid to ginger up the yeast.

Making parsnip wine

1. Scrub 7 lb parsnips and slice lengthwise. Place in a very large pan with 1 gallon of water and bring to a boil. Simmer until *just* tender – if you let them go mushy the brew will not clear.

2. Take a jellybag (if you do not have such a thing, a pillowcase is a good substitute) or large sieve, and support it over a plastic fermentation bucket. Tip in the parsnips and cooking water and leave to drip at their own pace. Do not press, squeeze or otherwise hurry things, or the result will be a cloudy wine.

3. Meanwhile boil 7 quarts of water, then leave to cool until just tepid.

4. Add the tepid water to the parsnip liquid in the fermentation bucket, with the juice of 2 lemons and sugar at the rate of 6 cups per 1 gallon of liquid. Stir well to dissolve the sugar completely, then add the yeast starter. This should be made up the day before, by half filling a clean bottle with tepid boiled water and adding a tiny pinch of citric acid and sugar, 1 teaspoon of yeast nutrient and 1 package of wine yeast. The bottle should be shaken, plugged with absorbent cotton and left in a warm place. After 24 to 48 hours the fermentation should have begun, shown by a cluster of bubbles on the top and a cloudiness in the water, and the starter is ready to use.

5. Cover the bucket and leave in a warm spot for 10 days, stirring well each day.

6. The fermentation should have slowed down after this prescribed time and the 'must' should be ready to move on into large glass jugs or jars. Using a jug and funnel, transfer all the must into as many jars as you require, and fit custom-built fermentation locks. For a first attempt at wine making, it is not essential to buy all the tailor-made equipment. Any large bottles you have will do instead of the proper fermentation jars. However, the latter are, of course, preferable, 1 gallon being the optimum capacity. Instead of commercial fermentation locks, you can improvise a simpler non-return valve system to release carbon dioxide with a plastic garbage bag or rubber balloon tied securely to the neck of the bottle or jar.

7. Slowly the active fermentation in the jars will cease, and the debris and yeast will settle in a solid layer on the bottom of the jar, and the wine will appear clear. To prevent sour flavors the wine must be siphoned off the sediment. Take a short length of plastic tubing, place one end in the jar taking care not to disturb the sediment, put the other in your mouth and take a sharp swig at it. This will bring the wine rushing down the tube. Stop it with your thumb, before directing it into waiting, sterilized bottles. Cap or insert corks (you will need a special gadget for this) and store in a cool place for 6 months or more.

7

4

5

6

Preparing the must

The must is the flavored liquid base of the wine, made up mainly of water. To extract as much flavor as possible the ingredients can be steeped in cold water for a day or two, with potassium metabisulphite added to prevent any natural ferments starting up. Or they can be simmered briefly. The cold water method is said to give a fresher taste, but it is not suitable for all ingredients. Flower wines use a combination of the two as a rule.

Ingredients should be sound, ripe and as fresh as possible – flowers in particular should be fresh, otherwise their scent fades. Hard ingredients – vegetables and apples – should be peeled, cored and chopped small to extract the maximum flavor. Use an electric blender where possible – metal should never come into contact with a must *after* adding yeast, but before will not hurt.

To make the must, simply combine the prepared ingredients and any other additions in the way of grape tannin, acid blend or pectic enzyme, with the correct amount of water, stir in sugar, and then add the yeast from the starter bottle. After stirring well for a couple of minutes, press on the bucket lid, and leave at room temperature. Within a day or two the ferment should have begun. A thick 'cap' on the liquid, composed of all the solids in the must, audible bubbling and a strong smell will confirm this. The must should be stirred vigorously at least once a day to aerate the yeast and any extra sugar added at the same time.

Fermenting the wine

After the prescribed time, when the ferment has slowed down, the liquid wine must be siphoned off – get a helper for this if you are tackling a large quantity of must. The quickest, easiest way to part liquid from solids is to tip the must into a large strainer, sieve, loosely woven cloth or jellybag, suspended over another fermentation bucket. Wring out as much liquid as possible, pressing the pulp by hand, spoon or whatever serves best. Now lift the full fermentation bucket onto a table and stand the sterilized glass jugs or bottles below on the floor, or a chair. Dip one end of the plastic tubing into the bucket, put the other in your mouth and suck sharply. This will bring the wine rushing down the tube. Stop the end up with your thumb, place it into the neck of one of the bottles and let it fill to just above the shoulder of the bottle. Stop it up again, and move onto the next bottle. Continue until the bottles are full, then fit fermentation locks or plastic garbage bags over the necks, and leave them in a slightly cooler place for the second phase of fermentation.

The bottles will ferment busily at first then, when the activity ceases, the debris and yeast will settle in a solid layer on the bottom of the bottle and the wine will 'fall clear'. When clear, it is a good practice to 'rack' it, that is siphon off the yeast layer into a clean jug, or sterilized bottles. If left on the sediment, the wine can become musty. The siphoning is done as before, but be careful not to disturb the sediment. Add a little potassium metabisulphite as a precaution and stabilizer ($\frac{1}{2}$ teaspoon crystals or 1 tablet per 1 gallon). The racked wine can now be stored in a cool place to mature – every month you leave it undrunk it will gain in distinction.

Wines

For convenience I am giving quantities for making 1 gallon of wine. The recipes are nearly all for wild flowers and fruit and they follow the order in which you would make them through the year.

Furze or gorse wine

Difficult to pick, because of the thorns, but the coconut scented yellow flowers make a wine of beautiful color and fragrance. Use a plastic jug for measuring, and do not squash the flowers.

12 cups furze or gorse flowers
1 gallon water
4 cups sugar
1¼ cups seedless white raisins
2 oranges
2 lemons (or ¼ oz citric acid)
⅔ cup strong tea or 8 drops grape tannin
2 heaping teaspoons all-purpose wine yeast
1 teaspoon yeast nutrient

Put the flowers into the fermenting bucket immediately. Boil half the water, half the sugar and the chopped raisins together for 1 to 2 minutes, then pour over the flowers. Thinly peel the rind from the oranges and the lemons, and add to the bucket. Squeeze out the juice and add that too. Add the cold tea or the tannin and stir thoroughly. Make up to 1 gallon with cold water, or cooled boiled water if you prefer. This should give you a tepid mixture, about right for adding the yeast from the starter bottle. Add the yeast and yeast nutrient, stir well and cover. Ferment for 1 week, stirring daily. After 2 or 3 days, when fermenting well, add the remaining sugar and stir to dissolve. Strain through a sieve or cloth (as explained in the method on page 238) and siphon into a gallon jug or bottle. Fill up to the neck of the jug with cool, boiled water, if necessary (the less surface area exposed with all wines the better), fit a fermentation lock or secure a plastic garbage bag with a rubber band over the neck of the jug. Rack when clear, bottle and keep for 6 months.

Dandelion wine

Another flower classic. Pick the dandelions on a hot day, and use *only* the petals, pinching them off and discarding the centers and the stalks.

8 cups dandelion petals
1 gallon water
4 cups sugar
1¼ cups raisins
3 oranges
1 lemon (or ¼ oz citric acid)
⅔ cup strong tea or 8 drops grape tannin
2 heaping teaspoons all-purpose wine yeast
1 teaspoon yeast nutrient

The method is exactly the same as for furze wine.

May blossom wine

Do not confuse may or hawthorn blossom with the white blossom of the blackthorn or sloe, which comes out a month earlier, before the leaves. Both bushes have thorns but may blossom is always out with its leaves.

8 cups may blossom
1 gallon water
4 cups sugar
2 lemons (or ¼ oz citric acid)
⅔ cup strong tea or 8 drops grape tannin
2 heaping teaspoons all-purpose wine yeast
1 teaspoon yeast nutrient

Method as for furze wine.

Elderflower wine

4 cups elderflowers
1 gallon water
4 cups sugar
2 lemons
⅔ cup strong tea or 8 drops grape tannin
2 heaping teaspoons all-purpose wine yeast
1 teaspoon yeast nutrient

Strip the flowers from the stalks as soon as possible after picking, as they are much looser then. The method is the same as for furze wine.

Rhubarb wine

Use the first young sticks of rhubarb to make this fresh, fruity medium sweet wine. Rhubarb needs no extra acid.

2 lb rhubarb
3 cups seedless white raisins
1 Campden tablet or ½ teaspoon potassium
  metabisulphite crystals
4 cups sugar
1¼ cups strong tea or 16 drops grape tannin
1 gallon water
1 package of Sauterne yeast
1 teaspoon yeast nutrient

Wipe and trim the rhubarb sticks, chop them small and crush or blend to a mush, saving the juice. Put this into a bucket with the chopped raisins, crushed Campden tablet or potassium metabisulphite crystals, half the sugar and the tea or tannin. Add enough water to make the contents up to 1 gallon (a little hot will give you a tepid mix), add the yeast and the yeast nutrient, stir well and cover. Ferment for 8 days, adding the remaining sugar after 3. Stir well daily. Strain into a gallon jug or bottle and cover, or fit a fermentation lock. Rack when clear. This wine can be drunk after a few months.

Gooseberry wine

Green gooseberries are one of the best wine fruit.

3 lb green gooseberries
1 gallon water
4 cups sugar
1 Campden tablet or ½ teaspoon potassium
  metabisulphite crystals
1 package wine yeast
1 teaspoon yeast nutrient

Top and tail the berries, put them in the fermentation bucket and crush them with the end of a rolling pin. Add the water and sugar – to make sure the sugar dissolves boil some of the water and stir it in. Add the crushed Campden tablet or potassium metabisulphite crystals dissolved in 1 tablespoon of water. Stir. Add the yeast and the yeast nutrient. Ferment for 1 week. Strain. Rack when clear. Bottle. Drink after 6 months.

Blackberry wine

2 lb blackberries
1 gallon water
1½ cups raisins
4 cups sugar
juice of 1 lemon
½ teaspoon pectic enzyme
2 heaping teaspoons all-purpose wine yeast
1 teaspoon yeast nutrient

Put the berries into a pan with about 2 quarts of water, and bring just to simmering point. Put the chopped raisins and the sugar into a fermentation bucket and add the blackberries and the water they were simmered in. Stir well to dissolve the sugar. Add another 2 quarts of boiled water and mix. When cooled to just warm, stir in the lemon juice and pectic enzyme. Add the yeast and the yeast nutrient, cover and ferment for 8 days, stirring daily. After 8 days strain the contents through a large sieve into another bucket and press the pulp in a cloth to squeeze out any remaining juice. Return to a clean fermentation bucket. Then siphon off into a 1 gallon jug or bottle, leaving behind as much sediment as possible. Fill the jug with cool, boiled water to the neck, fit a fermentation lock until fermentation is finished. Ready after 6 weeks.

Elderberry wine

Elderberries are so strong on tannin that they make a harsh wine, unless well matured – 1 to 2 years. Best made medium sweet.

3 lb elderberries
1½ cups raisins
1 gallon water
5½ cups sugar
1 package Burgundy yeast
1 teaspoon yeast nutrient
½ teaspoon pectic enzyme

Heat the berries and the chopped raisins in the water until simmering. Tip them into a fermentation bucket, add the sugar and stir well. When cooled add the yeast, the yeast nutrient and the pectic enzyme. Ferment for 5 days, stirring daily. Strain into jugs or bottles. Rack when the wine has cleared, and again after 3 months.

Liqueurs and cordials

Very attractive liqueurs can be made by the simple method of steeping fruit in spirits with sugar. Not cheap, alas, but worth making in small quantities for gala occasions to drink with a demitasse coffee after dinner.

Danish blackcurrant rum
(Solbaerrom)

1 quart white rum
2 lb blackcurrants
6 bitter almonds
3 cups sugar

Pour the rum into a wide mouthed crock, add the crushed blackcurrants and blanched almonds, cover and leave in a cool place for 1 month, stirring daily. Then drain the liquor off the currants, pressing out all juice, add the sugar and stir to dissolve. Bottle, corking well, and leave for at least 6 months.
Note: the remaining fruit can be used in pies.

Sloe gin
The best use for sloes, those tiny wild plums of the hedgerows. Made in the fall it will be ready by Christmas.

4 cups sloes
1 quart gin
1½ cups sugar

Prick the sloes, and pack them into a wide mouthed crock with the other ingredients. Cover tightly. Shake from time to time to dissolve the sugar. After 3 to 4 months strain, bottle, cork tightly and keep as long as you can.
Note: Use the leftover sloes to flavor pies, pasta sauces and casseroles – they keep for ages in a screwtop jar.

Raspberry cordial
Russians make this with wild berries. Use an equal volume of fruit to vodka. Combine them in a crock, leave for about a week, then strain the fruit out. Dilute the liquid with water, in about equal amounts, and add 2 cups of sugar per 1 gallon. Stir well, bottle and keep for several months.

This is another Russian method, which can be made with mulberries, loganberries and strawberries as well as raspberries. The berries are fermented in sugar. Half fill a 1 gallon jug or plastic bucket with berries then fill to the top with sugar. Cover and leave for 6 to 8 weeks to ferment. Strain the berries through a sieve, pressing out the juice. Strain the juice through a jellybag to clear it. Then add alcohol – vodka, brandy or rum, to taste – at least one part alcohol to three parts fruit juice.

Noyau
This dates from the 18th century, and is a potent liqueur made with beech leaves. Pack a glass bottle full of young beech leaves, then fill up with gin. Cover and leave for 2 weeks. Strain off the gin and to every 1 pint allow 1 cup of sugar which has been dissolved in 1 cup of boiling water. Mix well, add 1 tablespoon of brandy per bottle, and cork tightly.

Raspberry vinegar
Fruit vinegars are diluted with water or soda water before drinking.

1 quart white wine vinegar
4 cups raspberries or blackberries
sugar

Pour the vinegar over the fruit and leave for 4 days. Strain and add 2 cups of sugar per quart of liquid. Heat until just simmering. Cool. Bottle, cork tightly and store in a cool dry place.

Cherry shrub
Pick ripe Morello cherries, set them in a crock and set the crock in a pan of water (or cool oven) until the juice runs. Turn into a jellybag. Squeeze out the juice, sweeten to taste and add brandy – one part brandy to four parts shrub. Put the brandy in first, add shrub and shake.

Index